Homesteading in
New York City, 1978–1993

HOMESTEADING IN NEW YORK CITY, 1978–1993

The Divided Heart of Loisaida

Malve von Hassell

Contemporary Urban Studies
Robert V. Kemper and Estellie Smith, Series Editors

BERGIN & GARVEY
Westport, Connecticut • London

Library of Congress Cataloging-in-Publication Data

Hassell, Malve von.
　　Homesteading in New York City, 1978–1993 : the divided heart of
Loisaida / Malve von Hassell.
　　　　p.　　cm.—(Contemporary urban studies, ISSN 1065–7002)
　　Includes bibliographical references and index.
　　ISBN 0–89789–459–6 (alk. paper)—ISBN 0–89789–651–3 (pbk.)
　　1. Urban homesteading—New York (N.Y.)—History.　2. Puerto
Ricans—New York (N.Y.)—History.　3. New York (N.Y.)—Social
conditions.　4. Lower East Side (New York, N.Y.)　I. Title.
II. Series.
HD7289.42.U62N44　1996
307—dc20　　　　95–34582

British Library Cataloguing in Publication Data is available.

Library of Congress Catalog Card Number: 95–34582
ISBN: 0–89789–651–3 (pbk.)

First published in 1996

Bergin & Garvey, 88 Post Road West, Westport, CT 06881
An imprint of Greenwood Publishing Group, Inc.

Printed in the United States of America

The paper used in this book complies with the
Permanent Paper Standard issued by the National
Information Standards Organization (Z39.48–1984).

10 9 8 7 6 5 4 3 2 1

CONTENTS

Photos follow page 88

ILLUSTRATIONS

MAPS

TABLE

Acknowledgments

First and foremost I want to thank the homesteaders of the Lower East Side. I have tried to convey something about their lives and their struggles. If I did not succeed in this, that does not in any way lessen my profound debt to them. I want to mention several individuals in particular: Bill Antalics, Howard Brandstein, Virginia Ghazarian, Ayo Jerri Harrington, Margarita López, Robert Mercado, Amanda McMurray, Rosalia Mendez, Sergio Mendez, Maryanthe Siderelis, and Ruth Torres. Gabriel Boratgis became a friend whose kindness and willingness to share his knowledge were an immeasurable source of support.

I would like to thank individuals at the Lower East Side Catholic Area Conference (LESAC), the Housing Development Institute (HDI), the Department of Housing Preservation and Development (HPD), the Urban Homesteading Assistance Board (UHAB), and other organizations active in housing-related issues on the Lower East Side for their courtesy and helpfulness in responding to my questions. Carol Watson of HDI and LESAC, an inspiring leader and fighter on and for the Lower East Side, challenged me to think about the many facets of homesteading. Her sudden death in February 1995 was a great shock. I am grateful to Lynn Flint, anthropology and education editor at Greenwood Publishing Group, and Robert V. Kemper, editor of the Contemporary Urban Studies series at Bergin & Garvey, for their helpful editorial comments, and the production editor, Desirée Bermani, for her invaluable assistance. Marlis Momber generously shared with me her evocative photographic record of the Lower East Side and also her own experiences of living in the area for over a decade. My thanks go to Leslie Bernstein, Sally Booth, Jeff Cole, Anna Lou Dehavenon, Heinz Fritzsche, Rayna Rapp, Peter Suzuki, Hartmut von

Hentig, and Alisse Waterston for their support and advice at various stages of the research. David Maynard was a patient listener, encouraging voice, and critical reader; without his help I could not have completed the project. In my last conversation with Stanley Diamond, a few months before he died, I told him about my tentative research plans. He was as supportive as ever. It is my unending sorrow that I cannot show him the completed product.

1

INTRODUCTION

They shall rebuild the ancient ruins
The former wastes they shall raise up
And restore the ruined cities
Desolate now for generations.

Isaiah 61:4[1]

This quotation appeared in 1982 in a pamphlet about urban homesteading on the Lower East Side in New York City. Of another age, country, and culture, the quotation nevertheless evokes the depressed and deteriorating inner cities of late twentieth-century America, in which lack of safe and affordable housing, unemployment and underemployment, inadequate education, and inadequate health care are the defining factors. At the same time, these lines hold forth a vision of struggle and a promise for the future.

Sweat-equity urban homesteading on the Lower East Side was a community-based response to the shortage of affordable housing for the working poor. A grassroots effort by the working poor to rebuild their neighborhood, it not only endeavored to address the need for housing but other central factors contributing to poverty as well. The Lower East Side serves as an illustrative example of an inner-city neighborhood affected by the ongoing nationwide housing crisis and general urban crisis. Urban areas such as the Lower East Side have been especially at the mercy of the extensive and damaging legacy of the Reagan and Bush administrations at federal, state, and local levels, to date not effectively countered by a fragmented Clinton administration—and not likely to be countered, given the current political climate. An analysis of the grassroots effort to create safe and affordable housing and to reverse the conditions of poverty on the

Lower East Side must be situated in this wider context. The complex relationship between (1) local communities as nonautonomous and nonhomogeneous but active entities, and (2) local and federal governments, neither monolithic nor unified bodies of power, affects and shapes community development. Homesteading on the Lower East Side is one of several comparable locally based efforts that must be examined in order to create a basis for assessing problems and potentials of government-sponsored community development programs over the last several decades, most recently the Empowerment Zones of the Clinton administration.

The sweat-equity urban homesteading model, devised by activists and residents in cooperation with a local Catholic Church–sponsored organization, was inspired by an ambitious and visionary notion of community. Self-help sweat-equity urban homesteading involved the rehabilitation of city-owned abandoned buildings by low- to moderate-income men and women who were to become resident owners. *Sweat-equity* was the term used to describe the labor invested by homesteaders in the actual rehabilitation effort. This urban homesteading model brought together concepts of cooperative ownership, cooperative labor, and community integration. Resale of apartment units by tenants was to be subject to the control by building cooperatives and the community. Apartments rehabilitated through sweat-equity labor could not be sold for a profit and were to remain permanently available for low-income tenants. Further, the homesteading model envisioned that labor would be treated not as a commodity but as a community property to be shared and made available to those in need. Some construction work was planned as training and work experience for young men and women from the neighborhood. Disabled individuals, the elderly, and people from city shelters placed in the buildings at a later date were all to be treated as full members regardless of the amount of labor they contributed. Finally, the model was inclusive, extending beyond the control and management of housing to a broad-based alliance of community groups and interests. The objective was not the creation of property for a particular group of low-income people in doing the sweat-equity labor. Housing in conjunction with a variety of support services was to be created and made permanently available to a broad range of people, cutting across ethnic and racial lines and divisions based on age, health factors, and socioeconomic status.

The homesteaders were people living on or displaced from the Lower East Side. The majority were Puerto Ricans (70%); the remainder whites, Asians, and African Americans. Annual household incomes were less than the median household income in the area (in 1990, $20,007). Most homesteaders belonged to a population group that has historically been disadvantaged in terms of housing, employment, education, and health care. The notion of owning a home is little more than a dream for them. As a population group consisting predominantly of Puerto Ricans, homesteaders experienced life as a conquered class in a conquered place on many levels, as people from a country dominated by the United States, as Puerto Ricans in America with the worst socioeconomic status of all minority groups in the nation (Rosenberg 1992), and as residents in a neighborhood that is buffeted and torn by the forces of abandonment and gentrification.

The following organizations were central actors in the homesteading effort described in this study. One was the Lower East Side Catholic Area Conference (LESAC). It is a council of neighborhood churches that evolved from a small activist group with a multi-level focus on issues of poverty, housing, and related social issues into an organization that helped to spearhead the homesteading movement. Another was Nazareth Home, Inc., a nonprofit housing development organization founded and separately incorporated in 1983 by neighborhood housing activists and leaders of LESAC to serve the poor and displaced families of the neighborhood. The Housing Development Institute (HDI) was another key organization. It was formed by the Archdiocese of New York as an organizational unit to address funding and development issues in the realm of housing. In the early 1980s, LESAC, HDI, and Nazareth Home, Inc. entered the housing arena together by co-sponsoring one 16-unit building sweat-equity reha- bilitation project. LESAC's role was to provide construction management, Nazareth Home's to provide professional social services support, and HDI's to assist in fund raising and preparation of financial packages for individual projects.

A fourth important entity was the community-based organization known as Rehabilitation in Action to Improve Neighborhoods (RAIN). It was formed by activists and homesteaders during the early 1980s. Initially it was little more than a discussion group. Later it evolved into an organi- zation that oversaw a Community Land Trust. A Community Land Trust is a vehicle for holding title to the land on which buildings are standing and leasing it to the residents, in conjunction with restrictions on use of the land and thus the buildings. These restrictions attach a no-resale policy to a proprietary lease to ensure that the apartments remain permanently avail- able to low- and moderate-income people in the neighborhood.

My first impressions of homesteading on the Lower East Side of Man- hattan were gathered on a Saturday morning in the winter of 1989. On a bright, cold day in January I found myself along with ten other people filling buckets with wet and heavy debris in a windswept building on Avenue C. People associated with that building (whom I later learned to refer to as homesteaders) and volunteers were working on various floors of the building. We were all bundled up with several layers of clothes, and the battered hardhats that we were wearing made it difficult to distinguish homesteaders from volunteers. The building was filled with remnants of inhabitants from times long gone, pieces of furniture and children's toys in the air shaft, dark and narrow rooms separated by flimsy wooden walls, peeling wallpaint revealing a multitude of colors underneath, and old newspaper sheets sticking out from under fragments of linoleum tiles. On one floor all the walls were gone, leaving bare bricks and staring holes where windows had been. It was windy and the roof leaked. As we worked, individual faces and names began to emerge. There were several older women, several younger women, and a few men, none of whom appeared to be older than their mid-forties. The volunteers, in this case sent by a New York City charitable organization, had not been given much information other than that these were neighborhood people trying to rehabilitate abandoned buildings through their own labor with a minimum of assistance from the city, and that occasional volunteer labor would be appreciated.

By the end of that day we had moved accumulated debris out of one room and had begun to strip the walls and ceiling in another. The task ahead appeared daunting. We stopped working at four o'clock because it was getting dark. The homesteaders padlocked the building, and the volunteers left to return home; the homesteaders apparently were going to a meeting somewhere in the area.

Long after I had washed off all the dust and grime, I kept thinking about Dolores. A thin, tall woman in her sixties, she had worked almost silently throughout that day and had taken only occasional breaks to smoke a cigarette, perched on a window sill and having taken off her hardhat to reveal her short white hair. Another image had caught my eye that day, a sign hung on the front of the building proudly proclaiming it to be a member of RAIN. The images of Dolores and the sign, fleeting and hardly understood but associated in my mind with water in a barren land, intrigued me and filled me with questions. I continued to go back for many Saturdays to come, but my interest was caught that first day and remained the spur behind the research project on which this study is based.

Homesteading on the Lower East Side goes back to the early 1970s, when the first efforts were made to rehabilitate abandoned buildings—initially without city or state approval. In response to activism on the part of community-based organizations and also reflecting a shift in federal, state, and local policy directions, the city administration began providing some support and assistance to homesteading projects from the mid-1970s onward. In the early 1980s, the New York City Department of Housing Preservation and Development (HPD) accepted and incorporated the Urban Homesteading Program into its experimental "Alternative Management Programs." According to this model, homesteaders had to provide proof of support from a sponsoring local organization in order to receive support from HPD. The homesteaders committed to providing several hours per week of sweat-equity labor, and they contributed financially through monthly dues of $50 per homesteading unit (which may be one individual, a couple, or a family). They performed the nontechnical labor as well as some of the more technically skilled labor. Other work was contracted out. Eventually the city sold the building to the homesteaders at a nominal cost. Once rehabilitation work was completed, homesteaders held proprietary leases and shares to the building while assuming responsibility for paying a maintenance fee that also services the loans taken out during the rehabilitation process.

Two aspects are central to an understanding of the dynamics of homesteading on the Lower East Side. One was the arrangement made between homesteaders and the community organization associated with Catholic Charities. In return for technical assistance and financial consulting services, homesteaders agreed to allot some apartments in their building for use by the Catholic Church–linked program Nazareth Home, Inc., which uses them as transitional and permanent apartments for homeless individuals and families from shelters. These individuals and families were not themselves required to participate in the homesteading effort. The other aspect was the no-resale policy associated with membership in the RAIN Community Land Trust.

The housing program for the homeless associated with Nazareth Home and the Community Land Trust were the focus of most of the ideological conflicts surrounding homesteading on the Lower East Side. These conflicts arose from several interrelated issues that evolved throughout the process of homesteading—in particular contestation of gender roles and the concept of ownership.

In homesteading, normative gender roles were challenged and pitted against increasingly self-conscious notions of women's empowerment. Indeed, women played a predominant role in homesteading and occupied various leadership positions. However, the nature and significance of this predominance must be examined.[2] According to Ross and Rapp, the phrase "the personal is political" implies that "the seemingly most intimate details of private existence are actually structured by larger social relations" (1981: 51). This is borne out by the concrete reality of sweat-equity labor in which normative gender roles were reinforced even while they were being challenged.

The concept of ownership was at the center of ideological conflicts in homesteading. Normative middle-class notions of individual rights over property were reinforced in the course of housing rehabilitation, yet they also clashed with the homesteader-organized Community Land Trust's principal tenets of community ownership and control of property. In the process of acquiring ownership of real estate and a greater degree of control over their lives, the lines between haves and have-nots became more sharply drawn. There was a growing tension between a self-conscious shedding of connections to those even less fortunate and a simultaneous sense of shared identification as propertyless and powerless. These tensions and contradictions were played out in an ambivalent questioning of power structures and agencies that were perceived as being partly responsible for the homesteaders' plight. In the evolving resistance to any form of control from "above," the Catholic Charities organization and even RAIN were redefined from a helpful "brother/sister" with the same goals as the homesteaders into powerful, exploitative, and manipulative bodies, which, unlike city agencies and the political-economic structure of the housing market, were concretely visible.

Over the last decade, housing issues have come to be recognized as part of a complex package. This understanding has begun to reshape social science thinking and social policy.[3] In attempts to seek explanations for continued poverty, homelessness, unemployment, or other social and economic problems, the focus has shifted from consideration of a given issue to more contextual analyses. Policy planners and activists are also more inclined to believe that the provision of housing will not solve problems in a lasting fashion unless other matters such as employment, health care, and education are addressed.

Yet an analysis of homesteading on the Lower East Side indicates that in practice as well as in theory, housing is still treated as an isolated problem. This homesteading movement provides insights into the conceptual and actual split between housing on the one hand and a broad range of social and economic issues on the other. Sweat-equity labor, combined with the Community Land Trust concept, was envisioned as a bridge between processes of production through communal efforts and individual ownership of property. The reality of rehabilitating buildings and actually living in buildings completed through homesteading illustrates the futility of addressing homelessness or housing in isolation from other social and economic problems. This includes not only consideration of related economic issues such as the availability of employment and the affordability and availability of health care. One must also consider family dynamics, in particular with regard to gender roles. Formation, maintenance, and survival of such a movement and the directions taken by it can be properly understood only through consideration of the intersections of gender roles, family, and locality.

Hartmann (1981) questioned the concept of the family as an active agent with unified interests. She argued instead that the family should be seen as the locus of struggle over issues of production and redistribution, rather than primarily as a unit shaped by affect or kinship. After all, family members have differing interests that result from differing relations to patriarchy and capitalism. An analysis of homesteading, which straddles private and public worlds, domestic work, and production, must incorporate this concept of family. Equally important in this context, Hartmann pointed out that "capital and the state use the household but do not entirely control it" (1981: 393).

Finally, analysis of the urban homesteading movement provides a look into the dynamics and weaknesses of community organizations and the potential for effecting change through community-based programs. An assessment of this and other community-based efforts to address housing issues must incorporate the context of social policy developments at local, national, and federal levels. This study attempts to bridge the theoretical split between housing and other issues. Further, ethnographic fieldwork and research methods are combined with a social policy analysis in which the macro level of developments is the primary consideration. Explanations for particular developments on the Lower East Side with regard to homesteading must encompass the dynamics at the local level and those at the level of the society and the economy as a whole.

LOISAIDA

The area of the Lower East Side in which the homesteading projects of this research were located extends from Avenue A to Avenue D and from 14th Street to Houston Street (see Figure 1). This area, part of Community District 3 and bordered by the East Village in the north and west and Two Bridges in the south, is known as Loisaida. Street signs indicate the other name of Avenue C, Avenue de Loisaida, a Spanish rendering of "Lower East Side." Two Puerto Rican poets and activists, Chino Garcia and Bimbo Rivas, coined the name *Loisaida* in the early 1970s. This designation was formalized and officially recognized in the public record in 1984 when the Community Board voted to rename Avenue C as Avenue de Loisaida. Bimbo Rivas's poem "Loisaida" attests to the despair as much as to the determination to fight the destruction of the neighborhood.[4]

> Your buildings are
> burning up
> That we got to stop
> Loisaida, my love
> Te amo.

The designation Loisaida was used on the community newspaper and appeared with increasing frequency in various articles and documents from the early 1980s onward.[5] One such example is a film made in 1979 about early efforts to renovate and take control of deteriorating housing stock in the neighborhood. Entitled *The Heart of Loisaida*, the film breathes the idealism, hope and vigor of this movement in its infancy.[6] The heart that I encountered throughout the course of my fieldwork was troubled and torn. The image of a heart, vulnerable and in constant motion, conveyed a basic aspect of homesteading. Indeed homesteading is a fragile process of realizing an idea of home or even community in the face of overwhelming external constraints and internal fragmentation.

RESEARCH METHOD

Although there is an extensive literature on housing-related issues, homelessness, and tenant movements, little in-depth ethnographic work on homesteading has been done.[7] Throughout my fieldwork I was interested in gathering insights into individual personal constructions of homesteading and the way in which such constructions change over time. The main part of fieldwork for this study was done from June 1991 to March 1993. I began working on homesteading projects as a volunteer in January 1989. This work provided me with initial impressions and familiarity with numerous homesteaders. During my fieldwork I followed the actual labor process in homesteading projects through day-to-day exposure to rehabilitation work and through interaction with homesteaders in the course of such work and outside of it. I attended organizational meetings and community meetings. In addition to ongoing informal observation and interviews, I conducted formal interviews with homesteaders; with employees of LESAC, HDI, and various other organizations; and with officials at the New York City Department of Housing Preservation and Development (HPD). The time frame addressed in this study includes the years preceding my fieldwork. The first homesteading group on the Lower East Side was formed in 1978; however, similar efforts under different designations had preceded formal homesteading. The late 1960s and 1970s, when several self-help sweat-equity projects were realized, were formative years in the shaping of the homesteading movement and the vision of a community called Loisaida.

When I began the writing process I had to decide how to convey what I had heard, overheard, or been told in informal conversations and formal interviews by homesteaders and others over the course of the research. Any rendering of ethnographic fieldnotes is a construct; and voices reach the reader only after having been filtered, selected, and staged for best effect. Interviews recorded on tape or on a writing pad are as much the product of the interviewer's presuppositions and dominant concerns as of the respondent's words or silences. In short, I am cognizant of the problems involved when attempting to "repeat truthfully" what someone else has said, not to mention the fact that unedited spoken words when appearing on the printed page have an impact that may not have been intended or foreseen by the speaker.[8] However, I wanted to show to the greatest extent possible the reality of homesteading as I perceived it and as it was conveyed to me. For this reason I have decided to quote directly from my fieldnotes and interviews.[9] Individual speech patterns, repetitions, and incomplete sentences have remained as I heard and recorded them.

OVERVIEW OF CONTENTS

In Chapter 2, I outline the contextual setting for this study of urban homesteading. A brief background on housing and homesteading in the United States is followed by an introduction to the Community Land Trust concept and a discussion of the principal theoretical issues with which I am concerned. In Chapter 3, a historical background of the Lower East Side is presented. Chapters 4 and 5 provide concrete descriptive material about housing rehabilitation through sweat-equity urban homesteading and a discussion of the various issues that affect life in completed buildings. In Chapter 6, I return to this material in order to analyze its significance in terms of individual constructions of homesteading, family and gender roles, property, and community. In Chapter 7, I consider the changing roles of the various community organizations associated with homesteading on the Lower East Side over the years. This, in conjunction with some comparative material on other housing-related organizations in New York City and elsewhere, is the basis in Chapter 8 for an evaluation and assessment of the community-based housing movement in terms of comparable movements and in terms of the movement's significance to a broader set of concerns (e.g., local, national, and federal policies on housing and social welfare).

NOTES

1. This quotation, like others from the Bible quoted in this work, was taken from the *New American Bible.* Confraternity of Christian Doctrine (Washington, DC, and New York: Benziger, Inc., 1970).

2. The feminization of poverty has particular bearing on the understanding of community-based housing movements. See Hartman (1986: 19) on the increase of women as single heads of households and the significance of this trend with regard to housing issues.

3. "Housing studies have never been systematically integrated into the study of social structure as a whole. Much of the blame for conceptual confusion surrounding housing must therefore lie with those who have perpetuated the ghettoization of housing studies within sociology and social administration. The emergence of housing studies as a specialized field has been an unmitigated disaster for the understanding of housing tenure. The sooner housing studies become truly integrated into the study of the sociology of ideology, urban sociology, and the study of the welfare state, to name but a few other specialisms, the sooner are we likely to enrich our understanding of housing tenures" (Dolbeare 1986: 276); for a more broadly based perspective, see Bratt et al. 1986; Bratt 1991; Davis 1991, 1993; and Rosenberry and Hartman 1989.

4. Bimbo Rivas (John Bittman Rivas), a Puerto Rican poet, housing activist, actor, and director and producer of community theater who lived on the Lower East Side until his death in 1992, wrote the poem "Loisaida" in the 1970s. The excerpt is quoted here with the permission of Charas, Inc., New York; it is not

included in a version of the poem published in an anthology of poets from the Lower East Side (Algarín and Holman, eds. 1994). According to Chino Garcia of Charas, Inc., Rivas wrote the poem as a work in progress, continually adding to it in reflection of ongoing developments on the Lower East Side—in this case, the growing rate of arson.

5. A local paper, available free of charge in the neighborhood, is called *The Quality of Life in Loisaida/Calidad de Vida en Loisaida/The Lower East Side Magazine*. A bilingual community publication, it addresses issues of local interest. The publication first appeared in 1977.

6. *The Heart of Loisaida* was filmed and produced by Matias Bienvenida and Marci Reaven in 1979 (New York: Unifilm). The film covers a period in the late 1970s on the Lower East Side of Manhattan during which residents in the neighborhood organized themselves into tenant associations in order to repair and renovate their decayed and landlord-abandoned tenements and to provide services to their buildings.

7. For discussions of homesteading—predominantly from a sociological perspective—see, among others, Borgos 1986; Chandler 1988; Clark and Rivin 1977; Kolodny 1973, 1986; Listokin et al. 1985; Schuman 1986.

8. For a discussion of the crisis of representation in ethnography see Marcus and Fischer 1986.

9. Pseudonyms have been used throughout to protect the privacy of individuals who participated in this research project.

2

HOUSING, URBAN HOMESTEADING, AND COMMUNITY LAND TRUSTS IN HISTORICAL AND THEORETICAL CONTEXT

Housing clearance and housing shortage are alike related to the altered distribution of human settlement which has followed from a set of minority decisions about where work will be made available, by the criteria of profit and internal convenience. What are called regional policies are remedial efforts within these priorities rather than decisively against them. (Williams 1973: 294)

Cityful passing away, other cityful coming, passing away too: other coming on, passing on. Houses, lines of houses, streets, miles of pavements, piled up bricks, stones. Changing hands. This owner, that. Landlord never dies they say. Other steps into his shoes when he gets his notice to quit. They buy the place up with gold and still they have all the gold. Swindle in it somewhere. Piled up in cities, worn away age after age. Pyramids in sand. Built on bread and onions. Slaves. Chinese wall. Babylon. Big stones left. Round towers. Rest rubble, sprawling suburbs, jerrybuilt, Kerwan's mushroom houses, built of breeze. Shelter for the night. No one is anything. (Joyce 1961: 164)

The history of housing is inseparable from the history of economic cycles. The market economy in conjunction with the limited lifetime of inhabitable property provides an arena for conflict. Urban homesteading takes up only a tiny portion of this arena, but reflects many if not all these dynamics. This study of sweat-equity urban homesteading on the Lower East Side in the 1980s and early 1990s must be contextualized historically and theoretically. A brief background on the history of housing in America and in New York City is the basis for a historical overview of homesteading and a discussion of the Community Land Trust concept. The interrelationship of dynamics of class, processes of production, and the creation and maintenance of affordable and inhabitable property presents a starting point for an analysis of the politics and meanings of this housing initiative.

HOUSING IN THE UNITED STATES

The concept of owning one's home has always been an important part of the American Dream. The loghouse homestead built with settlers' own hands and the vision of the little house with a tree in the yard and a cat on the porch have lent enduring resonance to this dream. It combines the notion of an entitlement and historical right to a home of one's own with an image of self-reliance and privacy. Homeownership has become a symbol of reaching adulthood as much as a class marker. People in the United States generally have embraced homeownership as intrinsically desirable; thus, administrations have at times held out opportunities to become homeowners as a means to quell potential urban unrest (Bratt 1989b: 232). In America approximately two-thirds of all householders own their own homes. In 1993, the homeownership rate was 64.6%, unchanged from the rate in 1983 (U.S. Department of Commerce, Bureau of the Census 1994). However, for lower-income families the opportunities for homeownership have been limited, given difficulties in raising money for downpayments and closing costs, obtaining mortgages, and meeting maintenance and tax expenses. The focus on homeownership rates distracts from the obstacles confronted by poor and low-income families who rent their homes in the context of rising rents, inadequate housing, and insufficient incomes to meet expenses.

Key indicators such as homeownership rates among some sectors of the population, displacement because of mortgage foreclosures, rising property taxes, energy bills, health care costs, job loss, and increasing numbers of homeless in America attest to the fact that owning one's own home is more than elusive for poor and working-class Americans (see Blau 1992; Bratt 1989b; Institute for Policy Studies 1989). The rate of mortgage foreclosures doubled between 1980 and 1985. Rents skyrocketed during the 1970s and 1980s; between 1978 and 1985 median rents of all tenant households increased by 93%, for the poorest households—those with annual incomes under $3,000—there was a 147% increase. The high rate of conversions of rental buildings to luxury condominiums and cooperatives during the 1980s has further exacerbated the growing gap between the total supply of low-rent units and households needing such housing. During the 1980s, federal budget allocations for the construction of affordable housing continued to drop, from $32 billion to less than $8 billion in seven years (Bratt 1989b: 4). Meanwhile, middle-class mortgage interest deductions from taxes have come to total as much as $41 billion annually, a hidden form of housing subsidy that dwarfs subsidies to low-income and poor people.

There is an extensive and comprehensive body of literature on the history of housing in America.[1] The following remarks are not intended as a recapitulation of this history. Rather, I attempt to provide a background understanding of grassroots self-help efforts, citizen participation, and community control in the context of shifting dynamics of governmental centralization and decentralization with regard to housing and community development programs. On this basis the development of urban home-steading can be discussed.

According to Marcuse, a large part of the intellectual analysis of housing policy in the United States has been founded on a fundamentally flawed premise. That premise is the myth of the benevolent state:

In brief the myth is that government acts out of a primary concern for the welfare of all its citizens, that its policies represent an effort to find solutions to recognized social problems, and that government efforts fall short of complete success only because of lack of knowledge, countervailing selfish interests, incompetence, or lack of courage. (Marcuse 1986: 248)

Marcuse does not discount lack of knowledge, incompetence, and con-fusion among the factors affecting housing policy; more important, how-ever, he argues that the myth of the benevolent state obscures what he describes as "real categories" underlying the history of housing policies. Meanwhile, the myth of the meddling state that came to the fore during the 1980s was framed around the faith in a free private market and the belief that regulation of housing by the government is a counterproductive and unnecessary form of interference. The myth of the benevolent state, the ideological underpinning of the welfare state, placed the blame for policy failures on design and implementation defects, meanwhile "the myth of the meddling state is no longer concerned to deny the power relationships that the myth of the benevolent state ignored" (Marcuse 1986: 262).

Marcuse suggests a history of housing and housing policies in the United States that focuses on the following major components:

In a historical account using real categories, then, the origins of tenement house reform and housing codes would be found in five different chapters: on the economic role and social assimilation of immigrants; on the growth and arrange-ment of the physical infrastructure of cities, including provisions for handling the external consequences of that infrastructure (this, under the broader category of processes of production); on evolving techniques for the control of deviant individ-ual behavior (following Lubove's emphasis of environmental determinism); and on the devices for insuring domestic tranquility and social-political control of restive groups. (1986: 252)

Given these components, or "categories" (paraphrased here as economic considerations, appeasement, and social control), as a basic perspective, Marcuse indicates how various federal housing acts might be re-analyzed.

For example, with regard to the Section 8 program of the Housing Act of 1974, he argues that it is misleading to describe this program as a well-intentioned low-income housing subsidy program that has gone astray. Instead, this program has "permitted private interests to build, own, and manage housing intended for the poor, with no limits on profit whatsoever besides those nominally imposed by a requirement that rents be based on an administratively determined competitive level" (Marcuse 1986: 257).

Another view at the post–World War II history of housing policy is provided by Mollenkopf, who argues that the stage for the current disastrous state of affairs was set long before the 1980s. He contrasts the pro-growth politics of the Great Society era after World War II, particularly in the 1960s, with the New Federalism era predominant in the 1970s and 1980s. According to Mollenkopf, pro-growth politics and the New Federalism with its clear-cut agenda to reverse as much as possible of policies and programs from the preceding decades were both equally stymied by pre-existing complex webs of programs, making them almost impervious to efforts at reform, intergovernmental relationships, and diverse interest groups (Mollenkopf 1983: 258–259).

Both Marcuse and Mollenkopf point out that the Great Society era, shielded by the myth of the benevolent state, achieved different ends from those it was purportedly striving for—such as urban renewal and provision of decent housing for every family. In the years before 1980, important roadblocks were set for subsequent developments in the history of housing. Of course, it is important not to underestimate the devastating impact of the Reagan years on the state of housing in the United States in general and on community-based housing movements in particular. It is also important to recognize the amount of confusion and contradictions—whether they are the result of practical obstacles or ideological conflict—that diffuse the effects of any administration, be it Republican or Democratic. Yet this should not obscure the element of intentionality, or what Marcuse calls the "real categories," underlying the history of housing policy.

Analysis of federal, state, and local housing policy in the pre–World War II and post–World War II years provides insights into various levels of political agendas revolving around several key issues, employment and unemployment, circuits of capital accumulation in the real estate industry, and social control. For example, Bratt points out that the nation's first major subsidized housing program in 1937 was a strategy to reduce unemployment as a result of the Great Depression as much as it was to create safe and affordable housing for low-income people (Bratt 1989b: 55). Comparable agendas provided impetus for the Housing Act of 1949. The Act emphasized the goal of a decent home and living environment for every family. Efforts at slum clearance and the construction of public housing were thought to further the realization of this goal (Bratt 1989b: 37). At the same time, the increasing availability in the post–World War II period of mortgage insurance and guarantee programs provided a boost to the private housing market; public housing was relegated to the margins as housing for those defined as "permanently poor."

The concept of citizen participation, an ideological cornerstone of more recent housing policy, was included in the Housing Act of 1949 (Bratt 1989b). The Act stipulated that local governments had to ensure participation by citizens in their programs as a prerequisite for receiving federal funds. But over the next few decades no more than token attention was paid to this stipulation, amounting to little more than "citizen manipulation" (Arnstein 1969). Policy implementation was dominated by the notion—generally accepted by government officials—that attempts to accommodate the demands of local people affected by renewal programs were hardly compatible with accomplishing large-scale projects (see Bratt 1989b: 37–49).

The Model Cities program of the mid-1960s, a successor to the War on Poverty program, reveals the internal contradictions of governmental policies that strive for decentralization while at the same time attempting to assert control over local initiatives. The Housing Act of 1965 resulted in the creation of the Department of Housing and Urban Development (HUD), with the goal of having a more effective administrative body to oversee and manage housing programs. "A key goal of Model Cities was to coordinate the array of federal programs targeted to urban areas that had proliferated during the early 1960s. This focus marked the first major attempt to rationalize and centralize a locality's community development efforts" (Bratt 1989b: 43). Precisely how the program's aims were to be achieved remained unclear, particularly the attempt to provide citizens with the opportunity to participate in policymaking. Bratt's discussion draws attention to the unresolved issue of whether it is possible to have citizen participation as the result of a federal mandate. "Can top-down invitations or requirements for resident involvement ever amount to more than tokenism? Is it not true that 'community development,' almost by definition, has to be interwoven with a bottom-up effort?" (Bratt 1989b: 45–46).

In the 1960s it became harder to ignore the fact that urban blight, poverty, and inadequate housing problems continued to spread and that the number of low-income units continued to decline, federal programs for urban renewal and the War on Poverty notwithstanding.[2] There was increasing disenchantment with the bulldozer approach to urban renewal. Even though public policy makers continued to consider rehabilitation of neighborhoods more difficult and cumbersome than clearance and rebuilding, they began to perceive a centralized approach as the root of many problems. This distrust of large-scale efforts under centralized control augured the eventual shift away from the Great Society approach to urban problems to the New Federalism, which came to full flower during the Reagan administration. During the 1970s and 1980s, the federal government encouraged the private sector to increase its involvement in the production of low- and moderate-income rental housing by providing assistance to the mortgage lending industry, insuring and subsidizing loans to private developers, and providing production subsidies and tax incentives. At the same time, the government was gradually disengaging from the construction of public housing (Institute for Policy Studies 1989: 20). These actions, in combination with a withdrawal of most forms of subsidy for low- and moderate-income housing, did little to ameliorate the problem of housing in America while playing into the hands of developers, investors, and landlords.

The New Federalism also found expression in the Housing and Community Development Act of 1974, which shifted the focus from the federal government to state and local administrations and supported a policy in favor of decentralized decision making (Carlson 1978). The Act promoted the Community Development Block Grant (CDBG) program, which was supposed to supplant urban renewal as well as several other social services and environmental programs (see Carlson 1978).

During the 1970s and 1980s, a vast range of local housing programs attempted to meet the ever-increasing gap between incomes and affordable and acceptable housing. Among them were a variety of community-based self-help programs as well as urban homesteading. The desire during the 1980s on part of the administration to reduce holdings of public housing stock by selling off units and by demolishing others once they became unsalvageable through neglect and long-term deterioration (see Hartman 1986) coincided with and, indeed, helped to support the episodic flourishing of such local efforts.

The myth of the benefits of homeownership became the rationale for policy directions from 1974 onward. It was founded on the belief that homeownership was the key to maintenance of property and neighborhood stabilization. The unquestioning veneration in which homeownership has been held provided policy planners with the satisfaction of fulfilling the American dream for deserving Americans while potential homeowners were reaching out for the illusion of security. Kemeny sums up the principal myths associated with the concept of homeownership as "the psychological and 'natural' desire of owning, its inherent security of tenure (and by implication the inherent insecurity of other forms of tenure) and the capital asset which is produced" (Kemeny 1986: 272). According to Mollenkopf, homeownership is "such a righteous, uncontested ideal of the American Dream that alternative forms of housing tenure are not allowed the benefit of public debate" (Kemeny 1983: 297). Therefore, it is all the more remarkable that such debate has arisen repeatedly at the local level. Homesteading on the Lower East Side represents a fascinating union of conflicting ideological concepts; the notion of homeownership, achieved through individual sweat-equity labor, is joined to the concept of cooperatively owned and controlled housing to be attained and maintained through communal labor and community coalitions.

HOUSING IN NEW YORK CITY

It has almost become a commonplace to say that there is a housing crisis in New York City. Disinvestment, reinvestment, displacement, deterioration of housing stock, increasing discrepancies between incomes and rents, and fluctuations in the amounts of federal, national, and local funding for new construction, rehabilitation, and maintenance of housing stock are among the major factors contributing to the crisis. For instance, the number of new dwelling units completed in New York City in the post–World War II period reflects trends at the national level. Construction reached a peak around 1965 and dropped radically thereafter (New York City, Department of City Planning 1991a).

The most visible indicator of the housing crisis is the growing number of homeless people in New York City. Yet it is important to look beyond the illusion of the housing crisis as a very recent phenomenon. The term *crisis* should not be understood to mean that large-scale homelessness developed suddenly. In reality it has been of long standing, exacerbated by many factors in the last few decades. Data on homelessness serve as a chilling illustration of the extent of the crisis. In 1992 the Coalition for the Homeless counted 67,000 living on the streets of New York City and/or as squatters and 23,000 in city-run shelters. The 1990 U.S. Census, much maligned for severely undercounting the homeless as well as other population groups, found 23,383 in New York City shelters and 33,830 on the streets—and a total of 228,621 homeless in the entire United States, of which 49,000 were said to be living on the streets. In 1989, estimates of people living doubled-up in New York City ranged from about 69,000 to 103,000 (Weitzman 1989: 12). This latter figure represents an aspect of the housing crisis that is often conveniently overlooked. Many homesteaders live under such strained circumstances.

An important factor in the housing crisis is that many city-owned buildings are badly managed and continually deterioring (Weitzman 1989). In part this is due to an aging housing stock. Approximately 60% of New York City's housing stock was built at least 35 years ago. Nearly 40% of all renters live in tenements constructed before 1929, including 183,059 units in old-law tenements or 9.4% of all units (Stegman 1991). Old-law tenements are walk-up apartment buildings constructed before the passage of the Tenement House Act of 1901. New York City lost nearly 360,000 rental apartments between 1970 and 1984 through demolition, condemnation, fire, abandonment, or the merger of two or more apartments (Brower 1989). Fully 21% of low-rent units were lost between 1978 and 1987 (Weitzman 1989).[3]

The number of new dwelling units constructed in New York City on an annual basis is an indicator of and partial explanation for the continuing housing shortage. In the city the last high in new housing construction was reached in 1928; the number in 1989 was less than half of what was built in 1965, and less than a quarter of the total from 1928 (New York City,

Department of City Planning, 1991a). New housing construction continued to decrease during the 1980s, reaching the lowest level in the past 50 years. In Community District 3, known as the Lower East Side, which includes Loisaida, Two Bridges, Chinatown, and Little Italy, 947 new units were constructed in 1979; in 1989 the number was 563. In the years 1980–1982, construction of new dwelling units on the Lower East Side had dropped to zero. During those years, deterioration and abandonment of existing housing stock escalated. Ironically, in the same years the New York Department for Housing Preservation and Development (HPD) became involved in a decal program for abandoned buildings in the Bronx. From 1980 to 1983, 300 vacant buildings were decorated with decals of flower pots in windows and other indices of domestic felicity, which were visible to people driving by the area (Plunz 1990).

Frequently, even though funds are available in theory, bureaucracy, red tape, and sheer mismanagement block the use of housing funds. In 1991, according to an informal Housing and Urban Development (HUD) review of two major housing and community developments, New York City had accumulated $7.2 billion in unspent federal funds (Gruson 1992). Accusations and counteraccusations between HUD and HPD abound; the discrepancies between their administrations are compounded by differences on cost issues. According to one HPD official, between 1984 and 1992 the Department completely rehabilitated vacant city-owned buildings (4,500 units) at an average per-unit cost of approximately $65,000. The federal housing agency refused to finance projects that call for spending more than $57,856 to build or renovate a two-bedroom unit, making federal rules restrictive in view of the real estate and construction costs in New York City (Gruson 1992).

According to New York City's Ten-Year Housing Plan drawn up in the mid-1980s, fully 252,000 units were to be created or preserved by 1996; of these, 84,000 units were to be the result of new construction and 168,000 the result of preservation efforts. New York City committed an unprecedented and impressive amount ($5.1 billion) to the goal of improving the housing situation. However, only 9.3% of all new non-homeless housing may be affordable to those households in New York earning less than $19,000 annually (42% of all households) (see Weitzman 1989; Brower 1989). As a result, racial and ethnic minorities in New York City—including Puerto Ricans on the Lower East Side—will continue to suffer from the lowest number of housing opportunities and the greatest need.

HOMESTEADING IN AMERICA

The concept of homesteading has existed in America since 1842. It was adopted as a formal policy to assist settlers in Florida in becoming owners of land in the Armed Occupation Act of 1842, and it was further revised by the Rural Homestead Act of 1862 (see Clark and Rivin 1977). Congress encouraged families to settle in the western territories by offering them 160 acres of free land if they would build a homestead on it (see Jacobs et al. 1982).

The original Homestead Act of 1862 was based on the belief that every person has a right to a piece of the soil. This was a basic investment on which he or she could then build equity. Homeownership not only provides shelter and perhaps a source of pride, but it is an "equity accumulation device," according to Sternlieb. (Clark and Rivin 1977: 16; see also Sternlieb 1974)

Th Homestead Act of 1862 was based on several key assumptions. One was the notion that homesteading would help neighborhoods. Tenants were thought to have less incentive for maintaining their environments than homeowners, and renting was associated with transient people without roots in the neighborhood. The Homestead Act was based on the notion that homeowners would have a built-in incentive to improve their surroundings. The other assumption in the Act, that is, the notion of homeownership as an investment and "equity accumulation device," contradicts the first one. Selling a house is a way to realize the increased value a home may gain over time. Rootedness in and commitment to a neighborhood through security in one's own home are diametrically opposed to the view of housing as a marketable commodity. This contradiction escaped the notice of those who forged the Homestead Act.

The Homestead Act of 1862 became the legal precedent in the development of a homesteading program in post–World War II America. However, homesteading was only adopted for urban use in 1974. Its precursors were self-help and sweat-equity programs. The first mutual and self-help housing project in the United States was the Westmorelands Homesteads project in Norveld, Pennsylvania, in 1933 (it was completed in 1940). It comprised homes built by unemployed coal miners (Turner and Fichter, eds. 1972). In 1945 an Indianapolis settlement house initiated a sweat-equity program known as Flanner House; it resulted in the construction of family homes during the 1950s and early 1960s. In 1965 Better Rochester Living, Inc. (BRL), a private nonprofit organization in New York City, initiated a program of building rehabilitation in which tenants' labor was utilized.

In 1968 Congress called on HUD to prepare a study of self-help programs in the United States. The subsequent report found that self-help methods if properly applied could contribute to the production of housing and the elimination of poverty and homelessness. Nonetheless, HUD remained reluctant to actively support self-help programs, having little interest in programs involving relatively small numbers of housing units.

In 1968 Joseph Coleman, then planning commissioner in Philadelphia (and according to Clark and Rivin, the person "most often credited with first articulating the concept"), presented a paper on urban homesteading to the Philadelphia Planning Commission (Clark and Rivin 1977). In this paper, which presents urban homesteading as having great potential, Coleman stressed that it must involve all levels of government as well as the private sector in order to succeed. This indicated foresight. Seven years later, in 1975, it became apparent to some that official approval of urban homesteading did not necessarily result in constructive assistance. In a discussion of homesteading up to 1975, Davis has criticized the government for not providing much financial aid, technical advice or training. He argued that building rehabilitation through urban homesteading as it existed at that point basically placed the entire responsibility on poor and low-income people (Davis 1975). Furthermore, neither the federal government nor any of the state governments had initiated a comprehensive administrative and legal framework for urban homesteading. Hence, it was doomed to remain in an experimental stage.

Section 810 legislation, passed in 1974, provided for an experiment in urban homesteading to be implemented by HUD; it was initially designed to make use of vacant one- to four-family properties acquired by HUD through default on Federal Housing Administration–insured mortgages. The federal government would provide properties, but no funds for rehabilitation and administration of such properties. The Section 810 program defined limitations and requirements regarding urban homesteading program management, targeting of specific neighborhoods, and sources of funding that, among other factors, kept urban homesteading programs on a small scale across the nation. "Faced with such conditions, the subject cities did not have much room to maneuver. CDBG funds were overwhelmingly used to operate the program; a minimal number of neighborhoods, properties, and individuals could be helped" (Chandler 1988: 57–58).

The switch to an emphasis on local discretion with regard to allocation of funds occurred in the aftermath of criticism of Great Society programs. Urban homesteading was one of a range of self-help efforts that were developed during the 1970s and 1980s in conjunction with the Community Development Block Grant program; however, these efforts remained on a very small scale (Bratt 1989b: 180). Others included various forms of cooperative conversions of buildings with tenants living in their apartments. The Tenant Interim Lease program (TIL) is one such process whereby tenants take over the management of their building and later become cooperative owners. There have been various forms of local efforts at building rehabilitation for low- to middle-income tenants, not necessarily involving labor on part of these tenants. Rehabilitation of abandoned buildings is somewhat different from moderate rehabilitation of occupied buildings. Sweat-equity is not a component of all or, indeed, many self-help programs, and the total number of units constructed through sweat-equity programs is minuscule in light of the need for low-income housing (see Bratt 1989b).[4]

However, the concept of self-help has expanded the repertoire of strategies that can be utilized by community-based groups and organizations.[5]

Much of the vitality of early homesteading efforts was a result of local activism on part of grassroots coalitions and residents. This activism succeeded in turning the growing inventory of vacant federally owned houses, generated mainly by foreclosures of mortgages insured by the Federal Housing Administration (Borgos 1986: 431), into a political asset. It helped to convince city, state, and federal authorities to support urban homesteading. It was perceived as an alternative that was far more palatable, politically speaking, than the vision of energetic and noisy squatters demonstrating in front of boarded-up buildings or, even more embarrassing to the authorities, simply walking in and taking over.

ACORN, the Association of Community Organizations for Reform Now, has played a notable role in this history (Borgos 1986). Squatting was used by ACORN as an effective protest tactic. As Borgos puts it, the government's response was to "tame" squatting by "licensing it within a restricted context" and giving it an official identity as "homesteading" (Borgos 1986: 430). For HUD, the urban homesteading program was a tool by which to channel the politically volatile squatting movement. Meanwhile, the program remained small and tended to favor applicants who by virtue of their incomes were able to meet the criterion of having the "capacity to repair," the other criterion being "housing need." According to Borgos, "local officials concluded that providing homesteads to a tiny cadre of young, upwardly mobile families was a more prudent course than an ambitious low-income effort, and HUD did nothing to discourage this view" (Borgos 1986: 432). The "Guide to Federal Housing Programs" stated that urban homesteading families would have to have the resources to repair and maintain the homes, and therefore "the program may not be suitable for very low-income families" (Jacobs et al. 1982: 277). A HUD report in 1979 claimed to have found evidence that urban homesteading may even be "aggravating the problem of displacement of neighborhood residents." This is, after all, not a surprising conclusion in view of the fact that HUD policy on urban homesteading was aimed at middle-income families, thereby contributing to gentrification of neighborhoods and displacement.

The history of the ACORN squatters movement in the late 1970s in Philadelphia as presented by Borgos indicates a degree of success. In the course of several cycles of squatting and political bargaining with the city by increasingly sophisticated and organized ACORN activists, the so-called Philadelphia model of urban homesteading was developed. This model envisioned homesteading as a housing program rather than as a property rehabilitation program. The main components of the model as described by Borgos are (1) restriction of eligibility to low- and moderate-income families, (2) sufficient time to facilitate homesteads to meet housing codes, (3) financial assistance for rehabilitation, (4) production quotas dependent on a city's size, administrative capacity, and level of abandonment, and (5) aggressive solicitation of houses, that is, accelerating the tax foreclosure process of privately owned and tax-delinquent buildings or developing alternatives to it. During the early 1980s, squatting campaigns by local ACORN organizations in as many as 13 cities sparked reanalysis of local urban homesteading programs. A recurring obstacle was the Section 810 legislation as interpreted by HUD, which resulted in restricting homesteading to a few targeted neighborhoods. "HUD's regulations did not prohibit a more expansive approach to homesteading, but they strongly encouraged neighborhood targeting, as did HUD program literature and the agency's field officials" (Borgos 1986: 440). The ACORN campaign succeeded in bringing about a reshaping of this legislation and hence the entire federal homesteading program. Nonetheless, urban homesteading's impact on housing supply has remained limited.

Urban homesteading programs in Detroit, Philadelphia, and Baltimore among others were bedeviled by the disjunctions between federal guidelines and local requirements, despite discretion on many issues left to local communities. Wilmington, Delaware was the first city in the United States to incorporate urban homesteading into its housing program in the early 1970s. Subsequent programs in other cities were designed as small-scale pilot programs. Bratt points out that urban homesteading programs as well as sweat-equity programs have been difficult to implement.[6] Her less-than-sanguine assessment is corroborated by Chandler, among others:

Section 810 Urban Homesteading cannot be singularly charged with failing to improve low-income housing standards and upgrade neighborhoods. Its impact has always been limited by federal resource allocations, local conditions, and its own scope as a narrow-purpose program. . . . Even at its best, Urban Homesteading can be expected to have only a minor impact upon the complex housing problems of our society. (Chandler 1988: 147)

Although urban homesteading with its dominant theme of self-reliance may appear to have been tailor-made for the 1980s, fitting in superbly with the administration's approach and proclaimed set of values, it is important to remember that it grew out of the community activism of the 1960s. Bratt argues that the federal government made use of the concept of citizen participation not so much in order to make it a component of policy decisions but rather as an outlet for the burgeoning grassroots mobilization (Bratt 1989b: 35). Consequently, in the 1970s and early 1980s grassroots movements across the country were provided with some unexpected breathing space. Bolstered by the myth of the meddling state, the federal and local governments were glad to shift much of the burden for social programs—and, in particular housing—to community-based organizations. This did not mean, however, that bureaucratic regulations and stipulations were simplified or that a great deal of financial and other assistance to grassroots efforts was forthcoming. Nonetheless, local and publicly voiced outrage for continued problems and outright failures of housing programs could be rechanneled and blame placed on more immediate and visible local organizations rather than on city, state, and federal administrations.

During the early 1970s, planners and theorists associated with HUD asked several questions about the purpose of homesteading (Clark and Rivin 1977: 2). Was urban homesteading's principal role to provide a method for neighborhood stabilization, or to provide a way to recycle houses and increase a city's tax base? Was homesteading to perform an economic or a social role? This perceptual split between economic and social programs is revealing; it is central to an understanding of developments on the Lower East Side. Equally revealing, at that time policy makers, planners, theorists, and activists alike considered homesteading a tool of sorts, with the manifest goal of creating tenant-controlled housing not necessarily of primary importance. The stated goal, the creation of low-income community-controlled housing, reflected only one (albeit major) aspect of their agenda. Homesteaders found themselves trapped in between conflicting agendas. On the one hand, the city administration intended homesteading as a means to further the goal of neighborhood stabilization, recycle housing stock, and increase the city's tax base. On the other hand, activist groups considered homesteading a means for gaining control of housing stock in a neighborhood and for creating an empowered and politically active support base in a given locality.

Kolodny studied nine conversion projects of the late 1960s and early 1970s (Kolodny 1973). Each involved occupied buildings, and sweat-equity rehabilitation work was not an element in every one of these projects. However, Kolodny's assessments there are some parallels to actual and potential failures and successes of homesteading projects. According to Kolodny, a movement by tenants to gain control over housing through a cooperative model would have a chance of success if six critical conditions were satisfied:

1. continued tenant participation in the project's development;
2. availability of financing at below-market rates and with adequate speed in processing so that projects would not be held up in trying to put a financing package together;
3. a rehabilitation project calibrated to incomes of the tenants that are supposed to benefit from it;
4. avoidance of officially imposed neighborhood criteria on the project;
5. availability of professional and technical assistance;
6. a continued self-help, ad hoc quality of the project while not sacrificing efficiency (Kolodny 1973).

My study of urban homesteading on the Lower East Side illustrates the applicability of these criteria in that each of the points has been a source of difficulty. Kolodny further argued that officially condoned self-help sweat-equity projects could not only help in lowering costs of rehabilitation but would also channel independent efforts, which would otherwise continue without official input and hence run afoul of certification requirements. A more cynical way of putting this is to say that federally and locally approved urban homesteading was a way to domesticate independent grass-roots efforts that were seeking control over housing. The question to be considered in the following chapters is whether urban homesteading on the Lower East Side is indeed to be understood as little more than "tamed squatting."

Homesteading in New York City

In 1969 Father Robert Fox led a group of would-be tenants in East Harlem in the rehabilitation of two fire-damaged and derelict buildings on East 102nd Street. Father Fox initially funded the property acquisition out of the pockets of the would-be tenants; municipal loans were sought only in 1971 (Lawson 1984). This represents the prototype of sweat-equity housing rehabilitation. On the Lower East Side there were two early, trial sweat-equity projects. The first one in 1967 had not been cleared with the city; another one, at 522 East 6th Street, was started in 1972 and became mired in funding and administrative problems. In 1974 the first successful sweat-equity project was started on 519 East 11th Street. Three others on 11th Street followed in 1976. Housing rehabilitation efforts by the Harlem Renegades and Banana Kelly in the 1970s helped to make the concept of urban homesteading more concrete. In 1977 a waiver was obtained from HUD with regard to the Davis-Bacon requirement, according to which the receipt of federal funding mandates payment of prevailing union wages and use of union labor. This would have been incompatible with the premise of sweat-equity and voluntary labor used in housing rehabilitation to reduce costs (Lawson 1984). In 1980, HPD supported four urban homesteading demonstration buildings in Manhattan Valley between 108th and 109th Streets.

The Urban Homesteading Assistance Board (UHAB) played a critical role in New York City's urban homesteading program (see Laven 1984). UHAB is a nonprofit housing organization that was established in 1973. It has been active in providing advocacy and technical assistance services to self-help housing groups. UHAB's assistance was a central component of the urban homesteading program formally launched by HPD in 1981. Initially the program provided a budget of up to $6,000 per unit. Later that amount was increased to $10,000. In 1983 HPD announced the first public offering plan, a so-called Request for Proposals (RFP), an invitation to community groups to become involved and to draw on HPD resources for homesteading projects. Another Request for Proposals was announced in 1986.

The Department of Alternative Management Programs (DAMP) at HPD is an umbrella for several vehicles for the utilization of housing stock that the city has amassed.[7] These vehicles are based on HPD's position that it wants to manage the least number of buildings possible; the city considers building management too time-consuming, inefficient, and not cost-effective. DAMP includes the Tenant Interim Lease program (TIL), the Community Management Program, a program for moderate rehabilitation of occupied buildings, Mutual Housing Associations, and programs for vacant buildings, one of which is urban homesteading.

Between 1980 and 1991 DAMP sold 31 buildings with 261 units to various groups, and there were another 17 buildings with 120 units in progress. In the area of Community Board 3, a total of 15 buildings were sold by 1991. One HPD official also pointed out that not all buildings in urban homesteading are handled by DAMP. There are various departments within HPD, with a main split between the Office of Property Management and the Office of Development. Some of the buildings in urban homesteading are obtained from the Office of Development, others from the Office of Property Management. Hence, there is a certain amount of confusion and overlap. This is reflected in the problems experienced by individual projects.

Another HPD official drew attention to the experimental nature of the urban homesteading program as far as HPD was concerned. In 1991, out of a total workload of buildings managed by the city, the Urban Homesteading Program involved only 2.6%. To emphasize what a small and insignificant part homesteading is in the overall picture of housing in New York City, the official stated that in 1991 out of a total of 6,645 buildings managed by HPD, 2,800 were vacant and 3,850 were occupied. Of these DAMP handled 628 buildings, and no more than 17 buildings were being homesteaded at that time.

Essentially, HPD's position was that homesteading is not an effective way to solve the pressing housing crisis. There have been too many confrontations and antagonistic relations with various groups, although this was not the main issue according to the HPD official. HPD argued that too many requests for projects are not sufficiently persuasive in view of the time it takes to homestead a building and the speed with which HPD could, should and does "churn out" housing units. "We have to be a machine about it, keep churning out apartments, and when a little robot comes in our way, that should not stop us." Therefore, according to HPD, homesteading was not an appropriate method given the context of need and time constraints.

Further, the HPD official argued that HPD has been forced "to do more with less"—in 1980 the federal government allocated approximately $30 billion to housing nationwide; by 1992 this figure had shrunk to $7 billion.

The official claimed that HPD nonetheless managed to keep up production. New York City has tried to respond to the cutback by designating more money for housing—$5 billion in the Ten-Year Housing Plan of 1986—than the next largest 50 cities combined. Hence, homesteading with its focus on small buildings with four to five floors on the average is not considered to be of primary importance. HPD officials left little doubt that in their view urban homesteading was commendable in theory but hardly feasible in practice, and they were quick to point out that delays and problems in individual projects could invariably be traced back to local organizations' and/or homesteaders' actions or failure to act.

On the Lower East Side, urban homesteading has run its course for the time being. Thirteen buildings have been completed under the auspices of LESAC as sponsoring agency, and another 15 have been completed under the auspices of the Urban Homesteading Assistance Board. There are very few abandoned buildings available for homesteading; those that are vacant have been for the most part appropriated by other rehabilitation programs or deemed unsuitable for rehabilitation. The outlook for the future of completed buildings is disturbing, given renewed escalation of owner disinvestment and housing abandonment between 1988 and 1992—particularly in poorer communities—in New York City.[8] Even though the Lower East Side has experienced a period of relative stability as compared to other poor neighborhoods in the city, the early 1990s indicate renewed increases in the number of mortgage foreclosures and tax delinquencies (White et al. 1992).

COMMUNITY LAND TRUSTS

During a casual conversation with a homesteader about the Community Land Trust (CLT) concept, she said that this model of land tenure was successfully used before, somewhat sweepingly referring to the Middle Ages. I was intrigued by this claim of spiritual kinship with a land-holding structure in a very different time and location. Indeed, rural land-holding structures in Northwestern Europe before 1800 bound individuals and families in such a way that land held by them could not be freely disposed of (Smith 1967). Of course, although the affiliation with land provided a form of security in that it was inalienable, it also symbolized an inescapable bond the disadvantages of which my interlocutor may not have realized. The homesteader may also have been invoking the writings of the nineteenth-century politician and social philosopher Henry George, who is counted among the spiritual ancestors of the CLT concept. George argued that during the Middle Ages it was possible to have security in the use of land and its proceeds without having ownership:

Give a man security that he may reap, and he will sow; assure him of the possession of the house he wants to build, and he will build it. These are the natural rewards of labor. It is for the sake of the reaping that men sow; it is for the sake of possessing houses that men build. The ownership of land has nothing to do with it. It was for the sake of obtaining this security, that in the beginning of the feudal period so many of the smaller landholders surrendered the ownership of their lands to a military chieftain, receiving back the use of them in fief or trust, and kneeling bareheaded before the lord, with their hands between his hands, swore to serve with life, and limb, and worldly honor. (George 1979: 398–399)

On the basis of the concept of security in reaping "the natural rewards of labor," George, who saw land monopoly as a root cause of poverty in the United States, argued for a separation of use from ownership:

What is necessary for the use of land is not its private ownership, but the security of improvements. It is not necessary to say to a man, "this land is yours," in order to induce him to cultivate or improve it. It is only necessary to say to him, "whatever your labor or capital produces on this land shall be yours." (George 1979: 398)

The Community Land Trust model was conceived on this premise in the late 1960s by founders of the Institute for Community Economics (ICE). Cited among the sources that the founders of ICE have drawn on, are—in addition to George and R. H. Tawney, among other social thinkers and critics—(1) Vinoba Bhave's Gramdan movement, a "land gift" movement in India (a voluntary land reform effort initiated during the 1950s to create "village trusts" to hold land for landless farmers), (2) the Jewish National Fund, which owns a large part of Israel's agricultural land and leases land to rural communities, (3) the conservation land trust movement in the United States, (4) land-banking experiments in Scandinavia, and (5) Native American concepts of land stewardship.

The Community Land Trust model is a community-based homeownership initiative. The basic tenets of a Community Land Trust were laid out in the ICE handbook of 1982. A Community Land Trust acquires land by purchase or donation and holds it for the benefit of a community and individuals within it. The objective is to remove the land from the speculative market. Leaseholders may own the buildings on the land and any improvements made to them; however, there are restrictions on the inflation of such improvements along with the private market (Institute for Community Economics 1982: 18–19).

Community Land Trusts have been formed in rural areas in order to secure access to land and housing for low-income people, preserve family farms and farmland, and facilitate sound, long-term timber management. Urban Community Land Trusts have been formed to combat speculation and gentrification, preserve and develop low- and moderate-income housing, and maintain useful urban open spaces. More recently several trusts are being developed in highly contested second-home areas and prime vacation land such as in Jackson Hole, Wyoming, and in the southern Berkshires in Massachusetts (Mavrides 1993). Although housing is only one of the uses of Community Land Trusts, it is probably the most prevalent (Bratt 1989b: 180).

The goals of a housing program for the 1990s and beyond as set forth by ICE are threefold. One is to provide decent, affordable housing to those in need of it with the essential benefits of homeownership wherever possible. The second is to ensure long-term affordability by controlling transfer costs, protecting the gains made today from being lost to the market tomorrow. The third is to build an economic base in low-income communities, enabling residents to reinvest the fruits of their labor and benefit from their own economic development efforts. The Community Land Trust model addresses these three goals by providing the security of lifetime tenure, fair equity based on actual investments and home improvements, and a legacy for descendants and the future.

In 1993 approximately 70 Community Land Trusts were estimated to be in operation in the United States, with another 31 being developed (Mavrides 1993). Major cities with operating Community Land Trusts in varying stages of development include New York, Chicago, Dallas, Boston, Philadelphia, and Washington, DC. By 1994 in New York, the RAIN Community Land Trust on the Lower East Side and the East Harlem Homesteaders represent the only attempts to employ the Community Land Trust model, unless one includes various Mutual Housing Associations in this category.[9] The East Harlem Homesteaders represent an effort to form a Community Land Trust during the late 1980s, which eventually faded out of existence; some preparatory work had been done, but the effort fell apart when it came to the actual realization of building projects. The Community Land Trust RAIN has been in existence for little more than a decade. In the early 1990s it became nearly invisible as an active organizational body on the Lower East Side; the difficulties experienced by it are indicative of the potential weaknesses of others in urban areas as well as nationwide.

THE DYNAMICS OF CLASS, PROCESSES OF PRODUCTION, AND THE CREATION OF INHABITABLE PROPERTY

Homesteading—building a home through cooperative efforts of people in the neighborhood—is a powerful symbolic concept. It evokes the image of barn raising, an activity benefiting an individual family that requires the assistance of the community. The labor process involved, with attendant obligations and commitments for continued exchange of labor and assistance, encapsulates both the physical reclaiming of a living environment and a concrete realization of the elusive concept of "community." Barn raising, in its ritual and actual concretization of the interdependence of members of a locality, bridges the contradiction between private and communal interests. Homesteading carries the same symbolic power, embodying the ties that bind a locality into a community.

The process of homesteading, or housing rehabilitation through sweat-equity labor, enables us to understand the weaknesses of this and other housing movements. Its symbolic power is revealed as a cover masking not only the contradictions of private and communal purposes but also a split between processes of production on the one hand and the dynamics of housing on the other. In the context of a market economy, a none-too-helpful bureaucratic structure, and a powerful set of normative ideological concepts, homesteading through self-help sweat-equity labor—ironically presented by community-based organizations and local, state, and federal administrations alike as contributing to the creation of "community"—is transformed into a private pursuit. Communal labor gives way to individual accumulation. The end product, individual housing cooperatives occupied by low-income tenants who no longer feel part of a cohesive group, is again at the mercy of social and economic forces from which homesteading was supposed to provide a means of escape.

CONCLUSION

The following questions are starting points for an analysis of urban homesteading with regard to this particular local effort and to its viability on a national level. (1) What are the interconnections between the macro level of social, economic, and political dimensions of society and the local level? (2) What are the particular developments of this homesteading movement, and how should they be interpreted? (3) What are the short-term and long-term effects of homesteading on those involved in it?

Interconnections

A consideration of the interconnection between macro and micro levels must begin with a concept of social class, understood here as a "shorthand for a process" (Rapp 1987: 223).

Under advanced capitalism, there are shifting frontiers which separate poverty, stable wage earning, affluent salaries, and inherited wealth. The frontiers may be crossed by individuals, and in either direction. That is, both upward and downward mobility are real processes. The point is, "class" is not a static place that individuals inhabit. It is a process set up by capital accumulation. (Rapp 1987: 223–224)

The manner in which access to housing and control over one's living space is conceptualized and renegotiated reflects and embodies this process of class. Owning a home is tied to notions of social class identity. Loss of one's home, and ultimately loss of control over living space, represents one dividing line between haves and have-nots. Yet for all its ideological weight as a boundary between groups of people conceptualized as utterly different, the distance between homeowners or renters and those without a home—living doubled-up with increasingly resentful family members or friends, in a shelter, or on the street—is not so great. There is a powerful symbolism associated with becoming a homeowner in the ideological context of the American Dream. Homesteading affirms and strengthens normative values of ownership. At the same time, I suggest that the process of seizing control over one's neighborhood and one's housing involves a simultaneous questioning of normative values of ownership, power structures, family, and gender roles.

An analysis of homesteading helps to illustrate the ramifications of class dynamics at the local level. Homesteaders are situated socioeconomically and symbolically between various groups competing for turf in the neighborhood, (e.g., various categories of squatters, developers, and more affluent people buying into the neighborhood in the course of gentrification). Harvey's concept of displaced class struggle, "which has its origins in the work process but which ramifies and reverberates throughout all aspects of the system of relations which capitalism establishes" (Harvey 1978: 115), is particularly important as a dimension of housing conflicts. Housing movements are vulnerable because they are separated conceptually and in practice from processes of production, in terms of both housing production and the wider economy. Critics of urban sweat-equity homesteading, for instance in the city administration, tend to reduce problems experienced in any given homesteading project to interpersonal struggles—"in the privacy of one's home" so to speak. Yet these very struggles are enmeshed with socioeconomic class conflicts at the local level as much as with the dynamics of the market economy at a citywide and national level.

Another perspective on the interrelationship between the macro and micro levels of society is provided by Williams. In his discussion of the concepts of base and superstructure, Williams explores totality and hegemony. In his redefinition of base and superstructure he rejects a layered notion according to which base is seen in terms of a fixed economic or technological abstraction, and superstructure in consequence is perceived as having a specifically dependent content (Williams 1973: 6). Williams argues for a totality that breaks out of this static and layered notion. At the same time, he argues that the notion of a complex whole of social practices easily leads to leaving out processes of intention. "One of the unexpected consequences of the crudeness of the base/superstructure model has been the too easy acceptance of models which appear less crude—models of totality or of a complex whole—but which exclude the facts of social intention, the class character of a particular society and so on" (Williams 1973: 7). Williams lends a different dimension to the concept of totality by analyzing it in conjunction with that of hegemony.

As Williams interprets it, hegemony is not something imposed from above, an ideology that can be isolated. It is a part of social reality, continually adjusting to it and active within it, and deeply invading every aspect of our experiences. Along the same lines, according to Gramsci, "common sense," or what Linger calls "a mishmash of unreflective popular thought," can present a formidable barrier to the transformation of consciousness (Linger 1993: 4). In his study of an election and riot in the Brazilian city Sao Luís, Linger eventually arrives at a conclusion which implies how difficult it is to refashion common sense:

But alternative political arrangements receive only limited support in most são luisenses' sense of how the world works, which is to say in their intensely emotional experience of personal relationships in the domains of family, religion, and work. This experiential starvation of the political imagination, the correlate of hegemony's naturalization of the existing order, makes it hard to turn critical awareness of common sense into counterhegemony. The insights keep vanishing, and the cultural weapons forged get turned back on their makers. (Linger 1993: 18)

In the case of urban homesteading on the Lower East Side, ideological pressures are exerted from within the social context rather than as an outside force that can be resisted or struggled with more easily. Yet hegemony not only produces processes of internalization but also calls forth resistance. When we regard totality as something that involves hegemony and hence the presence of intention in processes of domination, we open up the possibility of finding an oppositional, emergent, non-incorporated culture in the face of a dominant one. In urban homesteading, various levels of internalization and reinforcement of dominant and normative value systems as well as various levels of resistance can be discerned.

In this context, Ortner has provided an illuminating discussion of practice theory (Ortner 1989: 11–18). According to Ortner, practice theory in its fully developed form considers both the external political-economic forces on a society's history and culture and the way in which these forces are internally mediated by cultural patterns and structures of various kinds as well as by social structural arrangements. There is a world of system and structure in which the actors are both acted upon and constituted by this world and at the same time thinking and acting agents, constituting that world on their own terms and investing it with meaning. In my study of homesteading on the Lower East Side, I am concerned with "actors who creatively used a world that was using them" (Ortner 1989: 18).

Interpretations

The second question, or set of questions, concerns an exploration of the developments of this particular homesteading movement and their interpretation in the context of other community-based housing efforts. It is important not to reduce a discussion of homesteading to an analysis based on a success/failure model. How is one to define "failures" and "successes" of homesteading movements and community-based organizations? In other words, why have urban homesteading movements continued to play a relatively minor role in providing solutions to the housing problem? Why did homesteading efforts not receive more support from federal and local administrations even though they appear to have fit in with the prevailing ideology of the 1980s? The works of Gilbert and Ward (1985), Collier (1976), Carmon and Gavrieli (1987), Castells (1978, 1983), Mollenkopf (1983), and Marcuse (1987), among others, suggest answers to these questions, framed around differing interpretations of the meaning and significance of community action, citizen participation, and self-help.

When we consider the history of community action, an image of autonomous communities defending their rights and asserting as well as improving their position in society is misleading. Instead, Collier points out that neighborhoods—and associated constructs of communities—must be understood as nonautonomous, and that the state is in no sense divorced from developments in such localities occurring as the result of community action (Collier 1976).

In a discussion of the role of state intervention in housing issues in three Latin American cities in Colombia, Venezuela, and Mexico, Gilbert and Ward (1985) argue that community action must be understood as forming an important component of "structures of anti-participation" developed by the state as highly effective methods of channeling and controlling participation. Community action is integrated into the state budget and bureaucracy—in other words, becomes institutionalized. Gilbert and Ward's perspective is based on a conceptualization in which the state intervenes on behalf of the poor only under three circumstances: (1) when they pose a threat to social stability, (2) when the state acts in order to foster capital accumulation and the poor benefit indirectly, and (3) when assistance to the poor furthers the interests of the state, for example, by broadening the tax base (Gilbert and Ward 1985: 242–243).

According to Gilbert and Ward, "whatever the virtues of 'urban social movements,' they seem to be thin on the ground" (Gilbert and Ward 1985: 182). They point out that many elements in local housing conditions derive fundamentally not from local decisions but from those taken at an international level. Encouragement of self-help movements became the conventional wisdom of the 1970s at a time when politicians and governmental agencies began to be aware of opportunities for new forms of social control and manipulation of low-income communities through "structures of anti-participation." Community action was encouraged as a way of diffusing unrest and providing an outlet for local activists that succeeded mainly in turning the problem back on itself. Influential support was provided by international funding agencies in the face of the failure of traditional approaches and policies to address the housing needs of the poor. At a national level this has in recent years translated into a growing role played by pro-active foundations in community organizations and community development.

Many self-help housing efforts in the Third World began not only without assistance from the authorities but as illegal operations. Only after some time did governments begin to recognize the benefits of this process and to intervene and legalize some of this activity (Carmon and Gavrieli 1987). Carmon and Gavrieli have a more positive interpretation about this development than Gilbert and Ward. They contrast the formerly predominant, institutionalized solution and the self-help solution sanctioned by the state. The latter provides people with the opportunity to transform themselves from passive users of services to active participants with a degree of control over their own lives. When analyzing these different interpretations on the role of the state in encouraging self-help efforts, one must remember that Carmon and Gavrieli talk mainly about the situation in Israel, and that Gilbert and Ward focus on Latin America. Although certain parallels may be discerned in the role of the state in these various settings, they are also characterized by vastly different political, economic, and social contexts. The same caution applies to transposing Carmon and Gavrieli's arguments to analyses of community action and housing movements in the urban United States.

Nevertheless, Marcuse among others has put forth similar arguments about the state's manipulative role with regard to community action. He says, "self-discipline is cheaper than external discipline, and neighborhood policy can be a cheap way to promote it" (Marcuse 1987: 285). He argues that decentralization when created from above tends to strengthen the power of central political leadership (Marcuse 1987: 282). Decentralization does not significantly alter the distribution of power or resources, but it can enhance feelings of self-confidence and empowerment by providing an illusion of power. Other writers such as Castells and Mollenkopf arrive at different conclusions. They argue—albeit from different perspectives—that community action in low-income communities can create a springboard for effective mobilization and a consciousness-raising "training ground." Castells sees urban social movements as originators of alternative political and cultural systems, although these movements themselves are not agents of structural social change, being limited and defined by their inevitable institutionalization within a dominant system (Castells 1983: 328). He argues that intervention by the state in grassroots movements does not regulate the process but "exacerbates contradictions and politicizes the issue" (Castells 1978: 174). He draws attention to the need for considering the realm of personal experience. According to Castells, grassroots movements provide a grounding in reality by returning to the local level of concrete, personal experience:

So, faced with an overpowered labour movement, an omnipresent one-way communications system indifferent to cultural identities, an all-powerful centralized
state loosely governed by unreliable political parties, a structural economic crisis,
cultural uncertainty, and the likelihood of nuclear war, people go home. Most
withdraw individually, but the crucial, active minority, anxious to retaliate, organize
themselves on their local turf.... Thus, urban movements do address the real issues
of our time, although neither on the scale nor terms that are adequate to the task.
(Castells 1983: 330–331)

Mollenkopf also asks whether communities act, and he answers this in
the affirmative. He argues that housing interests and a shared locality can
serve as a spur for action (Mollenkopf 1983: 14). There is more going on than
just "the danger of locality-based action in functioning not to reinforce class
struggle, but to divert, divide, obscure and suppress it" (Mollenkopf 1983:
23). According to Mollenkopf, localities have their own logic that is somewhat different and independent from the logic of class struggle. Although
capital accumulation plays a dominant role, there is a second set of relationships—one of social interaction and community formation—that causes
tension between distinct, unequal, and ultimately opposing logics of accumulation and community (see Mollenkopf 1983: 291).

In describing conflicts over housing and the struggle for homeownership, Mollenkopf speaks of the creation of a space for life outside capitalist
production that "can spur great leaps in political consciousness, forging
links of solidarity among disparate groups and distant neighborhoods and
pushing the conflicts of the place of residence out of the 'city trenches' that
protect the centers of power in capitalist society" (Mollenkopf 1983: 305).
According to Mollenkopf, it is possible to articulate a counter-ideology that
goes beyond the local level. However, concrete evidence for effective articulation of a counter-ideology beyond the local level is hard to come by.

Castells argues that grassroots movements are important not so much by
virtue of what they accomplish—which according to Castells is little—but
as dimensions of resistance. This perspective is problematic in that it can
obscure concrete reality through the emphasis on attitudes, interpretations,
and views on the local and personal level (i.e., relative states of poverty and
wealth, domination, and freedom to act are in the mind, or a matter of
perspective). Although I myself am interested in the local and personal level
of experience, I am at the same time wary of interpretations that are not
securely rooted in the contextual setting—the social, economic, and political
reality that partially defines and imposes limitations on consciousness.

Perspectives on an Assessment of the Short-Term Effects
of Homesteading

In order to break out of this theoretical dead end, I return to the local
level and consider what actual short-term and long-term significance

homesteading has for individuals, groups, and neighborhoods involved in it. Are the concepts of empowerment and self-help nothing but ideological traps to distract and occupy the restless poor? Is sweat-equity urban home-steading little more than the first stage in gentrification (see Feagin 1986: 111)? Where can one look for answers to these questions without getting lost in speculations about the level of personal experience on the one hand and abstract assumptions about the articulation of a counter-ideology at a wider social level on the other?

Homesteaders, employees of community organizations, and other inter-locutors repeatedly pointed out to me that every individual on the Lower East Side has a different story to tell about homesteading. I tried to keep this in mind in my portrayal, paying tribute to the validity of different voices. Yet their various perspectives, stories, and experiences also form a meaningful whole and help answer the above questions.

The urban homesteading movement on the Lower East Side offers lessons on the potential strengths and weaknesses of housing movements and community organizations. For homesteaders themselves, the experi-ence of homesteading shed light on the political and economic processes of housing production and the acquisition of property. At the same time, the concept of sweat-equity is of critical significance because it only *appears* to bridge the gap between housing and other central issues, for all that it affords homesteaders a potentially transformative experience with which to question normative conceptualizations of ownership, processes of pro-duction, and relations of power.

NOTES

1. Among others, see Bratt, Hartman, and Meyerson 1986; Dear and Allan 1981; and Bratt 1989b.

2. The number of public housing units produced annually reached a high of 91,000 units in 1971 (Bratt 1989b: 61). But a focus on the number of units produced in the late 1960s and early 1970s is deceptive, because this period of construction was relatively short lived. From the 1970s onward, production declined radi-cally—to a low of 6,229 units in 1977; a high of 44,019 units in 1979; and 10,415 units in 1987 (Bratt 1989b: 57). The private sector played an increasingly important role in the development of housing units; from 1965 onward, one-third of all new housing units was constructed by developers.

3. "In contrast to this decrease in low-rent apartments, the number of units renting for $500 or more per month affordable only to people earning $20,000 or above—the 1986 median household income for New York City—jumped by more than 93,000, or 26%. Units affordable to the top fifth of the population—those renting for $1,000 per month or more—rose by 11,000 units, or more than 30%" (Weitzman 1989: 42).

4. "In another group of cooperative conversions, *sweat-equity*—community people and tenants donating their labor to rehabilitate buildings—has been an important part of the process. Here, the goals of providing housing and tenant

ownership opportunities are merged with a potential for job training and employment. Despite the immediate appeal of this approach, sweat equity projects have been difficult to implement. As of 1981, between 500 to 1,000 units constituted the entire sweat equity, or urban homesteading, effort" (Bratt 1989b: 177).

5. See Kolodny for a critical history of the development of self-help strategies in the United States, which "include resident management of public housing projects and tax-foreclosed multiple dwellings, conversion of rental buildings to tenant-owned cooperatives, sweat-equity urban homesteading, and a number of variations on user-initiated and -controlled housing development and management" (Kolodny 1986: 447).

6. "In a second HUD demonstration, also based on New York City's experiences, six cities were selected to undertake sweat equity rehabilitation programs. Sumka and Blackburn (1982) found that the results of the demonstration were mixed, with only two cities establishing ongoing multifamily homesteading programs. Thus, while it is significant that HUD attempted to replicate locally initiated ideas, the multifamily sweat-equity and coop conversions programs were not easily repeated in other areas" (Bratt 1989b: 178).

7. According to a March 1993 Community Service Society report, there are indications of a new wave of building abandonments (Bach and West 1993). This assumption is based on increasing signs of financial distress exhibited by rental buildings. One out of six rental buildings in New York City was found to be behind in taxes or mortgage payments, or both. Most of the buildings in jeopardy were in poor neighborhoods, in many of the same areas that had suffered widespread abandonment previously. Although this report focuses on rental units, tenant-owned cooperative buildings with high mortgages as the result of rehabilitation work and high water and sewer fees are equally at risk.

8. "The cyclical downturn in the market is one of several causes contributing to escalating disinvestment and abandonment risks. Growing risks are also the result of overleveraged investment during the 1980s boom; a widening gap between rising operating costs (particularly water and sewer fees) and declining tenant incomes; growing disinvestment by institutional lenders; reduced tax incentives for rental investment; increased drug traffic in residential buildings; and concurrent reductions in public services and programs due to fiscal strains" (Bach and West 1993: x–xi).

9. A Mutual Housing Association is a vehicle for owning and managing several buildings in a cooperative manner. See Chapter 7 for a discussion.

3

PAST AND PRESENT OF THE LOWER EAST SIDE

Fieldnotes, November 10, 1991: Rod passed up buckets from the basement and I passed them on to José. Rod smoked cigarettes, tossed them into the debris, and then occasionally rummaged around in the dirt. He showed me some chicken bones that he found, saying that this tells a lot about what people ate; he showed me a ceramic marble and said that this was one of the few kinds of toys children had. He told me the building was built on a creek; that is why there is so much water. "Go look it up in the big library, the one with the lions, they have maps there which show the swamp and the creek." He told me that during the Civil War years much of the area was landfilled, as German and Irish immigrants came to New York City. Later we took a break. Dolores went to get something to drink. We sat on the crumbling steps outside looking at the dumpster. I asked whether anyone knew more about the swamp. José claimed the building was built on a cemetery. He went on to describe a friend's building a block away and said that they dug 12 feet down and found a boat dock. José used his hands to show the outlines of the dock which was shaped like a boat. "It blew my mind. They poured the foundation on top of this find, so it is still there."

Much of the Lower East Side is built on what is literally shifting ground. Indeed, a number of blocks are constructed on landfill. At times the history of the area surfaces and becomes tangible; in many buildings groundwater swells up into the basement and can only be controlled by installing of a pump. History is visible in the design of tenement buildings, dank, narrow, and poorly ventilated. History can be read in the yellowed pages of newsprint underneath old floor tiles. Just as the tenements were crowded to overflowing for many decades, the history of the Lower East Side is crowded with events and profound demographic, social, cultural, economic, and political shifts within a relatively short time.

Population figures illustrate this point. In 1645 there were no more than 500 people in all of New Amsterdam and none in what is today the Lower East Side. On the Lower East Side, population figures began to escalate in the early 1800s and peaked around the turn of the century; by 1910 as many as 540,000 people were crammed into the tenements of the Lower East Side alone (see Bromley 1910). According to the U.S. Census, by 1970 the population on the Lower East Side had dropped to 174,532; and in 1990 the total was 161,617, reflecting the contraction of the population in New York City and in this particular area. Beyond sheer numbers there were profound shifts of the ethnic, racial, and socioeconomic makeup of the population.

Gordon points out that the history of cities is marked by disruptions rather than continuities. "Urban history advances *discontinuously* [sic], instead of *continuously*, periodically experiencing qualitative transformations of basic form and structure. The current economic crisis and the related urban crisis, from this perspective, are just another in a long series of these kinds of transformations" (Gordon 1984: 22). In this context he describes three successive transformations—from commercial cities to industrial cities to corporate cities—with their attendant contradictions.

In the commercial cities, the poor lived outside the center of commercial and preindustrial activities. In New York the center of activities was on the lower end of Manhattan and along parts of today's Lower East Side. As the industrial city emerged during the mid-nineteenth century, property owners left the center and the poor and working classes were crowded into these centers. In New York this process began in the 1830s, as the first tenement buildings went up. Gordon argues that in the latter part of the nineteenth century, capitalist control over labor was breaking down and strikes were most intense in New York, Illinois, and Pennsylvania. This led to the development of the corporate city, as corporations began to seek other sites for industrial production and labor became decentralized. At the turn of the century, manufacturing moved out of the central cities. Gordon distinguishes between "old cities" such as New York, Pittsburgh, and Philadelphia, which reached maturity during the industrial stage, and "new cities" that could build from scratch, unhampered by the fixed physical capital of older cities (Gordon 1984).

It is important to recognize that the development of industrial cities and corporate cities *and* the development of recent urban crises are linked. The crises in New York in the mid-1970s and late 1980s into the present cannot be reduced to a simplifying concept of urban crises of recent standing. They are historically specific and the outcome of uneven processes of capital accumulation over long periods of time.

Demographic shifts and the fluctuations in population figures in New York City and on the Lower East Side reflect the transformations described by Gordon. The history of housing is an integral part of these transformations even though there are more specific explanations linked, among others, to shifts in federal policy over the last decade. For instance, since 1980 federal housing assistance programs have been cut by over 75% from $32 billion to $7.5 billion.

Tabb, writing about New York City's fiscal crisis in the 1970s, emphasizes the cyclical nature of the economy linked to the contradictions of capitalism. New York City's tremendous loss of jobs between 1969 and 1976 (542,000 jobs) is itself due to, among other factors, (1) the restructuring of the economy from an industrial to a predominantly service economy, and (2) the geographic mobility of capital (Tabb 1984: 333). Industry's quest for profit sought other, more favorable areas for investment. Government subsidies helped industry in this quest, and jobs followed capital and industry. Disinvestment by banks and other financial institutions in New York City's residential real estate market followed major capital shifts by industries that were withdrawing from the city. This was hardly a sudden development. Between 1965 and 1972, New York City had already lost nearly 16% of its jobs (Tabb 1984: 334). From 1977 to 1986, New York City lost 30% of its manufacturing jobs (Weitzman 1989: 30), in addition to 55% of manufacturing jobs between 1960 and 1975. A result of the restructuring of the economy was an increasingly critical mismatch between the job market and the labor pool. Vanishing low-wage manufacturing jobs, a growing need for office workers with more substantial education, and increasing dropout rates among New York City's public school students—as much as 50% in public schools in 1980 (Tabb 1984: 336)—meant fewer jobs available to growing numbers of people.

Puerto Ricans and African Americans were among the population groups particularly affected by underemployment and unemployment. Between 1977 and 1986, Puerto Rican relative income dropped from 50% to 40% of relative income of whites; and Puerto Ricans' real median household income dropped by 4.4%, as compared to a 2.2% drop for all other groups except whites (Weitzman 1989: 30). The effects of these developments and related ones, in particular the deterioration of the city's infrastructure and housing stock, were felt severely in poorer neighborhoods, as the history of housing tends to follow the flow of money and jobs.

HISTORICAL BACKGROUND OF THE LOWER EAST SIDE

Until the 1780s the Lower East Side, in particular much of what is today popularly referred to as Loisaida (Avenue A to Avenue D, and 11th Street to Houston Street), consisted of open marsh and meadowland with many creeks emptying into the East River. Most of Tompkins Square Park was part of this marshland and formed the tip of a triangular shape broadening toward the river to include 3rd Street and 13th Street. The area east of Avenue D, today the site of the East River Park and the FDR Drive, is built on landfill. Other marsh areas were located further south around Clinton

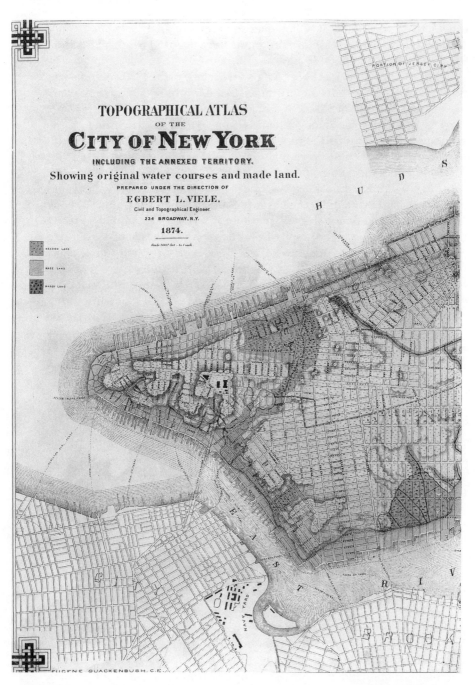

Map 1. Topographical Atlas of the City of New York Including the Annexed Territory Showing Original Water Courses and Made Land. Prepared under the direction of Egbert L. Viele. New York, 1874. On the map the Lower East Side area is a swamp.

and Jefferson Streets. The creeks and ponds in these marshy flats provided most of the fresh water in the early days of New Amsterdam. These sources of water later became cesspools of disease, before the ingenious water-tunnels bringing water to Manhattan from upstate were constructed. One such pond, called the Collect Pond, was used until 1817, when it was filled in and housing built in its place:

The neighborhood occupying what is now Chatham Square was founded as a suburb for the well-to-do, but it was built on the site of the filled-in Collect Pond, and the streets and houses soon began to sag as the fill subsided. By the 1830s the rich had fled. In their wake large numbers of the Irish immigrants were streaming into New York in pursuit of the job opportunities that had been created by the opening of the Erie Canal in 1825. (Sanders 1979: 3)

This episode is a paradigm for more generalized socioeconomic change; housing and related processes can be a revealing lens, both a reflection of and vehicle for these dynamics in the history of urban environments.

In 1651 Peter Stuyvesant, director general of New Amsterdam from 1647 until 1664, was granted a patent for a "bouwerie," a farm that included all the land east of the present-day Bowery, between 4th and 17th Streets.[1] Peter Stuyvesant's farm as well as other farms left their mark in street names of the area: the Bowery, DeLancey, Rutgers, and so on. Aside from the farms there were a few buildings near Corlears Hook and a few further inland around what is today Astor Place. The land directly alongside the river was the area first to be built up, providing housing and employment to early settlers, mostly Dutch and English. The mud flats were filled in over time, and the shoreline was lined with docks, weighing houses, and wharves.

By 1800 most of the landowners and wealthy residents—merchants and traders of the pre-industrial city—had moved out, and poor immigrants were moving in. Peter Stuyvesant's farm became the site of docks and shipyards; today there are garbage plants, incinerators, and power plants in its place. The change in building styles reflects the changing populations and their socioeconomic status. The wooden Dutch houses of the early settlers and farmers had begun to disappear from New York by the early eighteenth century. English red brick townhouses with tiled roofs were built in some areas during the eighteenth century and housed predominantly wealthy residents; only a few of these are preserved. The Great Fire of 1835 took a final toll. Until the early nineteenth century most of the area that today is the Lower East Side was still open land. However, as industry expanded and immigration to the area intensified, the density of housing increased rapidly. Already by the mid-nineteenth century the district was a notorious slum. Charles Dickens described it eloquently in 1842:

What place is this, to which the squalid street conducts us? A kind of square of leprous houses, some of which are attainable only by crazy wooden stairs without.

Map 2. Section Map of New York City showing stables, dockyards, and the like on the Lower East Side around 1879. Prepared by Matthew Dripps. New York, 1879.

What lies beyond this tottering flight of steps, that creak beneath our tread?—a miserable room, lighted by one dim candle, and destitute of all comfort, save that which may be hidden in a wretched bed. (Dickens 1978)

Historical accounts attest to overcrowding, poverty, and disease including cholera and typhus epidemics that ran rampant in the area (see Ford 1971). At the same time—and in a sense because of this history of extreme poverty, overcrowding, and unhealthy conditions—the area has given rise to a wide range of social reform efforts and movements, some of which continue to play an active part in the area today. Of particular interest is the history of settlement houses on the Lower East Side.

Settlements were private voluntary agencies, in the early years staffed predominantly by middle-class white women and financed through a mix of private monies and public funds. Settlements attempted to assist poor urban communities through a variety of services to the unemployed, homeless, sick, youth, and elderly. In fact, a settlement has been described as "a general practitioner" and "a creative instrument of social change" (Hall 1971: 61). It tried to combine the kind of assistance that social workers might provide with a support of local music, theater, and dance efforts. A central tenet of the settlement movement was that founders and fellow workers were to live in the neighborhoods where they expected to work. In later years this principle gradually became less important, although not abandoned altogether. The principle of "residence" was linked to the notion of creating a "homey" environment where poor people could relax and spend time. The notion of instructing the poor about a particular kind of domestic environment and a way of life reappears, albeit in contradictory agendas, in both activists' and city agencies' notions of affecting behavioral changes among homesteaders on the Lower East Side.

In later years settlements have taken on a more active role in social advocacy as well as in social research studies of unemployment patterns, housing issues, and neighborhood needs. The Neighborhood Guild, the first settlement house in the United States, was founded in 1886; it was followed by the University Settlement House and Society on 146 Forsyth Street and Grand Street Settlement. The Christodora House on East 9th Street and Avenue B, today a luxury condominium, was founded in 1897 as the Young Women's Settlement by Christina MacCall and Sara Libby Carson. In the 1920s it was one of the most active community centers in the city. Henry Street Settlement was founded in 1893 by Lillian D. Wald, a pioneering social worker, who also founded the Visiting Nurse Service, originally associated with Henry Street. Another famous social reformer associated with the Lower East Side was Jakob Riis, who wrote extensively and movingly about the conditions in the tenements in the late nineteenth century (Riis 1970).

Efforts at effecting social and economic changes have repeatedly found expression in and drawn strength from activities at Tompkins Square Park. This 16-acre park, initially constructed according to a formal layout along classical lines with a circle in the center and paths in all four directions, was described as a political hotbed as early as 1874. In that year it was the site of the so-called Tompkins Square Massacre, when a rally of unemployed workers was broken up with some violence by the police. No one was killed but many were injured, and the event became a symbolic milestone in the New York labor movement (Sanders 1979).

The park's most recent history has involved a series of increasingly acrimonious confrontations between (1) homeless people, squatters, and activists, and (2) the city administration, culminating in the closing of the park. Between 1988 and 1991 the city administration repeatedly attempted to forcibly evict homeless people from the park. On June 3, 1991, the park was closed to the public. After protests by neighborhood groups a few of the playgrounds were reopened, but the park remained closed, manifestly for restoration of the grounds and effectively to keep out homeless people and contain the increasingly heated political debate over the city's housing policy and its lack of solutions for homelessness. The park was enclosed by a high fence and guarded by a police contingent from June 3, 1991, to July 25, 1992. In subsequent months tent cities sprang up on empty lots east of the park. Again, a series of police raids followed; ultimately several lots were fenced off and the temporary inhabitants dispersed. Meanwhile, restoration work went on in the park, the bandshell that had housed a large number of tents was demolished, lamps and walkways were repaired, new grass was planted. The park was reopened on July 25, 1992. Since then an uneasy truce has been maintained with only a few demonstrations, a constant police presence, and wary community residents making use of the area.[2]

From the 1960s onward, the Lower East Side has provided a fertile environment for social movements and political activity on many levels. A New York City Planning Commission report from 1969 recognizes the high degree of activism and successful engagement of community organizations and the comparatively broad range of groups active on the Lower East Side. These include, among others, It's Time; Interfaith Adopt-A-Building; and the Joint Planning Council, a coalition of neighborhood organizations. Pueblo Nuevo; Charas, Inc.; Third Street Settlement; and Henry Street Settlement were among the organizations that were particularly active during the 1970s and 1980s. Further, Community Board 3 has played an important part in helping to shape developments on the Lower East Side.[3]

POPULATION SHIFTS ON THE LOWER EAST SIDE

The Lower East Side is remarkable for (1) its rapid population buildup in conjunction with construction of tenements within a very short period of time, as well as (2) its different original character when compared to other city neighborhoods. Whereas other areas north of the original city began as suburbs for the well-to-do, the Lower East Side from the outset housed primarily new immigrant groups that made up the poor to low-income working class in American industrial cities of the nineteenth and twentieth centuries. Continual in- and out-migrations of population groups in search of labor left their mark on the Lower East Side, carving out different neighborhoods in terms of race and ethnic background as much as in terms of socioeconomic levels. The Lower East Side is often used as an umbrella name for a number of different areas and complex histories, for all that these areas and histories overlap and are interconnected. Loisaida emerged as a distinct, separate, and self-conscious community in the post–World War II period. However, its history is inseparable from that of the entire Lower East Side.

The 1990 U.S. Census figures for Community District 3, provided in Table 3.1, are not broken down by neighborhoods; Loisaida, the area where homesteading occurred in the 1980s and early 1990s, is not separately identified. It is populated predominantly by Puerto Ricans; this is reflected in the fact that more than 70% of homesteaders are Puerto Ricans.

People from Ireland made up the bulk of the first large wave of immigrants to the area during the years 1846–1860. Most were employed in shipbuilding and construction trades. The years surrounding the reform movement in 1848 in Germany sparked another wave of immigration, bringing German Jews to the Lower East Side. Many of these went into manufacturing or established themselves as furriers or jewelers. By 1852 the Loisaida area was filled with tenements. Shipbuilding yards, dry docks, and ironworks on maps from that time indicate the major industries and employers. There were also a growing number of lumberyards, coalyards, and breweries (see Dripps 1852). Most blocks were densely built up, and there were few vacant lots. A map from 1879 indicates a shift to small-scale industrial enterprises (Dripps 1879).

The next large wave of immigration, in 1875–1882, brought Chinese to the area. Most of them stayed south of Canal Street. By the 1880s Italians, Russians, Poles, Ukrainians, Hungarians, and Rumanians began to arrive. In the years 1889–1914 more than 1.5 million Jews fleeing pogroms in Eastern Europe came to New York City, and many settled on the Lower East Side. During this time Orchard Street acquired its reputation as the "street of bargains," overflowing with shops and street peddlers. Photographs indicate various cottage industries such as cigarette making and sewing that helped to stave off utter destitution for many families in crowded tenements (Ford 1971).

At the end of the nineteenth century there were more than 300 synagogues on the Lower East Side. Many of these were not free-standing structures but were housed in apartments or tenement buildings (Israelowitz 1991). The

Table 1
Population Shifts in Community District 3

	1980	1990	Percentage of Population Group
White Non-Hispanic	154,848	161,617	(29.3%)
Black Non-Hispanic	14,813	13,387	(8.2%)
Hispanic	56,690	52,217	(32.3%)
(Puerto Rican)	(43,491)	(36,320)	(22.5%)
Asian, Pacific Islander	34,979	47,883	(29.6%)
Other Non-Hispanic	695	738	(0.4%)
Total Population	154,848	161,617	

1980 and 1990 census figures are from the New York City Department of City Planning, Population Division 1991b.

Population shifts in Community District 3 in recent years are reflected, among others, in changing classifications and the introduction of classification groups into the figures. For instance, census figures from 1987 for Community District 3 indicate that 44.7% of the population was White Non-Hispanic; 27.3% was Hispanic; 22.8% was classified as Other Non-Hispanic; and 5.2% as Black Non-Hispanic (New York City, Department of City Planning 1987). The classification of Asian and Pacific Islander, which plays such a prominent role in later census figures—29.6% of the 1990 population on the Lower East Side—does not appear in the 1987 figures. Further, in 1987 Census Bureau enumerators switched from classifying respondents by race to one of self-identification (Weitzman 1989). The U.S. Census Bureau uses the term *Hispanic*, which I have retained in this instance. I use the term *Latino* advisedly, being aware of the current debate within the Latino community as to whether *Latino* is preferable to *Hispanic*. There does not appear to be any consensus on this issue.

many different West and East European Jewish congregations that established these synagogues reflect the diversity in cultural and historical backgrounds of the Jewish immigrants alone. Immigration of Puerto Ricans in the second half of the twentieth century and most recently a growing number of Asians (Japanese, among others) have added more layers to an already complex and diverse neighborhood. Migration of African Americans from the South to the Lower East Side was negligible; mostly they moved to Harlem. Immigration to the Lower East Side leveled off after 1910 and was sharply curtailed as the result of U.S. immigration laws in the 1920s and shifts in the labor market.

From the 1940s onward, Latinos—predominantly Puerto Ricans—began to come to the Lower East Side and to Loisaida in particular. In 1950 there were 13,690 Puerto Ricans in the area (6% of the total population). By 1990 their numbers had grown to 22.5% of the total population in Community District 3, despite some contraction over the last decade.

Subsequent to World War II, there was a period in which immigration of Puerto Ricans into New York City was encouraged as a source of cheap labor. Many Puerto Ricans—in particular women—worked in the garment trades, sweatshops, restaurants and hotels, and small manufacturing. One homesteader described this in more personal terms:

I ended up here, because a previous generation of my family, part of it came to live here. Aunts of mine came many, many years before me, and they were looking also for economic improvement and surviving. When they came here, say it was 50 years ago, they lived here for say 35 years, worked like animals in the needle industry, that was the reason why they came here to the Lower East Side, because the Lower East Side was full of sweatshops. All those ladies, sisters of my mother, are—what do you call it—seamstresses. Here was where the jobs were.

As a result of capital flight and the contraction of manufacturing during the late 1950s, the city lost 55% of its manufacturing jobs between 1960 and 1975. Job loss was particularly severe in industries with large numbers of low-paid workers who had immigrated from the South and the Caribbean to find work. Puerto Ricans who had worked in the garment trades, small manufacturing, restaurants, and hotels were especially affected. "Puerto Ricans were no longer seen as valuable but as expendable to local economic needs" (Sánchez 1986: 213).

By the end of the 1950s, Puerto Ricans began to experience severe drops in employment. Puerto Rican females, in particular, were rapidly being squeezed out of the civilian work force. This restructuring of the economic role of Puerto Ricans, and of New York City's economy as a whole, had dramatic and unusual results on Puerto Rican housing conditions. A brief time of relative improvement in Puerto Rican housing in the early 1960s was followed by severe declines that have continued into the present. The forces rapidly shifting the New York economy toward corporate and personal services caused economic and population dislocations that proved only of temporary value to the ability of Puerto Ricans to meet their housing needs. (Sánchez 1986: 213)

A study on displacement pressures on the Lower East Side indicates a shift during the late 1970s and 1980s that applies particularly to Loisaida (DeGiovanni 1987). DeGiovanni distinguishes between long-term residents and residents who moved to the area during the last decade. According to a survey of 446 randomly selected households in 345 properties in the area, "respondents who had been in the area five years or less in 1984 tended to be white, young college graduates living alone or with an unrelated person(s) and earning a moderate level of income" (DeGiovanni 1987: 17). DeGiovanni argues that more recent migrants to the area are part of a wave of gentrification. The 1990 U.S.

Census data also indicate the growing number of Asians on the Lower East Side. This is due to (1) continued immigration to Chinatown, and (2) the growing popularity of the Lower East Side among Japanese who come to America temporarily (reflected in the increase of restaurants and shops catering to Japanese). The predominance of Puerto Ricans in Loisaida over the last few decades is significant in light of the fact that Puerto Ricans have the worst socioeconomic status of all minority groups in the United States (Rosenberg 1992).

SOCIOECONOMIC PROFILE OF THE LOWER EAST SIDE

In 1990 the median household income in Community District 3 was $20,007 as compared to $30,000 for New York City. The per capita median income in 1990 was $11,309. In 1989 27.2% of the population in Community District 3 received some form of income support, whereas in New York City 17.2% received such support (New York City, Department of City Planning 1992a). The median household income for Puerto Ricans in New York City was $21,000. In 1990 the poverty rate for Puerto Ricans in New York City was 40.6%. According to Rosenberg there are six factors, to be seen in conjunction, that account for the extreme deprivation of Puerto Ricans in New York City: (1) decline in manufacturing jobs, (2) increase in female-headed families, (3) circular migration between the island and the mainland, (4) failure of the public schools in New York City, (5) discrimination in the labor market, and (6) selective migration of the poorest Puerto Ricans into New York City (Rosenberg 1992: 27).

According to an analysis of the New York City labor market, Latinos and African Americans, including Puerto Ricans, did not benefit from the job growth following the 1975 recession (Stafford 1985: xiv–xvi). Although the total number of jobs in New York City increased between 1975 and 1982, unemployment among Latinos and African Americans increased. African Americans and Latinos have been tightly segmented in a narrow range of industries in the city's private sector. Latinos were predominantly employed in hospitals and nondurable manufacturing as well as in the apparel industry and in hotel and motel service industries. They have been virtually excluded from 130 out of 193 industries in the city's private sector, particularly finance, manufacturing, and cultural affairs. Yet those 130 industries had been among the leaders in job growth and accounted for almost 60% of the private sector workforce. In a shrinking labor market, Latinos and African Americans have been competing with an increased number of whites for nonsupervisory jobs in growth industries. Latino females have been concentrated on the lowest levels of the occupational ladder and have constituted a major share of operatives and service workers in lower-paying manufacturing and services industries. Many of these industries declined during the 1970s. Latino males have been concentrated primarily as nonsupervisory workers in the city's small nondurable goods industries, also in services to buildings, hotels, hospitals, and food service places as production workers, repairmen, craft workers, service workers, and laborers. The development of new office technologies has contributed to the displacement from office work. Most disturbing, a comparison of unemployment levels among high school graduates, college graduates, and those without high school diplomas implies that educational levels appear to have little or no effect on overall unemployment levels; this reflects continuing discrimination in the labor market in conjunction with the elimination of entire categories of employment in the course of the restructuring of American industry.

Labor market segmentation has an additional dimension. In private industries such as banking and communications, these population groups are employed predominantly in subordinate positions; within the public sector they are poorly represented in city agencies dealing with finance, intergovernmental relations, and budgets; and they are mostly employed in social service and educational agencies. Meanwhile, during the 1980s low-wage industries, notably "sweat shops," reemerged (Sánchez 1986). In sum, Latino and African-American unemployment has remained twice that of whites during periods of economic recovery and periods of economic downturn.

The effects of deindustrialization and those of a more time-specific urban crisis on poor and low- to moderate-income people on the Lower East Side are illustrated in a discussion by Sharff about the underground economy of the area (Sharff 1987; see also Abu-Lughod et al. 1994). Chronic underemployment and unemployment must be considered when looking at the high proportion of households on the Lower East Side receiving some form of income assistance and the high proportion of individuals making up for an insufficient income by engaging in various activities in the underground economy. This includes activities in connection with the numbers game and the drug market as well as stealing, mugging, robbery, and the like. The changes in the neighborhood over the last decade are critical elements in what Sharff calls "a rational, socioeconomic explanation of why a segment of the population *must* engage in unreported or unreportable work" (Sharff 1987: 47).

Large real estate companies began to buy up the area in the early 1980s at the same time as Reagan's budget cuts caused the benefits to plunge, and many families lost their benefits altogether. As the rents in the remaining tenements skyrocketed, families lost their shelter because of the lowered value of the benefits and the HRA's policy of "churning the caseloads" (Dehavenon 1985). The stage was set for the gentrification of the neighborhood. Some families moved (or more precisely, were removed) to the outer boroughs. Others doubled up with relatives in public housing on the fringes of the area. A few were lucky enough to remain in housing renovated through "sweat equity" (the investment of physical labor), while others became homeless and now exist in welfare hotels and public shelters. (Sharff 1987: 47)

Even as New York City lost a considerable number of jobs (over 50,000 between 1972 and 1981) in conjunction with the decline of the manufacturing sector, there has been a shift from legal manufacturing operations to illegal ones, benefiting from the ready supply of cheap labor.[4] Arguing that housing inequality is not a product of "pure housing market processes," Sánchez emphasizes the linkages between employment patters, housing, and treatment by local governments:

The imposition of productive idleness and redundancy on Puerto Ricans, starting in the mid-1950s, weakened their claims both to good housing and to government assistance. . . . Ultimately, these housing conditions help to make for a below-normal level of subsistence for Puerto Rican workers that reinforces reserve-labor status. This is supported by recent evidence that Puerto Ricans continue to supply labor for competitive capitalist sectors as well as for the current crop of sweatshops and other underground economic operations in New York City. (Sánchez 1986: 220)

Hence, the economic outlook in the 1990s for Puerto Ricans on the Lower East Side is not promising. At the same time, Puerto Ricans are especially affected by trends in the private housing market because they are more likely to reside in private as opposed to public housing (Sánchez 1986: 217). It is likely that Puerto Ricans will continue to be extremely vulnerable to a precarious and shrinking housing market, being locked out by inadequate incomes and limited availability of affordable and acceptable housing.

HOUSING ON THE LOWER EAST SIDE

Historically the Lower East Side was among the poorest and most densely settled areas in the city. In 1910 the population density on the Lower East Side was 234,000 per square mile as compared to 73,000 per square mile in Manhattan (Schwartz 1973:4).

The word *tenement*, the common name for an early walk-up apartment house, is now almost inseparably associated with notions of urban slums and with the history of the Lower East Side. Although there is some evidence for substandard housing construction for the poor on the Lower East Side in the 1820s, most tenement construction occurred during the second half of the nineteenth century (Abu-Lughod et al. 1994: 64). Charles Dickens eloquently described conditions in the tenements in the 1850s:

We could tell of one room, twelve by twelve feet, in which were five resident families, comprising twenty persons, of both sexes and all ages, with only two beds, without partition or screen, or chair or table; and all dependent for their support upon the sale of chips gleaned from the streets, at four cents a basket. . . . But why extend the catalogue, or why attempt to convey to the imagination by words the hideous squalor and deadly effluvia; the dim and undrained courts oozing with pollution; the dark and narrow stairways, decayed with age, reeking with filth, overrun with vermin; the rotted floors, ceilings begrimed and often too low to permit you to stand upright; the windows stuffed with rags?[5]

A recent photojournalism article in the *New York Times* pits the famous photographs taken by Jakob Riis at the turn of the century against photographs from the present (Roberts and Conrad 1991). Both series of photographs portray life in the tenements, and it is difficult to tell which ones were taken then or now.

Generally tenement buildings had four apartments on each floor, with toilets in the hallway shared among the apartments. Typically there were no bathrooms, showers, or baths. Sometimes there was a bathtub in the kitchen. However, for the most part tenants had to go to public bathhouses. From 1879 onward, a tenement building was required to have an air shaft. These air shafts generally measured 2 feet in depth. They were shaped to create a "dumbbell" design, hence the term *dumbbell tenement*. (When a building is gutted prior to being reconstructed in a rehabilitation process, these air shafts, once they are cleared of decades of accumulated debris, are quite useful for moving buckets up and down via ingeniously constructed rope-and-pulley systems.)

Tenement buildings were regulated in theory in the nineteenth century; the Tenement House Act of 1867 represented the first comprehensive housing law passed by the State Legislature that attempted to raise the standards of low-cost housing design. A regulation in 1879 decreed the required cubic footage per person; the allowable maximum coverage of a lot, which was not supposed to be more than 65%; and the fact that every room was to have a window with an opening at least 12 feet wide (Institute of Public Administration 1968). Thus, many rooms have openings toward the air shaft as an obligatory nod to these regulations. Actual enforcement was at the discretion of the Board of Health (Ford 1971). It was not until 1901 that tenements were officially deemed obsolete in design and inadequate in terms of standards of health and comfort. The Tenement House Act of 1901, also known as the "New Law" and hence the origin of the distinction between old-law and new-law tenements, set the national standard for tenement legislation. The dimensions of dumbbell air shafts were increased to courtyard proportions; there had to be running water and a water closet in each apartment; and every room had to have an exterior window. This latter point is pertinent in view of the practice of backbuilding in high-density neighborhoods, as a result of which windows were entirely obstructed by adjacent facades (Plunz 1990: 47–49). Nearly 50,000 new-law tenements were built between 1901 and 1929, housing 2.5 million individuals in 811,000 units.

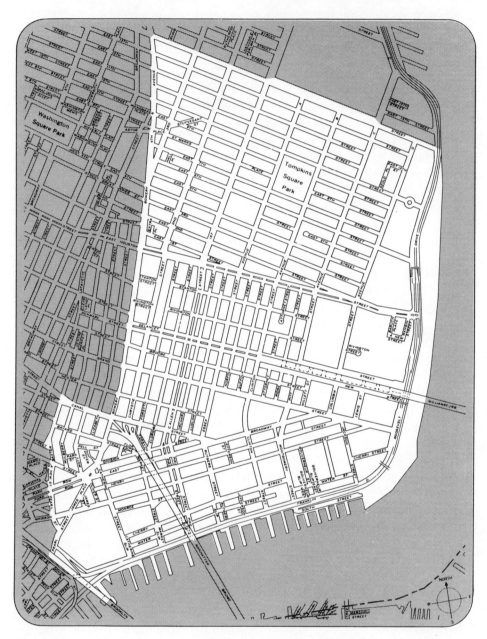

Map 3. Map of Community District 3. Courtesy of the New York City Department of City Planning.

A 1930 map based on U.S. Census figures indicates that the area between 3rd and 9th Streets and Avenues B and D had the highest per acre density in all of Manhattan, with 450-plus units per acre, as well as the lowest rents and comparatively high—if not the highest—infant mortality rates (Bromley 1930). This map also indicates that a large number of buildings were in bad condition, especially those in three blocks along the eastern border of Tompkins Square Park; these blocks were later to become the locus of a variety of struggles—abandonment and gentrification, squatting and homesteading—competing within one small area. However, housing abandonment, which in conjunction with waves of arson in the 1970s and 1980s caused the area to resemble a bombed city of rubble-strewn lots and empty buildings, was still in the future—there were then no more than 13 abandoned buildings in Loisaida.

The 1960 U.S. Census study of four census tracts on the Lower East Side found that 95.4% of dwelling units were in need of rehabilitation or replacement. Fully 75% of the population in this particular area paid less than $60 per month in rent. According to a New York City report, by 1960 "many buildings have been boarded up and removed from the market because of action by various enforcement agencies (Building Department, Fire Department or Health Department)" (see Institute of Public Administration 1968). The same report found that in 1965 nearly half a million families citywide were inadequately housed. Ironically this report pointed out that old-law tenements were slow to disappear from the housing market, attributing "a remarkable survival capacity" to these buildings and calling them the "sturdy backbone of New York's present slums" (Institute of Public Administration 1968: 7).

In 1969, abandonment and frequent razing of empty buildings were reflected in shifting patterns of density. The Lower East Side is shown as having medium to high density, or 111–141 housing units per acre (New York City Planning Commission 1969). From the late 1960s to the early 1980s incidents of arson contributed significantly to the destruction of potentially viable housing stock (see Bach and West 1993).

Against the background of New York City's crumbling economy in the early 1970s, its deteriorating infrastructure and housing stock, and the fiscal crisis in 1975, a concept of "planned shrinkage" began to influence governmental policy. Tabb describes the strategy of "planned shrinkage" in which the principal aim was the dismantling of services to lower-income communities and the reallocation of housing stock so as to better respond to the needs of the corporate city (Tabb 1984: 336).

Roger Starr, the city's Housing and Development Administrator in early February 1976, sent up a trial balloon. He suggested, as an alternative to continued across-the-board cuts in city services, that the city "thin out services" in certain slum areas: that the city close fire and police stations and curtail public education as a way of accelerating population decline. Such action would make whole areas of the city uninhabitable, and then the land could be bulldozed. By offering "inducements" for people to move elsewhere (hopefully out of the city?), the "city" could be saved. The acceleration of housing abandonment emerges as a major strategy proposed by some conservative thinkers for solving the city's crisis." (Tabb 1984: 337)

One homesteader put this more bluntly by saying that the long-term master plan of the city had been to raze the area and transform it into an area of luxury housing, thus making use of the Lower East Side's proximity to Wall Street. "But we [homesteaders] stopped them!"[6]

In 1970 the City Planning Commission issued a report entitled "Plan for New York City: A Proposal" (Alpern 1973). This report is revealing not so much in the actual results produced but in its implied intentions, the echoes of which can be seen today. The plan emphasized upgrading and maintaining of existing housing stock, whereas old-law tenements were deemed as posing insurmountable problems for rehabilitation. Substantial new construction was recommended only if federal or state subsidies would be forthcoming. The plan recommended turning over buildings wherever possible to nonprofit organizations and tenant cooperatives. This was depicted as a new approach to renewal with an emphasis on community involvement. In effect, new construction of housing was discouraged, neglect of buildings considered unredeemable was condoned, and responsibility for New York City's housing stock was shed and handed over to local organizations and nonprofit organizations that were not necessarily able to meet the challenge. In the years after this report was issued, few of the plan's components in terms of upgrading and maintaining the existing housing stock were implemented due to insufficient funding and administrative obstacles (Alpern 1973). The city focused primarily on rent regulation, and rehabilitation assistance as well as code enforcement were largely neglected. Meanwhile, "faced with a developing impasse in publicly assisted housing, the city has begun to develop measures to spur new low- and moderate-rent development without government funds" (Alpern 1973: 221). In the years after the report was issued the city was trying out various housing development programs, the responsibility for which was located outside the city administration in community organizations. The Urban Homesteading Program was one of these under the so-called Department of Alternative Management Programs (DAMP).

Even though the 1975 fiscal crisis served to rationalize further cutbacks in city services, it was evident as early as 1969 that the city had made a major policy change by encouraging the economic redevelopment of New York, particularly Manhattan, as a "national center"—for national and multinational corporations. This policy entailed, for the most part, a greater need for a "white-collar" workforce. As a result, the residual "blue-collar" worker was becoming superfluous in this changing financial climate, a fact related to shifting patterns of investment and disinvestment in neighborhoods such as the Lower East Side (Alpern 1973: 427–428; Turner 1984: 107–109).[7]

Marcuse used the phrase "treat and trickle down" for the city government's policy after 1975. It resulted in massive reductions of city expenditures in poorer areas, investment in areas supporting central business district activities and upper-income residential areas, and withdrawal from areas deemed past hope of recovery (Marcuse 1987).

During the 1980s the dynamics of gentrification took an additional dimension on the Lower East Side, the unfolding of the East Village art scene. "A working-class neighborhood for 160 years, the area has become in the 1980s the scene of a new art 'phenomenon': over forty commercial galleries displaying their wares to a clientele of corporate art consultants and wealthy international collectors" (Deutsche and Ryan 1984: 91). Art critics in the media celebrated this as a rejuvenation and renewal of the Lower East Side. Poverty and homelessness were transformed into a colorful and scenic backdrop to the aesthetic imagination.

In the image of the bum, the problems of the homeless poor, existing on all sides of the East Village art scene, are mythologized, exploited, and finally ignored. Once the poor become aestheticized, poverty itself moves out of our field of vision. Images like *Holbein and the Bum* [a large reproduction of a Holbein portrait of a figure facing in the direction of the bum in the doorway] disguise the literal existence of thousands of displaced and homeless people who are not only produced by late capitalism but constitute its very conditions. As a process of dispersing a "useless" class, gentrification is aided and abetted by an "artistic" process whereby poverty and homelessness are served up for aesthetic pleasure. (Deutsche and Ryan 1984: 111)

The increase of art galleries in the neighborhood was the prologue to "the ultimately successful battle which community groups waged to defeat Mayor Koch's Artist Homeownership Program" (Deutsche and Ryan 1984: 100). Initially the city planned to allocate $3 million in public funds for rehabilitation of vacant tenements for use by artists, but it was forced to abandon this plan in view of effectively voiced protest on the part of community organizations.[8]

During the 1980s the city repeatedly held auctions of abandoned properties on the Lower East Side as well as in other areas, despite vigorous protest on part of community boards and activists. A major objection to these auctions was the argument that such sales do not permit rational local planning and frequently resulted in properties remaining abandoned for some time as buyers defaulted. The city never published data on the number of defaults and foreclosures in connection with these auctions, nor on how many of these buildings were actually rehabilitated and occupied by owners or tenants (Brower 1989: 26).

Community organizations and activists also questioned the city's handling of the so-called cross-subsidy plan for 500 parcels of land that the city owns on the Lower East Side.[9] In the mid 1980s a community-initiated and

-endorsed development plan, based on a cross-subsidy mechanism, was prepared. This plan called for redevelopment of all city property for low- and moderate-income residents. Before the plan could be submitted to the city administration, the city announced its own cross-subsidy plan. It proposed to sell all vacant lots in the area to developers for market-rate housing and to use revenues (the amount of which remained unspecified) derived from these sales to subsidize the renovation of vacant city buildings, only 20% of which would be for low-income households. As a compromise the community suggested a 50/50 split of low- and moderate-income housing and market-rate housing. A version of this plan was eventually signed by the city and the community. When the first phase of construction was about to begin, the city decided on new terms for the cross-subsidy plan, according to which the city itself would fund, under a 10-year plan, every rehabilitated low- and moderate-income unit for which there would be a one-to-one match of luxury housing. "There is no longer any cross-subsidy, nor any rationale to link the luxury housing to the low- and moderate-income housing, except that the city simply will not allow its vacant buildings to be used for lower income housing unless the vacant land is used to produce luxury housing" (Brower 1989: 30). In view of this sequence of events, the previously mentioned auctions, and the proposed Artist Homeownership Program, the city administration's position on housing on the Lower East Side can only be described as ambivalent at best.

On the Lower East Side the number of housing units (housing one to three or more families each) decreased by .5% in the years 1980–1987, while in the Borough of Manhattan there was an increase of 4.3% and in New York City a slight increase of .7% (New York City Department of City Planning 1987). Another figure of interest in this context is the number of old-law tenements on the Lower East Side. In 1989 in New York City 1.2% of all housing land use was old-law tenement buildings; in Manhattan it was 7.1%; and on the Lower East Side, 27.7%. Walk-ups amounted to 12.3%. At the same time, even as federal funds are harder to come by, funding for neighborhood self-help has declined over the last decade. In this context the city's Ten-Year Plan announced in 1986, which has attempted to make up for the shortfall in federal funding, appears little more than a drop in the bucket.

The Ten-Year Plan, with a budget allocation of $5.1 billion, reflects the city's efforts to take responsibility for improving the housing situation. The plan was to produce approximately 84,000 new housing units and to preserve an additional 168,000 units over the coming ten-year period. Since then, however, the plan has been scaled back to $4.8 billion and production and preservation of a total of 138,397 housing units. This cutback has affected the Office of Property Management, the Capital Improvement Program, and funding for tenant organizing and community development in particular (Glazer 1991).

Community Board 3 stated in 1980 that the most urgent need in the district was for housing, both new and rehabilitated. According to Community Board meeting minutes, abandonment was extensive; figures indicated that over 25% of tax lots in the district had been in arrears for over a year. The area east of Avenue A between 14th and Houston Streets, otherwise known as Loisaida, was described as suffering from the most extensive abandonment and physical deterioration of buildings. In the 1970s and 1980s, cycles of disinvestment and reinvestment and ensuing tax forfeitures had disastrous effects on the area's housing stock (see Abu-Lughod et al. 1994). The 1992 and 1995 Community Board's "District Needs and Priorities" reports repeated the urgent need for affordable new and rehabilitated housing (New York City, Department of City Planning 1992a; 1995). The need is especially great for poor and low-income individuals and families.[10]

Concurrent with the process of gentrification, residents have been exposed to a variety of pressures that have furthered displacement and abandonment of buildings. Such pressures include excessive rent burdens in relationship to incomes, overcrowding, deterioration, suspicious fires, warehousing of vacant apartments, and tenant harassment by owners or managing agents (DeGiovanni 1987). Meanwhile, in 1992 there were 90 abandoned city-owned buildings east of Avenue A that—according to HPD—have been identified for various homesteading, cross-subsidy plans (under which a percentage of a building development is designated for low- to moderate-income people), and rehabilitation programs. There were 20 other abandoned city-owned buildings in this particular area of the Lower East Side that were occupied by several hundred squatters and for which there were no programs in sight (Senft 1992). According to HPD there were approximately 500 squatters living in 32 buildings on the Lower East Side (Nieves 1991). Problems in the neighborhood are further exacerbated by a relatively large number of shelters as compared to neighborhoods with higher median incomes (Senft 1992).

CONCLUSION

The Lower East Side represents a remarkable microcosm of housing history. Contested, fought over, abandoned, burned, demolished, publicly auctioned, salvaged, and rebuilt, it bears scars and testimonials to its diverse history. Populations on the Lower East Side, particularly Puerto Ricans concentrated in Loisaida, historically have been among the most disadvantaged in New York City in terms of the labor market, health care, education, and housing. Housing conditions in Loisaida are among the worst in Community District 3. The effects of disinvestment are still visible in the disproportionate number of deteriorating or abandoned buildings and vacant lots; equally visible are the effects of gentrification. Yet, ravaged by the effects of rapid industrialization and almost equally rapid deindustrialization, the Lower East Side has a tradition of activism and social movements that provides a complex and multifaceted counterweight to gentrification. In this context homesteading developed and flourished for over a decade.

A walk through the Lower East Side provides visual evidence of the diversity of the population and the contradictory developments over the last few decades. On Saturdays, on my way to one of the homesteaders' buildings, I crossed many invisible boundaries as I walked from Second Avenue toward Loisaida. I often passed by the branch of the Public Library on Second Avenue with its former name, "Freie Bibliothek und Lesehalle," still displayed above the door. The "Deutsches Dispensary" nextdoor, built in the same Victorian Gothic architectural style as the library, today appropriately houses the Gabrini Medical Center Polyclinic. Crossing First Avenue with its array of liquor shops, Japanese delis, and Polish butchers, I headed toward Avenue A. The Daffodil Cafe on 6th Street was quiet, and so was the Gladiator Gym. I went past the police station and the homeless men sitting at sidewalk tables across the street. On summer days locust trees carpeted the sidewalks with yellow snow, for a moment giving the lie to T. S. Eliot's tired, grimy, and stale mornings. Old women sat on stoops chatting. A lone violinist played to the universe at Tompkins Square Park. The park was quiet in the mornings, and it was too early for people to line up for food at Avenue B in front of the Park. With thoughts of café con leche at the Casa Adela on Avenue C, I walked past lampposts festooned with a multitude of ceramic tiles and glass at the corner of the park. I liked to pass by the community garden at Avenue B and 6th Street with its riotous assortment of flowers and vegetables. This garden was dominated by a lamppost sculpture. The lamppost was completely covered by an assortment of toys, boats, helicopter propeller blades, clocks, and teddy bears. Often a new item had been added to the collection. Then I went on to the recycling center on 7th Street; usually several people were at work sorting and cleaning up while others were bringing in their bottles and cans. In the early 1990s on that particular block there were vacant lots, burned-out buildings, a building being homesteaded, and a former synagogue dating back to 1905 that had been turned into a condominium. There were a squatter building, a soup kitchen at the corner, and three flourishing community gardens. During the summers of 1989 and 1990, when several buildings were actively being worked on, sounds of hammering and sawing filled the air, and people in hardhats and workboots walked around on the streets chatting with people from the neighborhood. Later, coming away from a day's work dirty, sweaty, and sore, I passed people sitting at tables on street corners playing dominoes in the evening, and people working in the gardens. At such times I was tempted to romanticize the entire scene. Yet the Lower East Side does not easily lend itself to this particular distortion.

Deteriorating tenements, empty lots, shanty-towns that are razed periodically, and abandoned buildings shoulder to shoulder with luxury housing are indicators of uneven accumulation of capital and uneven
gentrification of a neighborhood. Such processes are by no means unique
to this inner-city area. Yet the Lower East Side and Loisaida in particular
provide especially poignant evidence of the sharp discrepancies and the
ultimate interconnectedness of these processes within a relatively small
geographical area.

The old Chinese Noodle Manufacturing Company on Houston Street is
worlds apart from the new Japanese grocery on Avenue B. Bodegas and
Polish-American home-cooking restaurants are overshadowed by a multitude of restaurants offering anything from Italian to Thai cuisine. The
Nuyorican Poets Cafe on Sixth Street between Avenues A and B was a place
for Puerto Rican poets, musicians, and activists to meet during the 1970s
and 1980s. One observer viewed its reopening in 1990 on Third Street
between Avenue B and C as an indication of resistance and continuity (Maffi
1994). However, it can also be seen as an echo of continuing gentrification.
Described as a fashionable place on the Lower East Side in a *New York Times*
article in 1993, the Nuyorican Poets Cafe has become part of the "scene,"
although the art galleries "that transformed this area into a fabulous playground of the avant-garde in the 1980s have all vanished" (Jacobs 1993).
There is Mary House on Third Street, a women's shelter and soup kitchen
run by the Catholic Worker, with a house for men, Joseph House, one block
over. One homesteader with whom I walked along Avenue C pointed out
a building with a chop-shop on the ground floor. In 1993 this building was
gutted, and it is now being rehabilitated by a private developer. The
homesteader helpfully identified squatter buildings and warned me about
particular blocks on which drug dealers were congregating. On the "Plaza
Cultural," now a small park, a soup kitchen used to be operated by local
people who used donated food to prepare concoctions described as "rock
soup"; you start with a rock and water and keep boiling it in the hopes that
someone else will come by and contribute an onion, a carrot, or maybe even
a bone with meat on it.[11] A neighborhood featuring rock soup, costly sushi
and shiitake mushrooms as well as food care packages distributed under
the auspices of Nazareth Home, Inc. (a local charitable organization
founded in 1983 by the Catholic churches of the Lower East Side), does not
represent a gorgeous mosaic.

History has different faces. One homesteader, a woman in her early
seventies, told me that she had lived in the neighborhood for 50 years. She
moved out after the superintendent's son was found slain in her kitchen
under unexplained circumstances. She could not bear to stay in her apartment, so she moved to an apartment in Brooklyn. However, she described
this apartment as very unsafe; it was broken into several times. She hoped
to be able to return to the neighborhood through homesteading. Her sisters

still lived on the Lower East Side. She told me: "I knew the neighborhood when it was pretty; we had dances in the park, I remember ice-skating on the swimming pool."

History is reflected in one group of homesteaders' choice of a name for their building. "The Executive" is an ironic recognition of a time in which that particular building was a well-known shooting gallery and bore that name among the drug addicts in the neighborhood. Exhilarating and perplexing, the history of the Lower East Side has room for windmills. During the mid-1970s an "alternative technology" movement led to the construction of windmills and glass-domed greenhouses on rooftops. In fact, 519 East 11th Street, one of the first sweat-equity buildings, was the site of the first attempt to install a windmill. Attempts were also made to exploit solar energy for heating. Many of these efforts centered around Charas, Inc., an organization involved with vacant lot reclamation and youth organizing as well as the utilization of alternative technologies, with the overarching aim of reconstructing a community (see Chodorkoff 1980).

Yet another face of history relates to the increasing popularity of the Lower East Side among artists. During the 1970s and 1980s, artists came to the Lower East Side in search of an inexpensive place to live and an ambience of poverty amid stripped brick walls and rusty fire escapes. Indeed, 527 East 5th Street bears the name "Greenhouse Artist Residents Project," or GARP; 188 East 3rd Street is called "Free Living Our Way," or FLOW, attesting to differing strains of historical memory. A homesteader's description of her initial involvement in the neighborhood provides another insight into the Lower East Side:

I began observing the buildings, and I saw all these empty buildings. Empty! I cannot understand, I cannot figure it out. Why were they empty? I kept looking at them. Then I began seeing around the community fliers that were posted that were saying "Adopt A Building." I asked my cousin and my cousin said it was a movement to take over a building and then the city will sell it to us. I told my cousin: "Are you nuts, why would they sell a building to the community, that's private property, the heart of capitalism? Why would they sell property to low-income people, which would give me power to go to a bank and create my own economic base? Why? That does not make sense." My cousin said. "This is America. Contradictions are allowed." Now remember, I was coming from Puerto Rico, I see the enemy as the United States and white people are my enemy. Okay? Blue eyes, blond hair, what is called fair skin. I understand those are my enemy and they hate me and I have to protect myself from them, because any time they will hurt me. Never occurred to me until I moved to this country that white people like Malcolm X said were not the devil. He thought that white people were the devil, but then he changed his mind when he saw white people in Mecca. Now the same thing happened to me. I thought white people were the devil. When I got here I discovered they were not the devil. I guess I went to Mecca . . . in a way. This was my Mecca. The Lower East Side was Mecca for me. Let's put it that way. I saw white people who was more interested than even Hispanics or blacks to make things better for everybody across the board independent of the color of their skin. When I saw that, I thought: "Gee, am I in the twilight zone or what?" Not only that I saw white people supporting the right of Latin America to be free. I discovered the million-dollar thing that American government and American people are two different things. Big difference!

One person's Mecca may be another's hell. In winter things look different, and the cheerful graffiti suns and moons and shadowy dancing people painted on building walls seem so much mockery. Filling buckets with wet debris in a drafty shell of a building is bitter work. Yet homesteaders continued to work on their buildings, adding another layer of history to this area.

NOTES

1. Peter Stuyvesant's farm was the site of the original chapel of today's St. Mark's Church, one of the few buildings on Manhattan Island that have survived from the eighteenth century. Built in 1795, the church was almost completely gutted after a fire in 1978. However, it became the focus and catalyst for active community involvement. The church has been rebuilt and has provided a training ground in various construction skills for young people from the neighborhood.

2. For a comprehensive discussion of the recent as well as past history of Tompkins Square Park, see Abu-Lughod et al. 1994.

3. New York City's Community Boards were established in their present form in 1975, even though they were already incorporated into the City Charter in 1963. Community Boards address themselves to a variety of city land use and budgetary decisions. Their role is legally mandated but purely advisory. For a discussion of their limited legal power and the role of patronage, see Marcuse 1987.

4. "A recent New York State Department of Labor report (1982) indicated that there were 15 times as many apparel sweatshop firms operating today as in 1970, and, by the department's conservative estimate, these firms accounted for about 50,000 jobs, or almost all of the recorded job loss in the legalized apparel industry from 1970 to 1980. . . . The unmentioned yet critical element in this rejuvenation, whatever its actual size, is the long decline in working-class living standards, especially as related to housing. The desperation bred by these housing conditions made workers more willing to accept whatever work capital had for them" (Sánchez 1986: 218).

5. Charles Dickens, *The Sixteenth Annual Report of the New York Association for Improving the Condition of the Poor, for the Year 1859*, 45–46, in Ford 1971: 134.

6. The Lower East Side was not the first neighborhood in New York City to be considered dispensable. During the early 1960s, before the influence of writers such as Jane Jacobs began to be felt, urban planners still favored plans that treated entire neighborhoods as large architectural problems. This attitude, in conjunction with the type of planning propounded by Robert Moses (among others), would eventually have created "dead, stuffed cities" in the words of Jacobs (cited by Plunz [1990: 290]). During the Moses era the city bureaucracy promoted a view of Soho as a neighborhood that was essentially obsolescent. A plan by the developer

Ira D. Robbins involved razing all of Soho to free it for new development (Plunz 1990).

7. For a discussion about the intersection of the economy, the labor market, and housing as it has affected Puerto Ricans from World War II until the 1980s, see Sánchez 1986. Sánchez (1986), Marcuse (1982), and Davidson (1979), among others, discuss the shifts in New York City housing policy that have been described as "planned shrinkage," or "triage." "It can be argued that at least since the early 1970s, the allocation of city resources has developed into a policy whereby those areas considered not viable for capitalist investment and/or housing-related profit were deemed to be in decline and not worthy of additional public expenditures. The result of this 'triage' policy, the withdrawal of housing and community reha-bilitation funds, public transport, sewer and sanitation services, schools, and po-lice and fire services, has been to accelerate the destructive process of population and housing loss, which served as the initial reason for withdrawing city resources in the first place" (Sánchez 1986: 217).

8. In 1982 New York City proposed developing 120 loft-style artists' coopera-tives to be clustered on two blocks of the Lower East Side. The project was to be partially financed by the Participation Loan Program, in turn funded by the Com-munity Development Block Grant program, which mandated utilization of fund-ing for low- and moderate-income people. For a history of this episode, see Ryan 1984.

9. For an extensive discussion, see Abu-Lughod et al. 1994: 313–332.

10. "The number of units affordable to public assistance recipients declined by more than 60% between 1978 and 1987, and the vacancy rate for such units dropped from 3.6% to 1.1%" (Weitzman 1989: xi). According to Weitzman, 54% of Latino renters are in need of assistance. He defines households "in need of housing assistance" as all households living in physically inadequate conditions, or "at or below 125% of the poverty level with a gross rent-to-income ratio of 30% or more, or with a gross-rent-to-income ratio of 40% or more" (Weitzman 1989: 68).

11. A documentary entitled *Rock Soup* was filmed by Lech Kowalski and re-leased in New York City in 1992. It documents the history of the conflict over the future of the lot called "Plaza Cultural" and the soup kitchen in that space. The community was divided over whether or not to vote in favor of the construction of a senior citizens' home on that lot. Residents eventually voted in favor of the senior citizens' home; however, nothing has been built on the lot to date. Since 1976, people in the neighborhood have been attempting to turn it into a community park. On June 6, 1995, the block association was awarded an Operation Green Thumb lease to the park and the adjoining community garden.

4

SWEAT AND DEBRIS

Homesteader Prayer

We enter upon the threshold
of this discarded shelter
With hopes, perseverance
and the tools of labor
We toil to bring life back to these empty rooms
These rooms that held people
and their lives from the
elements of their existence
We bring the flesh and spirit
to the mortar and stone
fulfilling its purpose of shelter
As homesteaders we stand
together and declare this
building shall not die

The Homesteader Prayer was published in January 1990 in *The Homesteader*, RAIN's official newsletter produced by homesteaders (Pfandler 1990). The newsletter appeared for a short time in the mid-1980s and resurfaced in 1989. The Prayer captures the almost religious fervor and idealism that I encountered frequently when talking to homesteaders, in particular those who had not yet been actively involved for a long time. As a volunteer who came to work on buildings on weekends, I initially got caught up in this enthusiastic faith in the enterprise. The grueling work on a productive Saturday helped to provide a sense of determined and oddly exhilarating battle if not accomplishment; meanwhile, it obscured the complexity of the issue at hand. At the end of a day of homesteading there remained little thought beyond the satisfaction that one had managed to knock down all the ceiling plaster in a room or that one's back had survived lifting buckets out of a debris-filled airshaft; or maybe one was nursing blisters or a sore thumb caught under a few errant bricks. Greater awareness and growing understanding of the many obstacles to completing a building, not to mention altering the housing situation on the Lower East Side beyond a mere drop in the bucket, tempers this enthusiasm.

Readers of countless ethnographies, after working through various theoretical emanations, are sometimes relieved to turn to the reassuring chapter that describes "a day in the life of [the protagonist]." One has an approximate idea of what such a chapter will be like—the plot is basically the same, the ending happy or consoling; the protagonist arises early, the day is long, distribution of labor is problematic, much work is done, a lot of talk, various frustrations, and a dispute provide spice to life, food is shared or not shared to everyone's satisfaction, a few stories provide laughter and/or profound insights, a dance or music completes the evening, aside from some cicadas and a lovers' quarrel all is quiet during the night, the end. When writing about the day-to-day reality of homesteading, I found myself trying to slip into this mode of describing the "typical day," in other words, the kind of day on which—fatigue and tensions aside—things work and doubts and alienation from the process are laid to rest or serve to reinforce belief in the process. During my interviews with homesteaders I found that they also at times liked to describe homesteading in those terms, in a sense reconstructing the history of their involvement in the process into a composition with a clear plot, dramatic tensions, and a satisfying resolution. Negative aspects were woven into the storyline in the form of salutary lessons. The story of homesteading was turned into a test of moral fiber, endurance, and worthiness.

Issues of political and social relevance are often best illustrated by their concrete manifestations. Thus, it serves to look at the micro processes involved in homesteading. However, it is important to remember to make the connection between such processes and their context as well as the underlying causes, which are to be sought at the wider societal level of political, social, and economic dynamics. The crucial task of revealing the complexities of micro processes may turn into a trap, leading to a search for explanations not in the underlying causes but in their outcomes. The following description of homesteading is not an end in itself but rather a basis for subsequent analyses. Concrete processes in homesteading present a mirror, albeit distorted, for dynamics at the macro level. These dynamics are replicated and reinforced in homesteading. Yet the process of replication is by no means complete or total. Even as the hegemony of the market economy, coupled with a set of ideological rationalizations, asserts itself, contrary processes that question this hegemony occur and ultimately effect changes at the macro level.

WHO ARE THE HOMESTEADERS?

Homesteaders in the LESAC homesteading program were people living on or displaced from the Lower East Side. Over 70% of homesteaders were Puerto Rican, the remainder white/non-Latino (17%), Asian (9.5%), and African American (3.1%). There were 43 men (46.7%) and 49 women (53.2%). The number of women homesteaders slightly exceeded that of men. The proportion of homesteaders in their twenties and thirties clearly exceeded that of older people, less than 10% of all homesteaders over 50 years of age. There was an approximately 50% split between families and single people. Approximately 25% of single homesteaders had children, with more single women as heads of families than single men. The numbers were too small to be conclusive. Nevertheless, it is of interest to note that in 1990 in Community District 3, 20.6% of families were headed by single people, 16.3% of whom were women (U.S. Department of Commerce, Bureau of the Census 1990). Homesteading attracted people predominantly from the poorest population in New York City and the Lower East Side; further, it attracted a relatively large share of single female heads of households, despite the fact that homesteading was particularly difficult for single women with children.

A precise figure on the number of homesteaders on the Lower East Side is impossible to obtain for several reasons. It depends on whether one includes all buildings that have been or are being rehabilitated with the help of their future residents. There have been various kinds of homesteading projects under the auspices of different groups such as Habitat for Humanity and UHAB, several earlier projects that received assistance from Interfaith-Adopt-A-Building, and a few projects that to all intents and purposes were on their own. I focused on buildings associated with LESAC; the LESAC program in conjunction with the Community Land Trust represents the largest such effort on the Lower East Side and the most ambitious in seeking to integrate the construction of housing with community building. LESAC has been involved in a total of 17 buildings, of which 13 have been completed. Twelve buildings have joined RAIN.

One difficulty in obtaining a precise figure arises from the nature of the process itself. Estimates of the total number of active homesteaders past and present range from 150 to 200. Whether this includes people who have joined and later dropped out depends on the person being interviewed. There are no individual building records on how many people have been involved in the project and how many have dropped out over the years. Thus, reconstruction of figures depends on individuals' recall. It also depends on whether respondents were themselves part of a project from its inception and therefore would be in a position to say how many people have come and gone.

Another difficulty is linked to the fact that homesteaders sometimes moved from one building to another. The number I worked with, 94, is based on people actively involved at one time or another and not on the total number of individuals that currently live or will finally live in a homesteaded apartment.

The figures are further distorted by the reality of homesteading. Generally one member of a household assumed an active role while others in that household joined in the labor on an occasional basis or not at all. Women played a more prominent role in homesteading than men at a variety of levels; yet there was no discernible pattern on which partner in the case of couples would take on the majority of homesteading work. One woman continued to work while she was pregnant and reappeared a few months after having delivered her baby; her husband was not able to work on Saturdays because of his job as a cook in a Chinese restaurant. Among couples with children, some husbands and wives took turns; among others, one partner ended up doing most of the physical labor. One task performed more frequently by the males in the case of couples was security. For single men and women and single heads of household with children, homesteading presented far greater problems in terms of satisfying the required hours of sweat, especially with regard to security.

In 1993 LESAC had completed 148 units and 13 buildings out of an originally planned total of 196 apartment units and 17 buildings. The remaining 4 buildings were redesignated at different times for different programs.[1] Thirty units of those completed were designated by LESAC for homeless people placed in the buildings, 17 for the elderly and disabled, and 11 as commercial units. There is a total of 90 completed apartment units for homesteaders. The number of homesteaders (one per unit) in 1993 was 94; this includes several homesteaders whose apartment units were identified as units for the elderly or disabled. However, it does not include spouses or family members who actively contributed to the homesteading work in any one apartment unit. I spoke to and interacted with 35 homesteaders on a regular basis and conducted intensive interviews with 17.

I encountered the following occupations: administrative aid, child care worker, case worker in a city agency, carpenter, pressman, cleaning lady, cook, exterminator, mover, clerk, shipping clerk, office assistant, paralegal, secretary, teacher, office administrator, social worker in a local outreach organization, unemployed, part-time employed in various jobs. Some people were working in local advocacy organizations. Occupational histories of homesteaders reflect the occupational picture of Puerto Ricans in New York. They were concentrated predominantly in low-paying office service industries and in social work and the health care industries. According to RAIN and LESAC income stipulations, individuals applying to the homesteading program had to be employed at the time of application; their income was not to exceed 80% of the current median income on the Lower East Side as established by HPD. In 1990 the median household income in Community District 3 was $20,007, and the median per capita income was $11,309 (U.S. Department of Commerce, Bureau of the Census 1990).

The majority of homesteaders lived in overcrowded and substandard housing, doubled up with family members or friends. Several lived in public housing complexes on the Lower East Side. One homesteader who spent part of his childhood on the Lower East Side lived in Brooklyn with his wife and three children. He described the building as badly neglected and unsafe. At the time of the interview in 1991, Manuel had already been working as a homesteader already for five years.

MANUEL: Things are either not fixed or fixed with plastic or glue. It's ridiculous. Local winos are brought in to do the plumbing work. I'm embarrassed to invite people to my house. I'm scared to furnish my apartment. I am waiting to be either burned out or to have somebody break into the back to take whatever possessions I have. Living in this building affects everything. I don't even like using the bathroom. I have two daughters from a previous marriage. Because the apartment is so small, they are staying with my sister. The oldest is 16, and they are still waiting for this apartment that I'm supposed to be building on the Lower East Side.

There are no typical homesteaders. The following profiles are provided as a way of making these homesteaders less abstract.

Allan

Allan is about 30, of Puerto Rican descent, and single. He heard of homesteading from José, a friend involved in homesteading. Allan did not know whether José was still homesteading. Allan lived with his family in an apartment south of Houston Street. He expected to move to a temporary place shortly. He hoped the building would be finished by the time he had to move out of the temporary apartment. However, at the time of our interview the building was very far from completion; in 1994 the building was completed, and Allan was no longer with the program.

Allan has worked in a variety of jobs and has acquired a range of skills over the years. He has been a construction worker, ran a moving company, fixed air-conditioning units, laid tiles, and installed electricity in building interiors. He got laid off from his last job with a video production company. Allan expressed frustration with his role as construction supervisor in the building. He felt that too often the others left him to close up the building by himself. He was looking forward to the next building elections so he could relieve himself of this burden. Allan became animated when describing his plans for a tool shed on the ground floor and explaining what work still needed to be done on the building.

In a conversation between Allan, another homesteader, and myself, he expressed a certain degree of confusion over papers given to him so he could claim unemployment benefits. The other homesteader, Manuel, who works in a social services agency, gave him some advice on what to do. Allan indicated that he also found confusing much of the paperwork to do with the building, particularly with regard to legal and financial matters. He expressed anger with homesteaders in a neighboring building that has been completed for their unwillingness to extend help in any form now that they have moved in. He has been with the building since 1987. Work on that building began in 1986. Allan appeared alienated and detached from the political and bureaucratic aspects of homesteading and from the leadership in RAIN and LESAC; yet he was a regular member of the Saturday work team.

Marina

Marina is a single woman of Armenian descent in her late thirties. She has a health condition that prevents her from being physically very active. She works as an office assistant on a part-time basis. As a homesteader Marina was assigned duties that did not involve physical labor. Before she moved into her rehabilitated apartment she lived in a public housing apartment with her parents. Marina learned about homesteading through a leaflet that was pushed under her door by an outreach committee member in 1984, and she began homesteading in 1985. She felt it was important to be an active participant in a homesteading project.

Marina contrasted the building she was in originally to the one she finally was assigned. In the first building she was exempt from all physical labor because of her handicap and was encouraged by other building members to stay away. In the second building Marina was encouraged to participate as much as she could, even to the extent of helping with some of the lighter physical labor. In fact, her regular presence at the building during homesteading hours was demanded by the other building members.

Marina has been building director since the building was completed. She deals with city agencies, lawyers, maintenance companies, LESAC, and others and is knowledgeable about matters related to cooperative ownership, tax abatements, and housing assistance programs. She was encouraged to take a course on building management and since then has also been managing a city-owned building next to her own building.

Marina has been active in the community on a variety of levels. She has been an active member of RAIN; however, she expressed disillusionment with the politics and treatment accorded to individuals who are not part of the leadership of RAIN.

Eduardo and Maribel

Eduardo and Maribel are Puerto Rican, both in their late thirties. They have three children. Both are teachers. Both were born and raised on the Lower East Side. After their marriage the couple lived in Brooklyn, where they felt isolated as the only Puerto Rican couple in the neighborhood. They heard about homesteading from Eduardo's father. When they began homesteading, they did not yet have any children. The couple worked together on Saturdays. They came up with the idea of forming an outreach committee to let people in the community know about homesteading. Together Eduardo and Maribel went to churches and various local facilities to speak about homesteading. They interviewed prospective homesteaders in the early 1980s on behalf of LESAC and RAIN. They worked on several buildings before finally staying with one. As a result, they were full of anecdotes about the problems in these buildings. Maribel also felt that this time of being "gypsy homesteaders" was very instructive in terms of the personality and political problems that can arise. They homesteaded for six years.

Eduardo and Maribel expressed a great deal of ambivalence about RAIN and LESAC and foresaw problems for many buildings as well as for some of the ideas and concepts of RAIN. However, when they talked about their own building and their memories of working on it, they were full of pride. Eduardo took me on a tour of the building and pointed out the community room, the laundry room, and the bulletin board that is used for organizational purposes; and he repeated the sense of satisfaction he and his wife got from seeing the building finished. Both said that returning to the Lower East Side was like coming home.

Tana

Tana is an African-American woman in her thirties. She is single and has a 10-year-old son. She works as a fundraiser in a nonprofit organization. Tana spent part of her childhood in the East Village with her older sister. She came back to the Lower East Side when she found that it was difficult to find suitable housing as a single mother on a limited income. Tana initially got an apartment in a Mitchell-Lama building. She learned about homesteading through walking around in the neighborhood and noticing people working on buildings. She applied in 1986 and worked in another building before receiving her final assignment.

Tana said that for her, one of the biggest problems in terms of the actual homesteading work was doing security. She felt that it placed an undue burden on her. Tana was the only single woman doing security in the building. The other women were married and therefore could take turns with their husbands or get out of that chore altogether. Tana had to find someone to take care of her son from Friday night to Saturday evening when she was doing security in addition to working on the building during the day. She was involved in the administrative aspects of managing the building. She also was active in a number of conflicts between her building and LESAC. According to other building members and homesteaders in other buildings, Tana at times played a controversial role.

Tana expressed a great deal of cynicism about LESAC. She argued that one of the reasons there are so many problems with homesteading and with RAIN is that too many people are unwilling to take on responsibility and to play an active role in the process.

I have not conducted any intensive interviews with individuals who dropped out of the process. With a few exceptions the people I spoke to were all actively involved at that time; however, several implied that they were reconsidering their options. Several homesteaders whom I interviewed dropped out later on.

THE PROCESS

A building rehabilitation project through self-help, sweat-equity urban homesteading consisted of the following essential steps: forming a group of homesteaders, locating a sponsor to assist in technical and financial matters, finding a building, obtaining site control, formulating of a membership agreement and by-laws, preparing a financing and loan package, and actually performing the physical rehabilitation of the building. The sequence of these steps was not a given, and there is considerable overlap among them.

Formation of a Group of Homesteaders and Recruitment

The formation of a group of homesteaders through a variety of recruitment processes continued throughout the duration of a building rehabilitation project, depending on the size of the initial group and the dropout rate. The process of recruitment evolved from a haphazard one to one in which the attempt was made to screen homesteaders for their eligibility and commitment. In the early 1990s, recruitment efforts lagged because several projects were on hold and there was a general uncertainty about the future of homesteading as a whole.

Both LESAC and RAIN had equal say in matters of recruitment. Proof of eligibility for LESAC housing was determined in part by income level. An applicant also had to provide proof of some form of employment at the time of application, so that the paying of dues on a monthly basis was a realistic proposition. Further, applicants had to provide proof of residency in the neighborhood or of having been displaced from the neighborhood.

Homesteaders learned about homesteading through word of mouth, from family members, and from friends. A few individuals came to homesteading because they were politically active or consciously aware of housing and community issues. Others joined with little previous knowledge about the issues involved and were motivated by the desire to obtain an apartment. Some joined out of an illusion (which they shed quickly) that this would be a quick and affordable method of obtaining an apartment. One homesteader described his feelings upon initially committing himself to homesteading, in fact telling himself that a one-year commitment would not be so bad. He laughed when he told me this six years after making his commitment.

In the early 1980s, outreach committees tried to attract individuals to homesteading by (among other methods) pushing leaflets under people's doors and speaking at community events. Recruitment involved filling out an application, providing income documentation and proof of meeting the residency requirement, and being interviewed. After an orientation session, a new homesteader went through a so-called trial period. He/she was placed in a building for four to eight weeks. The trial period served as a screening process for the new homesteader's personal commitment and ability to work with others. In theory, the building then indicated whether the individual had been accepted as a new member, and RAIN and LESAC signaled their approval of the individual as a new homesteader. Alternatively, he/she worked in various buildings until a final assignment was made.

The process by which LESAC and RAIN would reach the conclusion that a particular individual was undesirable as a homesteader remained unclear. One homesteader described being puzzled about whether she had "passed" and been accepted into the program after having worked for several months on a trial basis. Finally someone told her that there was no formal acceptance or rejection procedure and that, instead, during this initial period potential homesteaders self-selected out or opted to stay with the process. The trial period was presented as an opportunity for the homesteader to reconsider and for LESAC and RAIN to reject him/her. I did not learn of instances in which an applicant was rejected outright. In part this may be due to the fact that during the first half of the 1980s, activists involved in homesteading were trying to attract as many people as possible in order to broaden their support base. Therefore, the screening process was cursory at best.

If a homesteader joined a building after it had been worked on for several years, the homesteader was required to perform a fixed minimum of labor hours, or sweat—if not in that building, then in another one. Once the sweat requirement had been met, the homesteader had the same rights as those homesteaders who had been with a building from the outset. Those who were not able to do sweat labor, such as elderly or disabled individuals, were expected to perform other tasks. Sometimes they acted as building secretaries or treasurers. In a few instances such homesteaders worked in the LESAC office; the time spent there was counted as sweat.

LESAC attempted to provide volunteer labor as a way of covering such individuals' sweat requirements. The sweat requirement of homeless people in the shelters who were placed in completed buildings was also supposed to be met by such volunteer work. This issue raised tensions among homesteaders, in that people from the shelter system were not required to do sweat even though they may physically have been able to do so.

Volunteers came from various backgrounds and areas. Some came from universities and churches across the country as well as from abroad. Some came from local charitable organizations. The socioeconomic level of volunteers generally was higher than that of the homesteaders. Most volunteers were middle-class professionals between 20 and 35 years of age with incomes from $25,000 upwards. Homesteaders regarded volunteers with some ambivalence and skepticism, which was reinforced by a constant turnover of enthusiastic volunteers who often did not return after having worked on a building once. Volunteers in turn frequently had confused notions about homesteading and homesteaders. The fact that homesteaders were predominantly Puerto Rican whereas volunteers were predominantly Caucasian contributed to mutual misconceptions.

The occasional use of Spanish in the presence of volunteers by home-steaders who also spoke English with each other appeared to be a symbolic reinforcement of identity and a way to emphasize the difference between insiders and outsiders. Occasionally, volunteers who used Spanish encoun-tered a barrier on part of the homesteaders, who acted as if they had not heard what volunteers were saying to them or as if they did not understand. Also complicating these dynamics was the fact that a majority of the volunteers were women. In some buildings, depending on the particular building's composition of homesteaders and attendance on a given day, a group of four or five women volunteers might be working with five women homesteaders and two men, whereas in other buildings the composition might be more balanced. Being a white woman anthropologist, I was more self-consciously aware of these dynamics. Simultaneously I was aware of the possibility that my own awkward position between volunteers and homesteaders distorted my perceptions of these aspects.

Reasons for dropping out were phrased in a variety of ways. Illness, family or marital difficulties, the wish to relocate, loss of a job, alienation from members in one's building, and disillusionment with the process were among the more specific causes listed for dropping out. One homesteader dropped out after three years of work. In view of the frequent readjustments of costs and the resulting future mortgage burden and rents (maintenance), she felt that the rent she would ultimately have to pay would be too high for her. Another homesteader dropped out after having worked on the building for five years. In his case, the decision was based on the fact that his wife was suffering from arthritis and would no longer be able to negotiate the stairs in the building (their apartment would have been on the third floor). His daughter took his place in the building.

My fieldwork data indicate a significant dropout rate. However, these rates varied from building to building, in part dependent on the size of the building and on the progress made by the building. One building with 11 apartment units, which had been worked on since 1986, at the time of completion in 1992 had only one remaining member of the original group of homesteaders. Sixteen people had come and gone since then. Two buildings were finally completed in the summer of 1993, two others in the spring of 1994. Homesteaders began working on one of these buildings in 1984. None from the original group of homesteaders is left in that building. On another building rehabilitation was started in 1986, with one original member remaining. Work on the two other buildings began between 1987 and 1988, and a core of the original homesteaders has remained with each building.

Homesteaders' involvement in the process was fragmented. Many homesteaders had difficulty meeting the various requirements in terms of time and money, frequently made erroneous assumptions about the amount of time it would take to bring a building to completion, and were often detached from the political and bureaucratic aspects of homesteading. Indeed, at times homesteaders appeared uninformed and confused about developments in their own buildings or homesteading generally. Some homesteaders became more active and conscious of larger social and political ramifications as a result of their involvement in homesteading. Others found the burden in terms of time as well as emotional, physical, and financial commitments to be too great a strain and dropped out.

Locating a Sponsor

A sponsoring community-based organization was of primary importance. In the case of a city-run homesteading program, the city could suggest a sponsor. The city's Urban Homesteading Program at HPD was handled through the Division of Alternative Management Programs (DAMP). The manifest goal of this division was to create alternative programs to return in rem (properties taken by the city as a result of abandonment, tax deliquency, or foreclosure) vacant residential buildings to private ownership. The Urban Homesteading Program, the Tenant Interim Lease program (TIL), the Community Management Program, and the Private Ownership and Management Program (POMP) are vehicles that have been or are being developed for this purpose under the umbrella of DAMP. All are based on the assumption that the city does not want to manage buildings because it is too time-consuming and neither cost-effective nor efficient. There is a great deal of administrative and financial overlap within the various divisions of HPD, and at times the lines between HPD projects and HUD projects are blurred. Non-profit organizations such as the Urban Homesteading Assistance Board (UHAB), Pratt Institute, Housing Development Institute (HDI), and Banana Kelly act as sponsors or local program administrators on behalf of the city in the realizations of these programs. On the Lower East Side, both UHAB and HDI have been involved in homesteading projects. In the case of HDI projects, with the exception of the first ones in the early 1980s, the sponsor's involvement predated formation of groups of homesteaders.

HDI was not involved in homesteading as an isolated organization. Instead it was one "head" of a multi-headed Hydra under the auspices of the Archdiocese of New York involved in homesteading projects on the Lower East Side; another "head" was LESAC. LESAC used to be a small, locally active organization connected to the Catholic Church. It operated on a small budget and was engaged in advocacy, social programs, and informational and educational efforts. Once the Catholic Church became active in housing in the early 1980s, LESAC's role was to provide technical assistance; HDI, as the development arm of the Church, was to coordinate sources of money and put together funding proposals. There has been a degree of confusion among homesteaders and other parties about the exact responsibilities of these various organizations. Matters are not helped by the fact that within HDI as well as HPD other housing programs ran concurrently and overlapped with homesteading programs. For example, the production of housing for the homeless, a matter of increasing political urgency for HPD and the Church as well as for local advocacy groups, has intersected with homesteading projects in various ways and has actually engulfed several buildings that originally were to be homesteading projects.

The role played by LESAC and HDI in homesteading projects has not been straightforward either politically and ideologically, or in terms of practical issues involved in the realization of these projects. One HDI employee, speaking of the relationship between HPD and homesteaders, said that it is a case of homesteaders not being able to live with HPD or without it. Here he exhibited a prevailing pattern of pointing outside the group or organization in search of explanations of problems. Similarly, homesteaders, when describing their relationship to LESAC and HDI, frequently sought explanations for problems outside their own group, just as HPD was quick to blame homesteaders.

In the fall of 1992, LESAC closed its office on Avenue C and to all intents and purposes abandoned an active role in the projects. Subsequently LESAC was mainly concerned with concluding its outstanding obligations and untangling itself from any involvement and its relationships with homesteaders, which in some instances had become acrimonious.

Finding a Building and Obtaining Site Control

Finding a building that is available for homesteading is not easy. Abandoned buildings that are owned by the city have been repossessed after the owner abandoned them or failed to pay real estate taxes. Such buildings can be found on the list of city-held properties. Because they are of no value as they stand, in theory the city may be open to plans that result in putting these properties back on the tax rolls. Another place to look for possible sites is the "Unsafe Buildings List" prepared by the Department of Buildings. These buildings are usually vacant although not always city-owned. Private owners may agree to sell, but their prices may be high.

According to an employee of HDI, one reason homesteading has come to an end is that there are no more buildings available. Yet as stated earlier, in 1992 there were 90 abandoned city-owned buildings east of Avenue A, which according to HPD have been identified for various homesteading purposes, cross-subsidy plans (under which a percentage of a building development is designated for low- to moderate-income people), and rehabilitation programs. Thus, the explanation for homesteading having come to an end is not entirely convincing, particularly in light of the fact that LESAC and HDI were beginning to withdraw from homesteading several years ago, when more buildings were still available. Nonetheless finding a building became increasingly difficult, in part due to prior appropriation for other programs, and in part because during the 1980s and early 1990s a lot of vacant and abandoned buildings on the Lower East Side were rehabilitated by the city, by housing developers, and by community organizations.

In the early stage of a homesteading project, it was advisable to hire a structural engineer or registered architect to prepare a thorough report on the building. This enabled the homesteaders to ascertain that they would not encounter major structural problems once they had invested considerable amounts of time and money in a building. Regrettably, homesteaders in several buildings encountered problems that might have been foreseen in a more careful preliminary study. At this point an architect was also brought in to draw plans and write specifications for the proposed rehabilitation; this helped determine the scope of work and cost estimates. Among all the professional people involved in homesteading, architects were the most vulnerable. They were the ones most likely to do work in vain. That is, their plans and drafts had to be completed and submitted before the projects could receive any funding.

Theoretically, before being able to begin working on a building, a homesteading group needed to secure site control. This is the legal permission for the group to control the property. Although it does not mean that the group owns the property, site control gives a group of homesteaders the legal right to work on the building. Obtaining site control essentially means clearing the project with the city and establishing that the building is available for eventual acquisition by the homesteaders. However, there are several buildings on which work was begun before site control had been obtained. In other words, some homesteading projects began as "squats" although the "squatters" did not live in the buildings.

Membership Agreement and By-Laws

At some point during the early stages of a LESAC homesteading project, homesteaders were supposed to draw up a membership agreement in which rules and responsibilities of members were specified in order to provide an organizational format to direct the day-to-day functioning of the group. This agreement specified, among other items, the procedure for accepting new members or removing old members, the policy for conflict resolution, the no-resale policy, the date for payment and the amount of monthly dues, and the amount of sweat per month for which each apartment unit was to be responsible (e.g., 32 hours of sweat per month per homesteader unit). In addition, the group had to draw up by-laws, which are more formal and less specific than the membership agreement. A housing cooperative needs by-laws for establishing a legal corporation for the purpose of buying, owning, and operating a residential building. In New York State, special laws were passed to allow the creation of Housing Development Fund Corporations (HDFCs), special corporations that can buy property from New York City. Certain procedures and legal papers have been standardized to make the creation of HDFCs easier. By-laws also help guarantee the group's eligibility for financial support.

Preparation of a Financing and Loan Package

The preparation of a financing and loan package was a major task at the beginning of a project and continued to be an issue throughout, especially if original cost estimates were too low. Frequently, members of a building that had been worked on for several years learned that the development budget had been vastly underestimated and that funds were insufficient to complete the work. In many instances the only option was to increase the mortgage. Consequently the maintenance to be paid by individual tenants upon moving into the building also increased. It was a bitter experience for homesteaders to see their future rents escalate to the point at which the apartments became almost unaffordable while the homesteaders were still years away from moving in, but had already invested many years in the project. Hence, funding for homesteading projects was a building block as well as a stumbling block.

Fund raising went on throughout the planning and construction period. The central component was the construction loan, which became a mortgage at the end of the project. Limited sources of city and state monies were available in the form of grants. Funds to purchase basic tools and to get interior clean-out and demolition under way came from what is known as seed-money, a combination of homesteaders' dues and money from various private not-for-profit groups, local church groups, and foundations. The Institute for Community Economics provided loans for nine buildings as seed money. New York City's Urban Homesteading Program at HPD used to provide financial assistance of $15,000 per unit in the form of a loan at 1% annual interest repayable over 30 years. Since 1990 this assistance has been an outright grant of $10,000. According to a UHAB employee, the city found that it was more expensive to administer and monitor a loan efficiently than to give money in the form of a grant. Following completion of the rehabilitation, the city agreed to sell the building to the homesteader group for a nominal sum, usually $250 per unit.

A person working for LESAC, and subsequently HDI, has called funding for homesteading "truly a patchwork affair." Site control and city funding helped to leverage other grants and loans. Some funds were also available from the Landmarks Commission, which was willing to finance certain aesthetic work on building facades. Each project used a variety of federal, state, city, and private sources. Furthermore, city and state programs are revised continuously. As a result, sources of money changed frequently; some loans became grants, and grants became loans.

In other cities with homesteading programs, financing as well as organizational aspects differed (see Bratt 1989b; Kolodny 1986). One city provided architectural services and a construction supervisor; in some programs there was greater reliance on federally funded, on-the-job training programs to provide labor, training, and supervision. On the Lower East Side the Department of Employment was offering a program for teenagers from the community who dropped out of school. Through this program, some labor on homesteading projects was available free of charge to the homesteaders. Aside from this, the only way in which homesteaders on the Lower East Side could keep labor costs down was by doing more of the work themselves. However, there were various regulations, both federal and local, regarding the amount of sweat an individual could officially contribute to a project. These regulations were based on the argument that participants in such programs should not be allowed to overextend themselves to the detriment of their jobs and personal lives.

Physical Rehabilitation: Demolition and Buildup

Demolition work was followed by the buildup process. Since LESAC first became involved in homesteading, the buildup process has changed considerably. Until 1991, LESAC acted as general contractor during the buildup process. Contractors hired to execute the work had to be approved and licensed by the city. The result was that the lowest bidder generally got the job. Then the city began to realize how much of the work was being executed in a shoddy fashion, thereby exposing the city to suits brought by completed buildings. From 1991 onward, homesteading groups were given the right to monitor the bidding process and to select their own contractors. Subsequently some groups have chosen to do so and have rejected LESAC as general contractor. Meanwhile, even prior to closing its office on Avenue C in the fall of 1992, LESAC began to pull back from homesteading projects. Some homesteaders presented this development as a choice on their part: "We have severed our relationship with LESAC." Others described it as another example of unfair treatment by LESAC: "They don't help us any longer."

Once rehabilitation was completed and a certificate of occupancy obtained, the homesteaders could move in. They hold proprietary leases and shares to the building. They assume responsibility for paying a maintenance fee (also referred to as rent), which is supposed to pay for the upkeep of the building and pay off the loans taken out during the rehabilitation process. Now the second half of homesteading, in many ways the more trouble-ridden one, begins: managing a building.

DESCRIPTION OF PHYSICAL ASPECTS INVOLVED IN REHABILITATING A BUILDING

There are two kinds of rehabilitation processes; one is called "moderate rehab" and the other "gut rehab." In gut rehab nothing but bare walls is left after demolition. In homesteading projects on the Lower East Side, the process used has been gut rehab. The buildings that have been rehabilitated ranged in size from small three-storey to five- or six-storey buildings. Some were constructed during the late nineteenth and early twentieth centuries; others are of more recent date. As a result the rehabilitation work differed somewhat, but the general process was the same. Projects progressed generally in accordance with the so-called sweat-contractor-sweat model. That is, homesteaders were responsible for the initial demolition and rough carpentry, some masonry, and the final work such as painting and cleanup. Contractors were hired for specialized buildup work, (i.e., major construction, plumbing, heating, electrical systems, and skilled masonry).

The first step involved clearing the building of accumulated debris. Second, the building was gutted from top to bottom. Window frames, pipes, floorboards, and some beams were ripped out; walls and ceilings were stripped; in some instances some of the masonry work was removed. Gutting and debris removal was done by homesteaders. Usually, basic structural renovation was necessary, such as roof work and beam replacement.

Once a building was an empty shell, the buildup process could begin. This was always a significant milestone. At this stage the need for technical assistance increased. Laying of cables, plumbing work, carpentry, and structural work required trained expertise. An outside contractor took over, even though the homesteaders continued to do some of the work. Through on-the-job training programs, homesteaders sometimes were able to do certain otherwise contracted work themselves. They could handle flooring, putting up sheetrock, and painting completely—or at least participate in it to keep the costs low. Work on the outside of a building involved repointing of masonry and renovation of fire escapes. Exterior decorative and structural elements such as lintels, roof overhangs, and front entrance steps could sometimes be considered of landmark value, and funding could be obtained for their repair or restoration; steamcleaning of the outside walls, an aesthetic improvement but not of structural urgency, also falls in this category.

Homesteaders' involvement in the rehabilitation work depended on the degree of technical competence required, either previously learned or acquired throughout the process. It also depended on the way in which a particular building was organized and able to maintain control of the process, ensuring that homesteaders themselves were trained to do as much of the work themselves as possible. The bulk of work done by homesteaders was manual labor, which required endurance more than technical expertise. In each building one or two homesteaders either brought previous expertise to the tasks at hand or were more willing than others to acquire the knowledge necessary for undertaking technically more demanding tasks, such as carpentry or blowtorching. Frequently, once a contractor began to work on a building, homesteaders' active involvement in the physical aspects of rehabilitation decreased; this often coincided with a withdrawal from other aspects as well.

Key days in building work were so-called dumpster days. On such days a building had ordered a dumpster and paid the expensive fee ($600–800) for it. The dumpster had to be filled with debris in a single day, lest opportunists in the neighborhood fill it during the night. Dumpsters were jealously guarded; if not filled up by evening they were carefully covered with wooden boards and weighted down as much as possible. Indeed, one homesteader gleefully described how in the "good old days" of homesteading in the early 1980s, when enthusiasm ran high and the demarcation lines between "us" and "them" appeared to be easily discernible, this homesteader and some others working on a large building made use of what he called "gentry dumpsters":

EDUARDO: Across the street there was a building being developed by Harry Sidel, who had dumpsters. We made "donations" of stuff to their dumpsters. They had contractors who didn't care, they weren't paying for the dumpsters, they didn't care if the dumpster wouldn't be filled up when Friday afternoon came around. So if they had an empty dumpster on Friday afternoon, we would fill it up for them.

On those days, buildings were particularly glad to have extra help. (Here I use the word *buildings* rather than *homesteaders* on purpose, because this is how homesteaders would speak in any instance where the building is viewed as a unit from outside and/or from within.) Together with the building's homesteaders, homesteaders from other buildings who volunteered, homesteaders who had not yet been assigned a building but were working off their share of required sweat-equity hours, and volunteers from outside the neighborhood helped to make up effective teams that could get a lot of work done in a single day.

The following incident illustrates the significance of dumpsters in terms of alignments of "us" versus "others," although in this case the "others" are less clearly defined. I was helping to fill a dumpster at a building when an older woman from the neighborhood, whom I had often seen walking with her dog and a cane, came over to talk to the homesteaders. She said that somebody had called her and complained that people were dumping illicitly in our dumpster. She had looked out of her window and recognized one of the people as a member of RAIN and therefore thought everything was in order, but decided to walk down the block just in case. The homesteaders thanked her, and she walked away satisfied. In this particular incident various RAIN buildings had been pooling their efforts and sharing the dumpster.

TENSIONS IN THE COURSE OF HOMESTEADING WORK

Homesteaders experienced many tensions throughout the physical process. Failure to do one's share of the work and to attend regularly was relatively easily addressed. The group could vote out a member who failed to improve after having been put on notice. However, a great deal of leeway was given. Also, recurring absentees often self-selected out, obviating the need for the group to vote against a member. The degree to which such an issue became a problem depended on (1) the particular member's rapport with other members in the building, and (2) the status of the building's rehabilitation itself. Losing one's temper was a regular occurrence and, depending on the degree of severity, was also fairly easily worked out. One homesteader described the outcome of an incident that occurred while he was construction supervisor. He had become very angry at the other homesteaders and had expressed this quite severely.

MANUEL: They were outraged. I resigned. That was right. I had lost my sense of how to treat people. Sometimes when you elect a president, the president really thinks that he is the president of the United States, so you have to remind them that you voted for them after all. Some people are very good construction supervisors, some very good presidents. Most of the time those who are reluctant to become president make good ones.

Other tensions throughout the physical labor process involved distribution of labor. Again, this was addressed on a case-by-case basis and generally did not result in confrontations. Although there was uneven distribution of labor, and although each building had one or two members who took on a larger share of the work, this remained an unspoken issue. Yet it was a powerful underlying element when confrontations did occur. However, during the actual work process the general tenor of interactions implied a continual reaffirmation that everybody was working toward the same goal.

Any problems experienced by homesteaders throughout the physical process cannot be separated from their personal lives. Trouble at work, loss of employment, or worries about family matters affected homesteading. Homesteaders with families experienced a variety of tensions at home. If one partner did most of the homesteading, the other partner might have felt that the division of labor at home was unfair. Homesteaders who worked during the week and then on Saturdays had difficulties in meeting family obligations on their only day off. One homesteader described tensions with his wife:

MANUEL: I have gotten jealous, angry, saying: "Hey, why don't you go do this!" She forgets how hard it is to work there, to come home all dusty at six or seven o'clock at night, and she can't understand why I can't take the kids out to supper.

Some spouses who did not participate in the homesteading work felt excluded and alienated by the process, in which they did not seem to be playing any role at all, while their husbands, wives, or partners were actively involved and appeared to be leading another life.

Homesteaders loved to describe the physical labor on the building, whereas talking about all the other components of homesteading brought out doubts, confusion, bitterness, and anger. The more outrageous the story, the happier they were in retelling it. The amounts of debris and garbage that were pulled out of buildings seemed to acquire almost mythical proportions, and descriptions of "the worst days" conveyed a tremendous sense of pride and a feeling of having passed through an arduous initiation.

LISA: Our building had been abandoned for nine years. It was like the neighborhood garbage dump. We pulled cars out of the basement. The garbage down there was impacted, packed so tightly. We did not have a roof; half the building had been burned away so the water would go right down there. We had to work with pickaxes. The garbage was like that on almost every floor except where there was no floor.

MARIBEL: The brickpointing came about just as the cold weather was beginning. It was so cold. First of all you had to stand still, and then you had to slosh this wet cement between the bricks; and you couldn't move around so your feet got terribly cold, the building was still open. Wetness gets into your bones, your gloves would get stiff with all this wet cement; it was so cold you would go up to the lightbulbs and hold them to warm up.

My fieldnotes contain many descriptions of days of filling dumpsters or carting debris out of a building, in retrospect making me wish I had devised a kind of shorthand for saying "mind-numbing, backbreaking labor":

December 9, 1989: The entire day was spent mucking out the basement, which was still partially flooded. The pump didn't work because it got clogged with mud. A LESAC employee was working on various pipes that had to be broken up and taken out, using a blowtorch in what seemed to me a blatantly careless and dangerous way in this narrow space, not using a cover for his face and burning himself frequently. He would swear and go on; the homesteaders got worried and tried to help. He got angry at them. Ramón, who rarely says anything, was just watching in evident exasperation. He complained to Jim that Leona had left the basement. In other words, there was no one there to carry out the buckets he was filling up. I didn't see him carry any at all, while the women tended to do both filling and carrying. Rodrigo came over to pick up some of the buckets, and then left again. With a great deal of display and horsing around he broke some pipes with a sledge hammer.

August 11, 1990: We cleaned out the ground floor room. José was loading the dumpster, standing at one end and meticulously arranging everything so that more could fit. He took buckets from people below and emptied them at the upper end of the dumpster, which had been divided off by makeshift walls, so the lower end was free for walking in and stacking big pieces. Anyway, at one point Jim started yelling at him as I was passing buckets up to him, saying that José should stop piling stuff up at the end, it would make the dumpster too heavy. José argued back and basically ignored Jim. I thought that José was more irritated because he was alone at the dumpster until I came over handing buckets up to him while Jim did not start helping himself, rather than by the critical comment re the dumpster.

October 12, 1991: After lunch I went back to the building. Ramona was not back yet, the two volunteers didn't come back. I joined Greg and Luis downstairs. They were emptying an air shaft crammed full with mattresses, dolls, dirt, bottles, books, a sink, shoes, and endless amounts of other junk. I filled and carried buckets upstairs. Concita was blowtorching in the boiler room. We worked fairly steadily, taking a few drink breaks. Greg and Luis were laughing and bantering constantly and seemed pretty well attuned to working together.

My personal low points were (1) pulling black and oily mud out of a partially flooded basement in which one could not stand upright, and (2) filling buckets with heavy, dusty debris and sending it down a chute into a dumpster with the dust permeating every fiber of one's being. Nor was it pleasant to work in a cold building on a winter afternoon, when the single lightbulb hooked up to the generator did little more than accentuate the gloom. Yet along with many homesteaders, I found that compared to other days in homesteading such days were the easier ones. The objective was clear; there was a sense of teamwork and of accomplishing something. This is not to say that such days were always tension-free or enjoyable, but they provided a concrete sense of the reality of the project.

ELENA: To tell you the truth, aside from the physical stuff, a dumpster day is one of the best days, a day when everybody works together; you pick up a rhythm, you all work together as one organism, no talking, no breaks, you just do.

It was ultimately far more draining to come to a building on a rainy winter morning to find that only two of the other homesteaders had shown up, and that therefore the work that should have been accomplished weeks ago would still not get done. It was draining to go to an unceasing number of meetings during the week and on Saturdays after a long day of homesteading. It was draining to come to a building and find that the toolshed had been broken into overnight and all the expensive tools paid for out of homesteaders' dues were gone. Worst of all, delays, uncertainty over funding, and uncertainty over the nature of support from the various community organizations involved in the process bedeviled each project at various times. Some buildings went through long periods during which no work was done at all. During such times, homesteaders associated with the building were forced to wait helplessly for an indefinite period and then, maybe as much as a year later, were expected to return to the project with the same enthusiasm as before. The resulting extremely high turnover rate among homesteaders exacerbated all difficulties.

A key problem was the length of time it took for a building to be completed. Some buildings have been worked on since 1979 and were finished only in 1992. Once a building was in the buildup stage and a contractor had begun working on it, chances were that it might be finished within two years. However, this would occur only if there were no delays of any kind. Four buildings nearing completion in 1993 illustrate different experiences with contractors. Two made very rapid progress once their contractor began work in the fall of 1992. The two others were mired in problems with their contractor; although the buildup work began at approximately the same time, they were at least four months behind, with attendant increases in cost and hence in the eventual maintenance charges to be paid by individual tenants. Each building had its own unique set of problems arising out of the nature of the building (size, structural difficulties, issues related to adjoining buildings or lots) and personality dynamics. Other complications arose in dealing with the city, obtaining site control, meeting HPD requirements, buying the building from the city, obtaining funding, working with a contractor, obtaining the certificate of occupancy, lawsuits brought by former owners of buildings, squatters occupying space in a building, and so on. The relationship that any given building had with LESAC and with RAIN affected developments in the building. To further complicate matters, both organizations underwent significant changes after initially becoming involved in homesteading.

It is instructive to look at individual buildings' records throughout a rehabilitation process (e.g., attendance sheets, daily logs, and reports on monthly dues and expenses). Regular attendance was not easy given the demands of family, work, or other personal matters. Sometimes attendance sheets listed the causes for failure to come to work, sometimes they would merely say "no show." Paying monthly dues ($50 per unit) was difficult for homesteaders with annual incomes ranging from $10,000 to $20,000, and the reports indicated that homesteaders repeatedly fell behind in their payments. Daily logs indicated the fragmentary nature of the process.

Sometimes work was broken off early or deferred because of low attendance or because of a building meeting. Each building had its own set of
problems and its own dynamics. Therefore, the problems common to all
(e.g., attendance, the paying of monthly dues, and the dropout rate) varied
in intensity from building to building.

In addition to dumpster days there were other milestones and associated
key tasks in a building rehabilitation. One milestone was the day on which
the roof was completely renovated or a new roof in place. This had practical
repercussions, because from that point on it was possible to leave material
for the buildup process inside the building.

In one building, wood for joist replacements had been stored inside the
building at a time when the roof work was imminent. However, due to
problems with funding this work was held up. One day the homesteaders
found to their dismay that a recent downpour had not only seeped through
the roof and transformed practically every floor into a mud flat but had also
soaked the new wood, which then became slightly warped. As a result, only
some of it could be used for its intended purpose.

Another milestone was the completion of demolition. Once demolition
had been completed and the buildup process begun, the need for guarding
the building at night increased. This presented a number of dilemmas.
Homesteaders took turns sleeping in the building. In some buildings, temporary sheds were constructed that could be locked and also could hold
some of the heat provided by a space heater. However, this placed a tremendous time constraint on everyone involved, particularly if the need for
safeguarding the building continued over a prolonged period. In theory two
people were assigned to do security; however, this did not always work out.

The local police were largely supportive of homesteaders. Once when I
was in a building with some homesteaders, two policemen came over. They
sat on the stoop and talked to the homesteaders for a while, asked about
the progress, and said the homesteaders should call them if they needed
anything. One of the homesteaders later laughed and said the police call
homesteaders associated with LESAC "the Church people" as opposed to
"squatters." In other words, in the eyes of the police "the Church people"
were acceptable and to be looked out for. Nonetheless, the police were not
in a position to prevent break-ins. As a result anyone doing security was
vulnerable. The following excerpt from my fieldnotes illustrates one older
woman's dismay over this aspect of homesteading:

> *August 24, 1991*: I saw Leona walking around outside, apparently taking
> a break. She talked to me about what they were doing in the building; and
> then showing a very strained and tired face, she talked about her fear re
> having to do security, that she was afraid, had been attacked twice, did not
> feel she could do this every night, not with a job, that the others did not
> understand, that she was afraid to say anything, that she didn't think she
> should have to do it.

Leona eventually participated in guarding the building at night. She was unwilling to elaborate on why she ended up doing so despite her profound reservations. She may have decided to do it because the peer pressure from the other building members was so strong. The same quality of sheer perseverance that helped her to stay with the building from the beginning in 1988 to its completion in 1993 may have carried her through this experience as well.

Like some other homesteaders, Leona emerged from the process embittered and angry. She felt manipulated if not by individual homesteaders then by the way in which the entire process had been set up. She described the job of security as the final and worst aspect of homesteading, robbing her of much of her initial enthusiasm. For single heads of households with children, doing security presented particular difficulties.

TANA: I was the only woman doing security. Most of the other people in the building are married or are men. It was rough. I had to do my own work, work on the building and do security, and take care of my child and everything else.

A member of the same building confirmed that in that particular building most of the units were occupied by couples, and in those instances the men tended to be the ones to do security.

EDUARDO: It was hard sometimes in that you had to stay by yourself sometimes, but I never had anyone break in on me. Except you just had to stay in the building and watch TV, and call the police if you heard something. We had a phone.

In some buildings a room was set aside for meetings and breaks. This often was also the room in which tools were kept and where a protective shed was erected for security. An old couch, a few chairs, a table, and a bulletin board with notices and leaflets about various aspects of homesteading lent an odd atmosphere of homeyness in the midst of buckets, piles of debris, and bare brick walls. It provided a sense of the building being inhabited. This was reinforced by the homesteaders' eagerness to point out which of the apartments would be their own, where the kitchen would be, and how many rooms they would have.

Two buildings approaching completion in the fall of 1993 had selected a contractor for the buildup process who not only refused to let the homesteaders continue working on the building but also took charge of security. As a result, this became another rehabilitation element in the building that had to be paid for by the homesteaders, adding to the cost and ultimate mortgage burden on homesteaders. A contractor's taking charge of security contributed to the increasing dissociation of homesteaders from the work of completing their buildings.

Doing security provided homesteaders with a way of laying claim to the building and making it their own. Once there was water in the building pipes, there was an additional reason for security beyond preventing vandalism and break-ins. In winter, the person doing security had to monitor a space heater that provided heat in the basement to prevent the pipes from freezing. I interviewed one homesteader in her future apartment for whom doing security had turned into a way of life and also a temporary solution for her housing problem.

January 8, 1991: The temperature was below freezing. Lourdes showed me the arrangement for keeping the temperature in the basement above freezing during the night. I watched her light a kerosene heater in the basement. While we were waiting to make sure that the flame was burning evenly and steadily, Lourdes showed me a deep water-logged hole on one side of the basement that used to hold the incinerator. Many buildings at one time had such incinerators before they were outlawed. She took me upstairs to the second floor, where she was firmly established in the space that will become her apartment. She assured me that it was quite warm because of another heater there. Lourdes had an arrangement of three mats near the door, where she carefully brushed her feet off, saying she was trying to keep the dust out. In the back she had a bedroom set up, two chairs and the heater sitting in the middle like a creature from outer space. She showed me her camping equipment stove, which she has been using for cooking and the arrangement with buckets, which she used to wash dishes and dump the waste water downstairs before she had running water. She described carrying water up in heavy buckets. She said she always cooked there because it was too expensive to go out. She showed me a narrow wooden table that she made herself. It had hooks on which to hang things, a narrow device with slots for knives, and she explained her system of cutting off the bottoms of empty coke bottles, hanging them upside down with the cap taken off so that silverware stuck into them could dry off and be stored there at the same time.

When I got ready to leave that day, Lourdes told me how to secure the plywood door downstairs so that she would not have to leave her cozy room. As I made my way out of the building and into the bitter January wind, I marveled at her ingenuity and endurance.

SWEAT AND RAIN

Sweat was a powerful symbol in homesteading. It occupied pride of place in the defining terminology of sweat-equity. The implication was that one buys shares with one's own sweat. The promise was held out that labor would receive its just rewards. Sweat also carried the connotation of worthiness. To do sweat was a way of proving one's moral suitability for receiving the privileges and rights of ownership. The notion of doing sweat implied a kind of learning period to prepare one for the attendant obligations and responsibilities of ownership. Sweat was the element that set off homesteaders from residents, it proved an individual's ability to make it, and it symbolized membership in the community of homesteaders.

Another powerful symbol was the name for the Community Land Trust organization, RAIN. "RAIN" was printed on T-shirts that many homesteaders wore, and the RAIN letters appeared on signs posted on buildings to signify that they belonged to the Community Land Trust. Water and sweat were central to homesteading, and their symbolic resonance was strengthened on a daily basis. During work on a building, sweat literally dropped onto piles of debris; homesteaders' faces were lined with sweat running over the accumulated dust and grime. Facemasks could be veritable hellholes when one seemed to be breathing nothing but sweat and dust. In summer, hydrants on the street provided welcome relief, and homesteaders helped each other in dumping water over their heads to cool off. Water from hoses attached to the hydrant at the corner was used to wet down dusty debris. Plastic jugs of water were passed around during breaks. Indeed, it was a big moment when a building was finally hooked up to city water.

In the language of symbols, sweat creates apartments and RAIN makes a parched community grow. However, a false dichotomy was created in that the sweat aspect of homesteading overshadowed or drowned out other aspects such as meetings and paperwork, which in consequence were often neglected. Glorification of physical labor as a way of taking control of one's housing situation and as a training ground for future management of one's property masked other forces and problems in the community, the housing sector, and the larger society. Thus, ironically it was a factor contributing to the loss of control. Meanwhile, developments in RAIN have contributed to friction, disillusionment, and alienation among many homesteaders so that this symbol of empowerment is turned into a sea of political intrigues and power struggles.

CONCLUSION

In the newsletter *The Homesteader*, one woman described her impressions and feelings after having been involved in homesteading for seven months (LaSalle 1989). She quoted from a journal in which she had noted her experiences and feelings on the first day of homesteading. On that day she helped to pull down wooden beams and throw them into the dumpster.

Joe told us to go to the second floor, climb out the window onto the platform, and help throw all the beams into the dumpster in the street. When people are doing this particular chore, no one is supposed to throw anything out the window until we're done, but about three times things were thrown down. Then we would scream up at whoever did it. It was kind of nerve-racking, but after a while we didn't worry about it. . . . I wrote that over seven months ago and I'm now a member of that same building. Now, seven months is not a long time for some of the older homesteaders, but it's long enough for me to offer this observation: No matter what difficulties arise, whether physical like cleaning out the "abominable" basement, or mental like trying to put together a proposal for some fund raising, or dealing with squatters or city red tape, etc. (you *do* get the IDEA, don't ya?) *whatever* comes up, I believe getting a home for yourself and your family, stabilizing, settling down, that's what the real deal is. So let's work together with this common goal in mind. That's what we're busting our buns for after all, isn't it? (LaSalle 1989)

This homesteader's enthusiasm and unbroken belief in the process contrast with another homesteader's comment in her contributing article in a later issue of the same newsletter. She voiced concern about homesteaders' tendency to become wrapped up in the material and physical challenges of a rehabilitation project while delegating decision making to others. She felt that if one is not "on automatic pilot" as far as the physical labor is concerned after the third month of homesteading, one hardly could meet all the other demands such as (1) dealing with paperwork, (2) attending meetings with other homesteaders, LESAC, lawyers, city officials, and others, and (3) most important, taking on responsibility in all these efforts. "A top-down structure is inevitably brittle and will be doomed to crumble, usually at a moment of extreme tension, when the work can least afford to be delayed by inter-group rivalry" (McMurray 1990). Her warning applies to the actual rehabilitation process and to the time after homesteaders have taken occupancy. According to this homesteader, struggles at the individual level accounted for much of the brittleness of homesteading projects. Indeed, such brittleness is equally if not more so a reflection of problems inherent in community movements within a society that has set up powerful obstacles at both material and ideological levels.

NOTE

1. As early as 1991 the four projects were already in question, largely as a result of funding difficulties and LESAC's changing focus on the Lower East Side away from homesteading. Two buildings side by side on 4th Street, on which initial gutting work had begun and where there was a group of homesteaders, have been given up by LESAC; their rehabilitation has been taken over by Coalition Housing. The history of the third building, 240 East 2nd Street, is described in more detail in the following chapter. It also was eventually redesignated for rehabilitation by Coalition Housing. The fourth, 206 Clinton Street, was redesignated at an earlier time for the construction of permanent housing for homeless families, with funding provided by the New York State Homeless Housing and Assistance Program. HDI continues to be involved; however, the local sponsor is It's Time Agency, a housing advocacy and social service organization on the Lower East Side. Nazareth Home, Inc., is supposed to provide support services. This building was completed in early 1995, and tenants have moved in.

Elizabeth Street tenement house yard, June 16, 1903, Jacob A. Riis.

Necktie workshop in a Division Street tenement, circa 1889, Jacob A. Riis.

Interior of a tenement, 1896, Byron Collection.

Rooftops, looking eastward from Avenue B and 9th Street toward the Projects and the East River, 1983, courtesy of Marlis Momber.

Empty lot on Avenue C, between 4th and 5th Streets, 1982, courtesy of Marlis Momber.

Manhattan skyline, view from the roof of East 4th Street showing 309 East 4th Street, 66 Avenue C, and 702 Avenue C, 1983, courtesy of Marlis Momber. The building at 66 Avenue C was the first LESAC building in the homesteading program.

Lower East side housing rally, 1984, courtesy of Marlis Momber.

Homesteaders in front of Eleanor Bumpurs Memorial Homestead, 304 East 8th Street, 1984, courtesy of Marlis Momber.

LESAC homesteaders on their way to a meeting after doing sweat, Avenue C between 7th and 8th Streets, 1989, courtesy of Marlis Momber.

Rosalía and Sergio Mendez, homesteaders, 1995.

Margarita López, homesteader, 1995.

229 East 7th Street, 1995.

El Jardín del Paraíso, between 4th and 5th Streets and Avenues C and D, 1989, courtesy of Marlis Momber.

5

THE DAY THE WALL FELL DOWN

And the land shall not be sold in perpetuity,
for the land is mine; and you are but aliens
who have become my tenants.

Leviticus 25: 23

This quotation expresses a central tenet of the Community Land Trust movement and strikes at the heart of the problem posed by the urban homesteading model devised on the Lower East Side. The implied notion of permanently decommodifying land and housing runs counter to the logic of capitalism and the market economy. In that logic, real estate is a commodity subject to the laws of supply and demand and the time-bound use life of building structures. The Lower East Side homesteading model in conjunction with the Community Land Trust was based on a profoundly different ideological concept, seeking to remove housing from the cycle of the market in order to ensure long-term security and affordability of housing for poor working-class people. The contradiction posed by such a model that attempted to survive in the context of a market economy becomes apparent when one considers the difficulties encountered by homesteading projects after completion.

The process of homesteading was not concluded when homesteaders received their certificate of occupancy and moved into a completed building. This may be an obvious point. However, homesteaders themselves at times forgot this fact. Individual homesteaders' perceptions and representations of homesteading got caught up in the process, leading homesteaders to seek explanations for various developments in factors immediately visible or tangible and to believe that housing problems come to an end after they have moved into their rehabilitated units. Such a preoccupation with homesteading as a compartmentalizable activity, the success of which is measured by the number of buildings completed regardless of their subsequent histories, is part and parcel with a tendency of city administration officials and homesteaders to seek explanations for successes and failures in single factors. Problems in completed buildings are rooted in the history of the rehabilitation process and are shaped by developments in the labor market and the increasing cost of living, and the cost of operating a building. The rising number of buildings in default is an indicator of continuing and future troubles in New York City's housing situation; low-income housing cooperatives are at particular risk of being recycled into the market.

Developments in buildings after completion involve three different categories: building management, financial issues, and relations with people from New York City shelters who have been placed in buildings. An understanding of these developments is a basis for analyzing how homesteaders' perceptions and attitudes are transformed over the course of homesteading. Further, dynamics at the micro level (i.e., individual buildings and their ongoing developments) illustrate the linkages between this level and the macro level of socioeconomic and political processes.

BUILDING NAMES AS SYMBOLS OF STRUGGLE

The contrast between active rehabilitation and life in completed buildings can be illustrated by the changing role of names assigned by homesteaders to their buildings. The powerful symbolic value of these names, which were created by homesteaders during active involvement in the process, reinforces the notion of homesteading as having a life of its own, with its own vitality and logic of development. Unfortunately, it also obscures and detracts from citywide and national developments with regard to housing and related factors.

Throughout the rehabilitation process, building names served as identity markers, as indicators of individual leadership associated with a given building, and as symbols of struggle. Once buildings were completed, the names were no longer as relevant; the locus of struggle had changed. This is one, perhaps seemingly superficial, change that occurred as buildings were completed and homesteaders moved into their apartments. However, when taken in context with other changes, the names and their ephemeral existence reflect important dynamics at work. Building names provide insights into homesteaders' constructions of the process they were involved in and the manner in which lived experience is encapsulated and transformed into stories. The waning importance of the names reflects parallel processes of withdrawal and disengagement on the part of homesteaders after they moved into completed buildings.

Buildings were referred to in different ways. During rehabilitation work, the street number was often used in an offhand manner: "Have you seen Chris?" "He's over at 229." There was only one 66, one 229, and one 721. Homesteaders frequently spoke about a building in terms of the home-steader who had played a leading role in the building. There was Jenny's building, Rose's building, Lourdes's building, Carmen's building, Manuel's building (pseudonyms). Most of the buildings were identified by the name of a woman homesteader, reflecting the prominent role played by women homesteaders.

Another appellation was the formal name selected by the homesteaders for their corporation. For example, "635 East 11th Street Archbishop Oscar Romero Memorial HDFC" was a resonant image of resistance against repression.[1] The name "Ahona Homesteading Cooperative" was based on the Taino word for "working women."[2] "641 East 11th Street 'Florisol' HDFC," translated approximately as "sunflower," has a hopeful ring. "239 East 2nd Street Joseph Cardona Memorial HDFC" is a reminder of a personal tragedy; Joseph Cardona was a squatter in the building before it was formally accepted into the urban homesteading program. A member of the original homesteaders' group, he died several years before the building was completed. His mother continued his work and is currently living in the building. "La Forteleza" sounds a note of invincible struggle.[3] A more sober and businesslike name is the "320 East 4th Street Limited Equity HDFC." The one-time shooting gallery "The Executive" retained its name after rehabilitation, illustrating that the past reaches into the present in many forms; another shooting gallery, "The Toilet," was demolished before it could be turned into a homesteading project. A sense of shared injustice is reflected in the name "304 East 8th Street Eleanor Bumpurs Memorial Homestead," or "Bumpurs" for short; sometimes the building is affectionately referred to as "the old girl."[4] Some buildings are referred to by characteristics that set them apart from the others. For example, there is the building above Pedro's coffeeshop and, most infamous, the building where the wall fell down.

This building, a four-storey unit, is located next to a rehabilitated build-ing that was completed in 1990. LESAC had planned this building to be another homesteading project. In 1990 LESAC began to do some work on it and invested approximately $6,000, but homesteaders had not yet been assigned to the building. During this time, sources of federal and local funding for homesteading projects were drying up. Several buildings that already were being worked on were experiencing severe difficulties in raising necessary funds. Meanwhile, the city was increasingly unwilling to support new projects. As a result, LESAC stopped all work on this building. In February 1991 the entire back wall facing Houston Street collapsed during the night. Rubble spilled into the backyard, and the side wall of the adjoining building was exposed. Attempts were made to secure the remaining structure and to make sure the adjoining building did not suffer structural damage. Blue plastic sheets were hung on the remaining wooden beams on the building's back side in order to contain loose bricks and debris. Flapping in the wind, these sheets quickly became shredded and made an odd contrast to the neatly painted adjoining building and its clean backyard. Despite assurances from LESAC, residents in the adjoining building were extremely upset and continued to worry that their building would be affected.

As far as the homesteaders in the neighboring building were concerned, the issue was not resolved in a satisfactory manner. Homesteaders in buildings undergoing active rehabilitation viewed the event with greater equanimity. It was added to the many stories of "battle" and was mentioned with a certain enjoyment. The reality of living in a completed building was distant at best; many homesteaders had an idealized image of life after the completion of rehabilitation, akin to the notion of an uncomplicated reward or a feast at the end of a day's work. The problems experienced by homesteaders in completed buildings seemed minor compared to the pain and effort of rehabilitation. Among homesteaders in completed buildings, however, the incident of the collapsed wall reinforced an increasingly pervasive feeling that accountability was an elusive and slippery concept, particularly as problems with completed buildings were becoming more apparent. The collapsed wall became a metaphor for the general precariousness of living in a rehabilitated building. During rehabilitation work, the notion of controlling one's own housing situation appeared concrete and tangible. For homesteaders in completed buildings, faced with financial and administrative problems and the effects of defective construction work, control over their own housing situation once again was subject to doubt and at danger of being swept away altogether.

MOVING IN AND LIVING IN A COMPLETED BUILDING

Receiving a certificate of occupancy was a high point in the rehabilitation process. However, it was hardly an insurance of happiness. One homesteader in a completed building emphasized that she believed the real trouble of homesteading would begin after the building was finished. At that time the need for understanding all the legal and financial documents becomes apparent. One can no longer avoid the people one is living with. The homesteader felt that this was particularly important when one has a child and wants the child to be able to play with others in the building and on the block. She said that many people in her building were not ready to face the tasks of running a building and preferred not to get involved. Another homesteader put this more concretely:

LISA: For the homesteaders themselves, there is no transition period between lifting buckets, filling dumpsters, and running a building. And no one who is a member in any of these buildings has ever been a member of a shareholders' corporation before, and never owned anything before, never owned anything of value, so there has been no transition, no education, no training.

Managing a building as a housing cooperative is a complex proposition. Homesteaders face many tasks once they move in. These tasks involve financial, legal, and technical problems. The budget of operating expenses contains a daunting list of items to be considered such as gas and electricity charges, maintenance and repair costs, taxes and insurance fees, not to mention servicing the debt. The fact that many of these costs will increase over the years becomes apparent to many homesteaders only once they actually confront it in the form of unpaid bills.

Seemingly minor matters have begun to create irritations and unnecessary costs in completed buildings. For example, during a meeting of homesteaders one individual mentioned a problem concerning warranties on practically all systems and appliances in her building (e.g., stoves, refrigerators, and boilers). In that instance the warranty cards had been mislaid and not properly mailed in at the time of installation. If any of these costly appliances break down, residents in this building might have no recourse. Again, this raises the issue of accountability. Who should have checked to make sure the warranty cards were handled properly? Who was responsible for ensuring that a building kept thorough financial records throughout a rehabilitation process in order to prevent nasty surprises at a later stage? Is LESAC to be held accountable for things going wrong? Is HDI to be held accountable? Is the city—or, more specifically, HPD—to be held accountable?

Over the course of a homesteading project and in the years after taking occupancy, homesteaders moved through various stages of leveling accusations at one or another party. This process of fault finding suggests conflicting processes of increasing alienation from homesteading and increasing combativeness as understanding of the complexities involved grew. In other words, there were concurrent processes of personal disempowerment and empowerment.

Some completed buildings were already in dire financial straits in 1993. In talking about one such building, one homesteader said that buildings should have had an accountant but were hardly in the position to pay for one. One building had an accountant do the work on a *pro bono* basis, but the homesteader bitterly stated that this was of no help to the other buildings. Here a pattern became apparent: completed buildings began to act increasingly as isolated units. While active rehabilitation was still going on, demarcation lines between individual buildings were not as clearly drawn. Another homesteader expressed surprise about the cost of the annual audit of the building and pointed to another future issue that may embroil many of these buildings in unexpected expenses: faulty construction work.

LISA: These buildings were not really built with long-term stability in mind. They got the cheapest contractors and they had no supervision, so you had cheap contractors doing unsupervised work on these buildings. A lot of stuff slipped by, which is going to cause a lot of trouble in the future.

FINANCIAL MATTERS IN COMPLETED BUILDINGS

In most buildings the accounting procedure throughout the rehabilitation process was not thorough, and errors made as long as six, seven, or eight years ago are reflected in problems experienced by buildings after their completion. One homesteader argued that some problems were due to the homesteaders' failure to assume responsibility for the process.

DAVID: That's another point where homesteading is a real education. When the money starts flowing in, when the checks come in, what you really need is good oversight, accounting, keeping track of where it goes. What happened to us was basically there was one person doing it, now we are finding that out. We're paying the price. Costs were underestimated. Accounts were kept very sloppily, records were not kept well. Everything has to be accounted for, invoices kept. When someone says I have to have every invoice related to this or that right now, all of a sudden we have to start reorganizing because the guy before didn't put so much time into it.

Several homesteaders held LESAC partly accountable for these difficulties.

TANA: A lot of the questions I had were about why are you paying these bills with no backup, why are you paying these salaries out of our account for men working on this building? . . . They work on our building sometimes and on other buildings at other times, and they would charge our account. These are LESAC employees and day laborers.

Some buildings considered suing LESAC for misappropriation of funds. One building in fact sued LESAC in the early 1990s; the case was settled out of court and a sum of money awarded to the building. Hardly anyone imputed self-serving motives to LESAC, but homesteaders do fault the organization for acting in an unprofessional and even underhanded manner.

ELENA: I mean, the point is nobody went to Baden Baden with this money, nobody bought a fleet of Cadillacs or went on junkets to Vegas to gamble. They were all . . . the road to hell is paved with the purest of intentions. This is an example. There was no accounting, nothing was run in a businesslike fashion, which the head of LESAC has got to be responsible for. No accounting was put into place, there was apparently no recognition that you cannot play around with millions of dollars this way, all of which needs to be reported on and documented and filed and done in triplicate. And it is a scandal basically that homesteaders are later saddled with surprise bills for $10,000 or whatever the hell it is, especially in these hard times.

Funding and Other Sources of Entrapment for Completed Buildings

Money from the city and state governments played an ambiguous role in homesteading throughout the active rehabilitation process and after completion. In some of the stories told about homesteading, such money at times takes on the appearance of flypaper on which hapless homesteaders got stuck. The city provided a basic amount per unit ($10,000) as a form of seed money to provide the homesteaders with leverage to raise other funds. However, as homesteaders put it, the city then drowned homesteading projects in a sea of requirements and bureaucratic red tape. At the same time, the city blamed the homesteaders for failing to raise more money and to make progress on the rehabilitation.

In one case, homesteaders in a building assumed that a certain sum of money had been given to them in form of a grant. However, to their great dismay they were informed several years later that this money would be treated as a mortgage to be paid back with interest. Originally the source for this funding had been a $1 million Housing Trust Fund grant administered by the state in the mid-1980s. Administration of the grant was taken over by the city and divided in half: 50% was left as outright grant money, 50% became a low-interest loan administered by the city. Hence, 50% of the money originally received by a particular building in the form of a grant turned out to be a loan, albeit at a low interest rate (1.2%), to be added onto the original mortgage.

Section 8 Assistance

Another form of city money is the so-called Section 8 assistance program, which was created in 1974.[5] It provides assistance for payment of maintenance and rental charges for eligible low-income tenants. The program has not been discontinued; however, in December 1994 it stopped accepting new applicants. A tenant is eligible for Section 8 Housing Assistance Payments if the new rent is more than 30% of his or her total family income, or for the Senior Citizen Rent Increase Exemption (SCRIE) if the tenant is 62 years old or older and the new rent is more than one-third of his or her total family income. A tenant who is eligible for Section 8 will pay approximately 30% of his or her income as maintenance or rent. The remainder of the maintenance or rent will be paid to the co-op corporation by the city. SCRIE rent assistance is provided in the form of a deduction from the amount of real estate taxes owed by the co-op corporation to the city.

Initially, the Section 8 program subsidized rents in the form of payments to private developers and owners on behalf of low-income tenants for new construction and rehabilitation.[6] Later it was changed to provide rent subsidies directly to an individual or a family. The burden of finding an apartment that meets federal quality standards within the stipulated four-month time limit upon being accepted for Section 8 assistance is borne by the recipient. 1994 guidelines for Section 8 certificates state that a three-bed-room apartment cannot cost more than $993 a month, not including gas and electricity; and the maximum amount for a two-bedroom apartment is $785. Given the high cost of housing in New York, it is very difficult to find an apartment that meets these guidelines. For homesteaders relying on Section 8 assistance to meet their future rent bills, this presents a problem. Due to increasing costs of rehabilitation and miscalculations, building mortgages and projected rents have increased frequently over the course of rehabilita-tion work and hence bring the apartments perilously close to the designated limit.

One homesteader in a completed building who receives Section 8 assis-tance said that this program was still an untested element in homesteading. The same homesteader claimed that it also might be the element that would keep this building afloat, because it would be politically far more problem-atic for LESAC to let a building "go under" if it has Section 8 residents. She seemed to believe that LESAC would step in to help the building in the event of a serious difficulty, but she was not able to offer any concrete suggestions about how LESAC could help. Budget cuts proposed in early 1995 would cut HUD's fiscal year 1995 budget by $7.3 million, or one-third of its total budget; if this package became law, it would affect Section 8 assistance. Another homesteader calls Section 8 an artificial subsidy.

MANUEL: We are nonprofit, we are not a landlord, we do not look to public manage-ment and money to help us out. In our building, the projected costs of the building have been worked out and the rents are skewed to reflect different income levels. We don't need Section 8.

Manuel argued that because homesteading was intended for low-income people and should have affordable rents to begin with, Section 8 assistance should not be necessary. He also felt that the introduction of a group of people receiving housing assistance would create two kinds of residents while placing the building into a dependence on outside assistance. Manuel described the Section 8 program as a giant tax-evasion scam. He talked about developers obtaining tax write-offs for buildings with Section 8 subsidies in order to get buildings done; and he pointed out that once Section 8 subsidies expire, the apartments revert to the open market. He drew my attention to the Manhattan Plaza sequence of events described by Schur (1986).[7] In doing so Manuel taught me a lesson not only about the Section 8 program but also about the extent of knowledge exhibited by homesteaders regarding their own situation and the economic and political context. For all that sometimes I was reminded of the stereotypical image of the hapless, uninformed, and passive victim, I repeatedly encountered the exact opposite in forceful, active, and informed individuals.

The J 51 Tax Abatement Program

The J 51 tax abatement program has led to unpleasant surprises. The program was created in 1955 and provided tax abatements to those who would buy up decaying housing stock and rehabilitate it. As a result of the abatement, the taxes on the building would be frozen for 12 years. According to Tabb, this was in effect a subsidy program to underwrite gentrification. "There is a huge incentive involved, one that has prompted many unscrupulous landlords to illegally harass the lower-income and elderly tenants who occupy converted apartments" (Tabb 1984: 338).

In the case of homesteading projects, a tax abatement is granted to a building under certain circumstances. A building may qualify if less than 25% of a rehabilitation project is new construction. Several buildings had projected future operating costs based on the assumption that the buildings would qualify for the tax abatement. In these buildings, J 51 applications were being held up for a variety of reasons. In one building the complete complement of permits necessary for filing an application was not available. Another building had difficulty in proving that it qualified for the abatement. A building member claimed that the building even received a notification stating such qualification from HPD. However, it turned out later that the building did not qualify for the tax abatement because it was completely rehabilitated and has an outside wall that was newly constructed in its entirety. This meant that real estate taxes would go up significantly, in turn increasing building maintenance to levels hard to meet by the homesteaders. (Ironically, in 1992 this particular building experienced structural problems with that same wall. Moisture seeped through the wall into the building.)

Several years after completion of the building, the homesteaders abandoned the issue. This was due in part to general exhaustion; a homesteader said that the building had not been having meetings on the issue. Further, financial considerations played a role. There was not enough money available to pay for the legal fees necessary for effectively pursuing the abatement. The building's funds were tight. One tenant was undergoing a divorce and had fallen behind on maintenance payments. The building had a reserve fund but understandably did not want to touch that unless there was a dire emergency.

According to a report on New York City's early low-income housing cooperative conversions, many buildings do not receive J 51 abatements because of technicalities rather than for concrete reasons that would make them ineligible for the abatement (Lawson 1984). For instance, if a building fails to meet a deadline for getting a certificate of occupancy, it becomes ineligible for the abatement. Therefore, those buildings that could benefit most from the abatement are often the ones that fail to get it.

Another building, which was completed in 1989, encountered an unexpected difficulty in trying to apply for its J 51 tax abatement. The homesteaders could not get the contractor to sign off on the plumbing work. Therefore, the building was not able to file all the papers necessary to apply for the tax abatement. The reason for the contractor's refusal was that his bill had not been paid. LESAC argued that the building should pay the plumber the $10,000 in question; the building's homesteaders were upset about being saddled with a bill months after they had thought everything was completed. Further, the group felt that LESAC mishandled funds. Instead of paying any particular building's bills with the money raised for that building, it was using funds wherever they were needed. Several homesteaders have argued that LESAC's bookkeeping has been chaotic and haphazard at times, although no one has seriously implied a misappropriation of funds. Nonetheless, buildings found that funds, which they had believed to be available for their rehabilitation project, had been spent elsewhere. There was ongoing confusion about how much money had already been spent by a building. As a result, it is not so surprising that a particular bill became the center of a drawn-out argument. A terse statement in the RAIN Annual Report for 1990/1991 indicated another building group's dismay about a situation with regard to unexpected bills:

We found out that they [subcontractors] had not been paid for work done in our building. Since LESAC had full control of our monies, we were unaware of the situation until the notice. We put our trust and our home in LESAC's hands; they have lost our trust.

Water and Sewer Tax Rates

One out of every four formerly city-owned buildings sold to community groups and low-income, tenant-run cooperatives is on the brink of fiscal collapse, and could be returned to city ownership in the future, a study by City Limits reveals. The properties, a major bulwark of the city's affordable housing strategy, are so deeply in debt and owe so much in back taxes that the city has placed them on a list of properties up for reclamation. (White et al. 1992)

This dire statement is the conclusion of a discussion about the egregious consequences of a 182% increase in the city's water tax rate between 1984 and 1992, which now completely overwhelms the budgets of many low-income buildings. The city increased its water tax rate in order to raise money for expanded sewage treatment, sludge disposal, and a new water tunnel. The installation of water meters to encourage conservation has exacerbated the problem. It affects low-income buildings disproportionately in that such buildings have less efficient plumbing systems, are generally more crowded, and hence use a lot of water. In response to the outcry by community organizations, the city administration has been making efforts to address the crisis. One such effort involves giving buildings that had meters installed by the city a credit for future water bills. This plan would cost the city about $20 million in the short term, but it might help prevent buildings from being seized by the city for unpaid bills. Housing advocates and politicians have supported the drafting of a bill that would prevent increases in the New York City water rates for as much as two years, while a new rate structure is worked out.

Buildings that have been completely rehabilitated and consequently have new plumbing systems are less likely to waste water needlessly through leaks and dripping faucets and less likely to have an inflated water bill as the result of such waste. Nevertheless, water rates are far higher than had been foreseen at the time rehabilitation work on the buildings on the Lower East Side was begun, and these rates were not figured into the budgets. During rehabilitation some homesteaders were aware of this problem, which their buildings would face upon completion, but optimistically believed it would be manageable.

THE NO-RESALE POLICY AND NAZARETH HOME

During the active rehabilitation phase, two central ideological issues in homesteading on the Lower East Side—the no-resale policy, and the so-called Nazareth Home people—were embraced or, at worst, ignored. Once several buildings were completed, these two issues became the subject of increasingly acrimonious debates and conflict. Both are discussed in greater detail in Chapter 6; they are mentioned here to illustrate the many levels of problems confronted by completed buildings. Furthermore, the change in outlook and attitudes of homesteaders vis-à-vis the entire process is linked not only to building management issues but also to changing ideological notions.

Buildings that joined the RAIN Community Land Trust formally agreed to a set of restrictions that in essence attach a no-resale policy to a proprietary lease. The purpose of the no-resale policy is to ensure that the apartments remain available to low- and moderate-income people in the neighborhood. As a holder of a proprietary lease, a homesteader may not sell the apartment for a profit; instead, he/she is only permitted to sell it back to the Community Land Trust for the approximate monetary equivalent invested over the course of rehabilitation.

Some buildings initially were included in the group of buildings receiving assistance from LESAC and were expected to join RAIN. They backed out at the time when they would have had to formally join the Community

Land Trust by selling the building land to RAIN. In consequence, LESAC no longer provided them with assistance. A few of these buildings managed to complete rehabilitation; others were effectively stuck and experienced difficulties at all levels, in particular with regard to funding. In buildings that joined RAIN, particularly in completed buildings, the no-resale policy has been debated and questioned. Many homesteaders now residing in their new apartments are ambivalent about the fact that they cannot sell their apartments at a profit.

The Nazareth Home issue is also the subject of debate and questioning. Homesteaders made an agreement with LESAC at the inception of homesteading. In return for financial assistance, consulting services, and construction assistance by LESAC, homesteaders would allocate several units in each homesteaded building for the use by Nazareth Home for placing homeless, disabled, and elderly people in transitional and permanent apartments. So-called permanent units are supposed to revert to Nazareth Home for reassignment when they become vacant after the respective tenants have departed or died.

There are three types of problems regarding Nazareth Home units in completed buildings. First, most Nazareth Home people in the buildings have not been involved actively in the rehabilitation process. Nazareth Home people were not themselves required to participate in the homesteading effort, although if they wished to do so, they could. One woman was scheduled to receive a Nazareth Home apartment because she was an elderly lady displaced from the Lower East Side. However, she acted as building treasurer and was involved in the administrative and political aspects of the rehabilitation of her building. In another building the person who eventually occupied a permanent apartment had been selected during rehabilitation. She was not herself able to participate in homesteading; however, her nephew volunteered in her place. One homesteader who used to live in public housing was defined as a Nazareth Home person by virtue of her being disabled and not able to do sweat. She also participated on a number of levels. But these are exceptions. Generally, Nazareth Home people have joined buildings as virtual outsiders. They do not have a shared history with other residents in the building. As a result, it is difficult for them to become accepted as full members in the relatively tightly knit community.

Second, homesteaders define Nazareth Home people as somehow different from themselves in terms of their need for housing. This perceived difference is exacerbated by difficulties experienced by individual buildings with Nazareth Home residents. Although any such difficulties—infringements against building rules in one form or another—are certainly not restricted to Nazareth Home people, their background as people from New York City shelters has been cited as explanation for their actions.

Third, in completed buildings the question of who actually owns the apartments in which Nazareth Home people have been placed has been subject to heated debates. One position argues that Nazareth Home people should not be made shareholders in the buildings, and further that the apartments eventually should be controlled by the individual buildings. The other position argues that Nazareth Home people should be given full shareholder rights including a proprietary lease for the time of their tenancy in the building, and that vacant apartments should revert to Nazareth Home for new assignments.

The following sequence of events in a completed building illustrates the way in which RAIN, Nazareth Home, LESAC, and outside sources of funding are inextricably enmeshed. A resident had died in December 1990. His apartment has been at the center of a conflict involving various factions among the homesteaders in the building, LESAC, RAIN, and Nazareth Home. After the resident's death, Nazareth Home wanted to place someone from the shelter in the building. LESAC supported this effort, saying that the apartment had originally been designated as a Nazareth Home unit. Homesteaders argued that they were unaware of this and that they could not be forced to accept such a resident. RAIN was ambivalent, reflecting the fact that there has been tremendous internal debate in RAIN about the Nazareth Home units. A homesteader in the building explained that the resident who died had been given shares in the building by the homesteaders. They claimed that at the time they had known that Nazareth Home had helped him, but they denied knowing that the apartment was designated as a Nazareth Home unit. LESAC meanwhile claimed that in return for funding the building had made an agreement with the Housing Trust Fund of New York committing the building to help the homeless in the area—that is, to provide several Nazareth Home units for a period of ten years. Homesteaders argued that their understanding was that the commitment was for seven years only. The homesteaders also claimed that part of the documentation in this agreement had been forged. Mutual accusations did little to clarify the issue. This provided more fuel to the debate within RAIN about long-term control over the units. The eventual outcome, not to say resolution, has been that Nazareth Home chose to relinquish the unit rather than engage in a long battle, possibly in court.

BUILDING MANAGEMENT

The Urban Homesteading Assistance Board (UHAB) has produced informational brochures, working manuals, and literature to assist tenants in managing their buildings. UHAB places a lot of emphasis on post-rehabilitation building management and provides training sessions on how to repair leaking faucets, how to deal with the building's lawyer, how to handle tenants in arrears of their rents, and even how to write a check. One manual is entitled "How to Manage Your Lawyer," hardly a sentiment very pleasing to lawyers in question. Nevertheless, it alerts homesteaders to the need to look at everything and everyone with a critical eye. LESAC did not become actively involved in this aspect. One HDI employee explained that until 1989 LESAC used to run training classes and that the expectation was that RAIN would take over this function. This, however, has not happened. The HDI employee implied that there are diverging opinions within RAIN and LESAC on this matter. The Catholic Church has been ambivalent about active involvement in homesteading. The given ideological rationalization that homesteaders should be encouraged to run their buildings themselves and seek information and assistance on their own initiative in order to remain in control of their living situation is little more than a smoke screen for this ambivalence and ultimate withdrawal. The same argument is applied to the question of whether homesteaded buildings should seek an outside agent for building operations and management.

This notion has been anathema to LESAC and HDI and to RAIN as well, despite the fact that neither LESAC nor HDI have been willing to become actively involved in building management. The objection to having an outside agent manage the building for homesteaders was that it would remove any incentive on their part to remain actively involved in the building—that is, that homesteaders would thus be retransformed into passive and ultimately disempowered tenants. Whether this is indeed the case is not the point here. Rather, I was struck by the irony that ideological notions about empowerment were not applied to ensure that homesteaders have the wherewithal to manage the buildings on their own.

Having a building managed by an outside agent adds to the financial burdens on the tenants. One homesteader in a building that was approaching completion in 1993 explained that the homesteaders planned to manage the building themselves because it is too expensive to hire an outside agent.

An outside agent was brought in for one building: Pueblo Nuevo, an organization active on the Lower East Side for over a decade. This building was caught between conflicting interests on the part of LESAC, the homesteaders, the Chinese American Staffworkers Association, RAIN, and the city. Each party had a different account of the events that lead to an impasse over several years and repeated unsuccessful arbitration efforts. In brief, the conflict involved a debate over whether a commercial tenant and member of the Chinese American Staffworkers Association had shareholder status and voting rights in the building. Currently the building is being managed by an outside agent while there is no acting board of directors. The city has attempted to resolve the situation through arbitration. Some homesteaders have said that in order to broaden support for homesteading and to obtain sweat labor for the building, LESAC made a deal with the Chinese American Staffworkers Association without consulting the homesteaders at the beginning of construction. They further argued that LESAC has been mishandling their funds and has been trying to force them to accept the situation by withholding support for continuing the rehabilitation.

According to homesteaders and others involved in homesteading, nothing is as detrimental as stopping work on a building for an extended time; hence, LESAC's decision to withhold support at a point when the building was nearing completion can well be interpreted as a form of blackmail. A homesteader from another building explained that according to papers signed at the beginning of the rehabilitation process, homesteaders get a 3% interest rate on their mortgage from HUD as long as the space is residential only. If a building includes commercial shareholders, the interest rates go up to 9%. This homesteader argued that LESAC was pushing the homesteaders to accept the commercial party, "because many years ago when LESAC was just getting off the ground they made some deals with people in the Chinese community in order to try to get them also involved in the homesteading." LESAC meanwhile claimed that the homesteaders were aware of the commercial tenant from the beginning and were satisfied to receive the share of sweat labor that was being provided. LESAC further said that because the homesteaders failed to assume responsibility and become more actively involved, the representative of the Chinese American association, not himself a tenant, was doing them a favor—he was taking the time to go to meetings and to represent the building on the homesteaders' behalf. Therefore, according to LESAC, homesteaders were not justified in deciding that the commercial tenant, whose interests had been represented by this individual, should not be a shareholder.

The issue does not become clearer when we look at the situation vis-à-vis RAIN. RAIN did not like to admit that any building may have been forced to join the Community Land Trust, particularly because RAIN had taken the stance that it was independent of LESAC and hence would hardly need LESAC to act as enforcing agent. Both organizations, however, insisted that this building just like any other building was fully aware that it would have to join RAIN in return for receiving support throughout the rehabilitation process.

In the fall of 1991 the residents of the building brought a lawsuit seeking a third arbitrator to be named and disqualification of the respondents' arbitrator (named by the opponent group). The residents' group also brought a suit against RAIN. The RAIN lawyer refused to discuss the case. Accusations are leveled against everyone involved, individuals are called anything from "neurotic" to "egomaniacal," and stories about a particular player's abusive behavior abound. Amid all the accusations, the central points of conflict are obscured—that is, the increased mortgage interest rate, the no-resale policy that is a part of RAIN membership, and the question of who is in control of the building. In April 1995 the conflict was still unresolved.

In the coming years, homesteaders will face other potential legal struggles. Many of these involve questions about ownership and rights as shareholders. For example, there is no precedent on how to resolve a situation in which a couple in a shareholder's apartment divorces and disagrees over disposition of the space. As far as future legal issues are concerned, homesteaders are heading down an uncharted road without the benefit of effective support from LESAC, RAIN, or even other buildings.

PROBLEMS OF COMPLETED BUILDINGS IN CONTEXT

None of the completed buildings are trouble-free. Some have difficulties in terms of their past and present accounting procedures. One building is experiencing unresolved internal struggles about whether a particular party is a shareholder with attendant rights in the building. In several buildings problems are looming on the horizon with regard to the building's ability to pay the bills. In one building a homesteader moved out of the city without informing the other residents in the building and giving them time to decide what to do about the suddenly vacant apartment. Homesteaders claim that in several buildings residents are in arrears on rent payments. For instance, in a building with relatively few units, a couple is going through divorce proceedings and has not been keeping up with rent payments; the other tenants have so far been reluctant to confront them.

Some problems were foreseeable during rehabilitation. One homesteader during the final stage of her building's rehabilitation described several future residents. In this seven-unit building, two units were going to be occupied by single men with one child each; both were unemployed at that time. The implication hung in the air that this would be a problem once building members would have to begin making mortgage payments. Given the economic situation in New York City and a population particularly vulnerable to fluctuations in the labor market, the problem is likely to worsen. There is a disjunction between (1) people's ability to pay for the price of housing, based on their income, and (2) the cost of housing, determined inter alia by the real estate market, the construction industry, the materials industry, and finance capital. This disjunction is exacerbated by the particular financial and other problems of a homesteading project.

Other problems have begun to emerge after completion. Each building is supposed to set aside 1% of its total maintenance payments for emergencies. In 1991 none of the buildings had such a reserve fund, small though it would have been. According to a RAIN director, the reason for this was miscalculation of budgets by LESAC; as a result the fees for the reserve funds had not been raised. Some completed buildings began to build up a reserve fund as late as a year or two after the homesteaders moved in. Lack of adequate financial reserves is a serious issue in view of problems already experienced by completed buildings, such as a leaking water heater or a drainage system that backs up sewage into the basement.

When buildings are in trouble, who steps in to help? In theory, RAIN. One idea behind the formation of RAIN was to prevent the loss of buildings to the community due to internal conflicts, inability to pay the bills, and more generally the vagaries of the market economy. According to one RAIN director, RAIN has the option to cure defaults. She explained: "If a building goes into foreclosure because the budget exceeds what the building can raise in maintenance fees, RAIN can step in and help to work out a payment plan." RAIN is also supposed to act as arbitrator in certain internal situations. Further, RAIN has instituted an emergency reserve fund with which it could theoretically help out if a major repair had to be undertaken in a building that was not able to pay out of its own reserve fund. However, given total assets in 1991 of approximately $55,000, there are limits to what RAIN can actually do. In a number of cases RAIN was not able to resolve the situation. Moreover, RAIN has not developed to the point at which it could effectively step in to help; and it has been undergoing internal and external difficulties, further limiting its ability to act.

The precarious economic context, as it affects the entire neighborhood and impinges on homesteaders and RAIN in the most mundane issues, is illustrated by the following item discussed during a RAIN meeting in 1991. Many homesteaders had savings accounts at the local credit union, and RAIN also had placed its money in that financial institution. In 1991 the credit union, operating on the principle of shared profits and losses, did not pay any interest on savings accounts to any account holders, justifying this action by citing the difficulty experienced by the credit union in collecting loans. During the subsequent discussion, homesteaders and RAIN board members debated whether to withdraw their money and place it in another bank, but they were confounded by the presumed minimum deposits (homesteaders' estimates ranging from $200 to $800) required on savings accounts in order to have free checking privileges.

In any given problem there are multiple actors and a variety of complicating political and ideological issues. Until the beginning of the 1990s, LESAC was in a position to exert a fair amount of influence on homesteaders; subsequently the Archdiocese and, consequently, LESAC withdrew from homesteading with an effect akin to abandonment. Homesteaders were divided into several factions, some of which were reflected in RAIN. Other actors included other organizations on the Lower East Side, the Community Board 3, and HPD. There was a process of fragmentation and disintegration that weakened the homesteading movement as a whole. People living in completed buildings were distancing themselves further and further from their original reasons for becoming involved in homesteading.

TRANSFORMATION OF HOMESTEADERS' PERCEPTIONS AND ATTITUDES

One homesteader complained about her sense of alienation from other homesteaders once actual rehabilitation work had been completed: "Beyond homesteading we have nothing in common." Homesteaders' reservations about individual members' future ability to pay the rent were more easily put aside during the rehabilitation process. Similarly, reservations about a given member's lifestyle could be turned into jokes as long as that lifestyle did not yet in any way affect the building. The possibility of a member running out of money or bringing drug addicts into the building became a serious issue only after homesteaders took up residency in their building.

Differences more easily glossed over during the rehabilitation process acquired new dimensions in completed buildings. Some individuals found that their particular personal situation (e.g., marital status or sexual orientation) further isolated them from other homesteaders. Differing familial and/or marital status—together with cultural markers, individual language use, employment status, and occupational history—act as dividing lines among homesteaders in completed buildings and spill over into ideological differences and questions of leadership in RAIN and in the community.

Changes in active involvement, levels of commitment, and interaction with other homesteaders occurred after homesteaders began to take occupancy of the rehabilitated units. Some changes are the result of individuals resuming their private lives. Others are rooted in the financial and political history preceding building completion. Finally, changes occurred in the face of the unmanageable fiscal reality of running a building on limited incomes, given mortgage payments, water and sewer taxes, and a precarious economic environment in which tenants often cannot pay their bills. The effects of patterns laid out long before these particular homesteading projects began (e.g., the system of taxation and subsidies; federal, state, and local policies relating to housing; and water and sewer charges) were felt as an ever-tightening net in which homesteaders floundered, while looking toward notions of empowerment and self-help to extricate themselves.

Once people moved into their apartments, the sense of unity in battle was lost. People found little in common beyond a shared history as homesteaders, and even this may well be subject to further differences of presentation: "He talked a lot but didn't want to do any of the work"; "I always thought she really wanted to sell her apartment"; and so on. Alienation set in especially when buildings begin confronting new and unexpected problems. In the course of acquiring ownership in a society that places a premium on ownership, a transformation from propertyless individuals to property owners occurs with attendant changes in outlook. This transformation shaped homesteaders' relationship with others, particularly with those who are not owners. The transformation is an ongoing process that does not begin on a specific day. It is significant, particularly because it presents a contrast to the goals stated at the outset of projects. This process of transformation and the way in which it is rationalized by homesteaders tells us as much about the workings of the wider society as it does about this relatively small number of people and their homesteading movement.

CONCLUSION

Buildings' financial, administrative, and interpersonal problems illustrate how precariously situated these newly created low-income housing cooperatives are. Further, they provide insights into the dynamics affecting homesteaders' changing perceptions over the course of rehabilitation and after moving into completed buildings. However, it is important to keep in mind that the problems experienced by completed buildings are rooted in direction markers for the most part set during the rehabilitation process, as much as they were shaped by socioeconomic factors at both citywide and national levels.

NOTES

1. Archbishop Oscar Arnulfo Romero of El Salvador was internationally renowned as a voice on behalf of poor people in his country and for courageously speaking out against repression perpetrated by an extreme right-wing government and its military. He was shot while celebrating mass on March 24, 1980. The government denied having played a role in his death and equally denied any responsibility for the massacre that followed during his funeral on March 30, 1980.

2. The Taino were an Arawak people of the Greater Antilles and the Bahamas; they became extinct under Spanish colonization during the sixteenth century.

3. "La Forteleza" is named after the El Morro Fortress in San Juan, Puerto Rico. It was built in 1631. In 1797 the fortress was besieged by British forces, which withdrew after one month.

4. In October 1984, a 66-year-old African-American woman, Eleanor Bumpurs, was shot to death in her New York City public housing apartment by a police officer who was attempting to restrain her while Housing Authority officials evicted her for nonpayment of rent. The incident raised many questions and considerable controversy over the appropriateness of police behavior and procedures, underlying racial dynamics, and the role of the city's social service agencies in handling Mrs. Bumpurs's case prior to the eviction action.

5. Section 8 was created as a part of the Housing and Community Development Act of 1974, promulgated to encourage the maintenance and production of low- to moderate-income housing through rent subsidies and tax shelter sales. See Chandler (1988) and Bratt (1989b) for a description.

6. For a discussion of the devastating effects of the Reagan administration policies with regard to the Section 8 program, see Hartman 1986.

7. In a description of the Manhattan Plaza project in the mid-1970s, Schur analyzes the way in which the Section 8 program has been abused by government officials and developers in New York City in the interest of private profit making and the local government's redevelopment schemes while only incidentally contributing to the creation of housing. Furthermore, much of this housing by no means remained securely available for low-income people in need of Section 8 assistance. As income levels of residents originally eligible for Section 8 changed, those apartments shifted to market-rate levels (Schur 1986).

6

CONFLICTING CONSTRUCTIONS OF WORK, GENDER ROLES, OWNERSHIP, AND COMMUNITY

Nosotros tenemos meetings con las cucarachas
que son las cucarachas en la casa de las
cucarachas que visitan los vampiros para
chuparle la sangre a los ratones en el 538
east 6th st. que es mi casa y beben
cerveza con sangre.

We have meetings with the cockroaches
who are cockroaches in the house of cockroaches
who visit the vampires
to suck the blood of the rats in 538
east 6th st. which is my house, and drink
beer with blood.[1]

INTRODUCTION

LOURDES: It is not an easy thing. It is very hard. Do you think that I would not like
to own this apartment? I would like it very much. And I would like to think
to be able to go and get a mortgage and then get money to buy another house
somewhere. I want to have things like everybody else has. I want to have a
million dollars in the bank if I can. It is not that I don't want to. It is not that
I don't like money. I like good shoes like any rich person would like good
shoes [stretches out her legs and points to her pair of polished black walking
shoes]. I like the stuff that comes in this magazine [shows me an issue of
Architectural Digest]. I like it. It's not that I don't like it. But I also have a brain
and a soul. And I am a combination of those three things. I am not one thing
only. When I sit in my house during the night, I think about it: "If I have twenty
pairs of shoes, it is because nineteen other people don't have any shoes." After

all, I have only two legs, don't I? For what I need twenty pair of shoes? Then logic tell me some things, my body and my moral tell me other things, and it is a struggle every human being go through every day in their life. I could tell you right now that for me it would be great to own all this property [points at the bare walls in the room where she is doing security] and to think that this is mine. But that is not who I am only. I am also a person who has a conscience, a person who know that the only reason I am here today is because there were other persons before me and it is a question am I going to live in peace with myself or not. Then I have to make a balance. So I do some compromising. I like this pair of shoes. I buy a pair. One pair. I would like to have twenty. Different colors. Yes. But my moral let me do it, let me live in peace? Because happiness is not only having a lot of money. I don't say it doesn't help, but is not the only thing. But in my opinion if you are a human being it is a combination of things that create a balance, that balance that give you peace is what make happiness, make you a happy person.

For Lourdes, balance is a fluid and dynamic construct and individual people are filled with contradictions. Using Lourdes's homily as a starting point, it is useful to remember that value systems contain contradictions and that processes of change are not easily labeled or fixed. There is no demarcation line separating before and after. The outcome of actions is not determined; practice, departing from stated value systems of a particular social movement, can lead to different outcomes. Practice and concrete events can shape something that was not contained in the ideas underlying the social movement. At the same time, a movement is defined if not limited by the same ideas and normative values that are being contested.

Contestation of the concepts of work, gender roles, and ownership represents three central dynamics in homesteading that overlapped and informed each other. Transformative processes involved both a reassertion of pre-existing values and the creation of something new. Some dynamics with regard to work and ownership were foreseen and even furthered by activists involved in homesteading. Others, particularly with regard to contestation of gender roles, were not foreseen; and their impact on the course of homesteading was not expected. I am not claiming that home-steading profoundly reshaped gender roles. Indeed, various normative values have reasserted themselves, and women have been subjected to difficulties because of their sex. However, the contestation of gender roles has been of central importance in the development of homesteading.

WORK

When considering the work of homesteading from the point of view of value transformation, three areas become apparent. First is the manner in which material resources and labor power were shared by homesteaders. The second involves the various styles of work. Third, the concept of teamwork was constantly put to the test. These areas are subject to contradictions and developments that can be illustrated by the concrete work of homesteading on its day-to-day basis.

There are three major categories of work associated with homesteading. One is unskilled labor, for the most part debris removal. The second can be described as skilled labor. The third involves paperwork, logs, record keeping, management of forms and schedules, handling of financial matters, and participation in administrative and political activities and meetings involving the building in particular as well as other buildings.

Each building had four elected positions: president, secretary, treasurer, and construction supervisor. The president's role was the least clearly defined and the least critical in day-to-day work. Each building was supposed to have regular elections. Certain matters required voting by a quorum of building members. Buildings were supposed to maintain attendance logs in which the amount of time put in by volunteers was noted. At meetings, procedures were to be governed by Robert's Rules of Order and to follow a formal agenda.

In practice the various categories of work were handled differently. Each building had an individual style that largely depended on the personalities involved. Generally the process has been more informal and haphazard than the above description suggests. The beginning and end of a work day depended on tasks to be completed, as well as on the weather and amount of daylight. Sometimes breaks were called by the construction supervisor, at other times a member complained and requested a break. Attendance was not always recorded; similarly, volunteers were only occasionally asked to sign an attendance sheet. Moreover, daily logs for noting work accomplished and expenses incurred were not kept very rigorously, a fact that eventually came to haunt homesteaders when questions about expenditures arose. Again, the degree to which these tasks were executed varied from building to building.

Problems and tensions internal to the building were worked out on a semi-familial level rather than through formal structures. One homesteader described his building as lackadaisical when it came to observing building rules and by-laws, but he assured me: "We have been getting along okay." Unless problems were intractable, formal procedure was mostly used to lend a stamp of legitimacy to a decision after consensus had been achieved through an informal process.

Once I went to a building on a Saturday morning to find that the homesteaders were attempting to hold a building meeting. Manuel, an original member and a leader in the group, was trying to get the others to start the meeting by saying that he could not be in charge of it that day, because he would have to leave early. The others seemed passive as he tried to jolly them along. He said: "Come on, you have to help me with this, I can't do it today; who's going to chair the meeting, how do we start, what is the procedure?" Then it turned out that nobody was prepared to take notes. The building secretary was not present. Manuel tried to get Allan to write something down and promised that he would type it up afterwards, that he only needed something in writing. Allan appeared unhappy and confused about having to do this. One of the items on the meeting agenda was the preparation of a construction report, which required a description of the work done over a period of several months. The building members tried to reconstruct this from memory, an attempt that was not very successful. In addition to the fact that formalities were here viewed as a peculiarly painful ritual, this incident reflected a degree of confusion about the process that some homesteaders in other buildings shared. In other words, there was a great deal of misinformation and uncertainty about many aspects of homesteading and the wider political process involved.

The third category of work associated with homesteading, paperwork and everything related to it, was handled in the least equitable fashion. In each building there were only a few people who from the very beginning familiarized themselves with the administrative and bureaucratic aspects of homesteading and acquired greater knowledge of the political process. Although handling paperwork was very time-consuming, it gave those homesteaders a greater understanding of the obstacles they were encountering and a position of greater authority in the group. Most homesteaders remained removed from this work category.

In one building a homesteader showed me a large, dust-covered binder. It had evidently lain in a corner of the building for some time. In it the original members had kept photographs of the building's opening and other proud testimonials to their struggle. There were newsletters and publications about homesteading and the Community Land Trust concept. There also were daily logs and attendance sheets for several years in the mid-1980s. These papers represented a fragmentary record at best; further efforts to maintain a record on the building had been abandoned, almost as something the homesteaders had outgrown.

Homesteaders were proud of their growing expertise and expanding construction terminology. Sheetrocking, debris, hacksaws, chutes, brick pointing, steam cleaning, and joists—all these terms and others were used with gusto. Skills increased throughout the rehabili.ation process, although generally only a few building members actively pursued any of these skills through further instruction, training, or licensing. Some individuals had prior carpentry or electrical experience, but most homesteaders had no such background.

At times, construction supervisors made a show of assigning work to various individuals; however, to a large extent involvement in particular tasks was self-selected. Invariably a few homesteaders worked harder than the others, but this was not commented on. Those who did not work as hard had little desire to draw attention to that fact, and others for the most part were operating with the understanding that the balance would right itself over the long term. As one homesteader put it, "We are all in this mess together."

In the execution of tasks there was a flexible, make-do approach that recognized that the appropriate tools might not always be available and that conditions for work were far from ideal. Solutions to some technical problems were devised with a great deal of ingenuity. If one thing did not work, something else was attempted. Homesteaders improvised.

This flexibility extended beyond individual buildings during those years when homesteading activities were at a high and several buildings were actively undergoing rehabilitation. Tools, materials, and labor moved back and forth among the buildings. One building might have a dumpster but not enough buckets to create efficient bucket lines. Someone with a truck or a van—frequently an old and fragile-looking van lent by Nazareth Home—helped to ferry some buckets from one building to the one in need of them. A dumpster would be shared if one building was not able to fill it. Wheelbarrows were among the more expensive construction tools that buildings shared as much as possible, because monthly dues were not sufficient to buy complete sets of tools for each building. Undamaged bricks, which one building had carefully salvaged and stacked up during demolition and later had no use for, were ferried to another building. Gravel in the basement of a completed building was loaded into buckets and brought to another building whose foundation was about to be poured. Like reusable bricks for which careful accounting was not required, volunteers also moved from one building to the next depending on the need for their labor.

Labor was shared in ways that cut across generations and buildings and beyond the immediate homesteading community. Some work was done at no cost to homesteaders by young men and women from the neighborhood, sponsored by the Department of Employment in a so-called Youth at Work program (it provided young people without a high school degree with construction training and experience). One woman worked on behalf of her grandmother, who was going to be the occupant of the apartment and would not have been required to provide sweat labor. A pregnant woman had her nephew work in her place. One homesteader took the place of her father, who had been homesteading for many years and was forced to give up because of health reasons. She had previously been volunteering on another building, because her best friend was the daughter of one of the homesteaders there. One woman's boyfriend worked alongside her on the project. Some homesteaders continued to work on other buildings once their own had been completed. I learned of one incident in which homesteaders suspected a building member of having paid a relative to work in her place. Because it was not proven, it was tolerated, however grudgingly. In similar situations, homesteaders did not like to take action against a building member unless the particular behavior was impossible to ignore and directly interfered with the building's viability.

Once buildings were completed, concepts of sharing, flexibility, and teamwork changed; homesteaders' tolerance of each other turned into more critical scrutiny of neighbors and potential neighbors. Willingness to become involved in the problems of those buildings still under construction decreased, and tensions between buildings developed. For example, two buildings had access to a common backyard. During rehabilitation homesteaders from both buildings had worked on clearing the yard of accumulated debris. After one building was completed, the yard became contested ground and was claimed as the property of the completed building. Another example relates to the need for electricity. Homesteaders in one building still undergoing rehabilitation were angry that the neighboring building rejected their request to be hooked up to their lines. The homesteaders did not understand what had changed and considered the rejection to be mean-spirited at best; and the homesteaders in the completed building were no longer interested in dancing precariously on the margins of legality.

After LESAC was no longer supervising construction activities, the buildings were more isolated from each other and the flexible, "can-do" approach gave way to an almost businesslike style. The choice of contractor reinforced this change. In 1992, four buildings finally had managed to put their financial package together, so that the build-up process of their buildings could begin. Two buildings decided to work with a contractor who agreed to have homesteaders do some of the work as a way of keeping costs down. The two other buildings selected a contractor who preferred not to have homesteaders involved in the work at all. Hence, not only was communication among homesteaders within the latter buildings no longer tied to the completion of concrete tasks, but also communication between buildings dwindled away. In the other two buildings, homesteaders continued to work on weekends in addition to doing security in the building every night. Their relationship with Nazareth Home, which was going to place several families in each of the buildings, was kept alive through volunteer labor provided by Nazareth Home.

Over the course of a decade the work of homesteading has been characterized by a premium placed on sharing of material resources and labor power, flexibility and willingness to improvise, and a powerful sense of teamwork. However, it also became apparent how these characteristics, which seemed to connote a communal work environment, were frayed at the edges and even became a liability once buildings neared completion. During rehabilitation, homesteaders considered the haphazard treatment of building matters (such as record keeping) a necessary flexibility to get through hard times. At completion, this same behavior was regarded as negligence and sloppiness, which could potentially create endless problems for buildings. Moreover, as buildings disengaged from other buildings, the need for teamwork was no longer apparent. Sharing of material resources and labor acquired the characteristics of actions out of the ordinary—in other words, actions that were no longer part of a web of reciprocal relationships. Reciprocity and cooperation broke down because the need for it, present as before, was no longer rooted in concrete day-to-day activities. It had become abstract. Meanwhile, dominant ideological notions of private ownership obscured the ultimate vulnerability to market forces of poor and low-income people as owners of apartments.

GENDER ROLES

There are three areas of particular significance in the relationship between gender roles and homesteading. First, gender roles affected the division of labor and the manner in which work was executed. Second, various forms of harassment illustrate how men and women were affected differently by homesteading. Finally, leadership in homesteading has been the most complex touchstone of contestation of gender roles, evolving over time and linked to the development of the homesteading process.

Although women homesteaders outnumbered men only by 7–10%, in conversations among homesteaders ten of the buildings were identified with one of the women in the building. In each building the composition of men and women was different; in some buildings women outnumbered men, in others there was rough parity, and in others men outnumbered women. However, the latter situation was less frequent. Homesteading groups, here seen as analogous to work environments, presented an unusual near-reversal of what one would find in most blue-collar work environments. Not only were there as many women as men actively involved in homesteading, but they were identified as leading members in most buildings. Among original building members, homesteaders who were with the process from the start and finally moved into a rehabilitated unit, the number of women far exceeded that of men.

When one looks at individual buildings, the issue becomes more complicated. Division of labor in each building was shaped to a degree by sex, but age and education cannot be discounted. The racial and ethnic composition was different in each building; in some buildings Puerto Ricans were in the majority, with whites making up the remainder; in others there were more whites or African Americans; in one there was a large contingent of Chinese Americans. Numbers are too small to reach any conclusions on whether the particular racial and ethnic composition in buildings was a significant factor in the division of labor.

Precise figures on the number of hours spent by men and by women on various tasks are impossible to obtain, given the fragmentary nature of the work process and irregular attendance by many building members. However, a few general characteristics emerged. Women did a greater proportion of certain unskilled labor tasks than did men. They filled buckets and carried them, swept, carried miscellaneous items such as wood and broken-up pipes out of the building, and scraped fire escapes and stairs inside buildings. As far as unskilled labor tasks were concerned, men were more likely to break up pipes with sledgehammers, knock down beams, set up the debris chute, and pack the dumpster. Construction supervisors generally were men; an exception was a building in which all the homesteaders were women. More men than women came to homesteading with previous skilled labor experience. This was reflected in the distribution of labor during rehabilitation work.

Men and women homesteaders exhibited different styles of working. Generally speaking, when men were working on any particular task, they could not easily be interrupted to help out elsewhere and then resume. Women did so more frequently. This reflects the nature of domestic labor crossculturally, here carried over into a work environment that can be described as domestic only in the broadest sense of the term.

Age was a contributing factor, in addition to individual personality. In some buildings older homesteaders, in particular older women, were engaged in long and arduous shifts of heavy but unskilled labor, whereas younger members were more frequently engaged in a variety of tasks throughout a work day. Another factor that influenced this division of labor was the role played by the particular individual in the group—that is, how active and vocal that individual was in the group. Those with more influence in the building ended up performing a greater variety of tasks and some of the skilled labor tasks during homesteading, whereas those more passive and/or lowest in status and power vis-à-vis other homesteaders were more acquiescent about performing rote manual labor, physically demanding but tedious, over long periods of time. Younger women who also happened to be in positions of leadership in their buildings and in RAIN engaged in a greater variety of tasks than did other women. They performed skilled labor tasks and became involved in aspects of construction supervision such as directing work and moving from one work area in the building to another to help out wherever necessary.

One younger woman took over the job of blowtorching. Concita explained to me that no one else in her building wanted to do it because they were afraid. She had taken a course and was trying to get licensed. She had already been fined once for starting a small fire in the oil tank and working without a license. The building could not afford to hire someone to do this work and also could not afford another $1,000 fine. Concita was one of two original building members who had been with the building since 1985; the building was completed in 1994. When the building members described the incident of the small fire and the amazed comments of the fire department when it came to the scene, they expressed pride about their self-created brush with disaster.

There were various forms of harassment in homesteading. One related to a display of machismo during homesteading work that I noticed in many buildings. The following excerpt from my fieldnotes portrays a fairly typical work scene.

December 9, 1989: Ramón complained to Jim that Leona had left/was no longer there to carry the buckets he had been filling up. I didn't see him carry any at all. Rodrigo picked up several at times, but with an appearance of "helping the weak women." With a great deal of joking masculine display, he broke up some pipes with a sledgehammer. Rodrigo also kidded Jim about not doing any work. Ramón snapped several times at Jim that he didn't want to do something, that Jim should ask Rodrigo to do it.

Another excerpt illustrates the frequency of this type of situation.

December 14, 1991: I noticed a kind of one-upmanship on how many buckets to carry at one time, the attempt to show me that they (José) are men and can carry those filled to the top and also three at a time. José yelled to Carmen to fill the buckets to the top, because now he would be carrying them out; but his frequent breaks meant constant backups of buckets in the hall. A few times, when Rita came out with them, he got upset, said: let them pile up, I'll get them.

Another version of this dynamic occurred when a homesteader had recently given birth and three months later returned to work. In this particular building there were more men than women, and none of the women were in a position of leadership. The men treated this woman with a great deal of affectionate concern. They tried to keep her from picking up heavy buckets. But at the same time they insisted on filling the buckets all the way so that they would indeed be too heavy for her.

One area of homesteading in which several women felt particularly vulnerable involved the task of guarding the building. Several women, in particular older women, expressed discomfort with the notion of having to spend night after night in an empty building in order to ward off intruders. They felt vulnerable and afraid. In some instances this reluctance to do security became a source of conflict between homesteaders. Doing security was held up as the mark of a true homesteader and of genuine commitment to the building. In one case, the woman's reluctance to do security isolated her further from other building members, who had been at odds with her over other building matters.

Some homesteaders encountered sexual harassment by other home-steaders in their own buildings, adding another dimension to the concept of domestic abuse. I was aware of only a few such occurrences. I mention them not to divulge confidences by homesteaders, but because the way in which such a matter was handled reveals something about the various groups involved in homesteading. Neither the homesteaders in a building involved nor RAIN or LESAC were willing to address the issue openly. One incident occurred at a time when homesteading on the Lower East Side was at a high point. At that time LESAC and RAIN had no interest in acknowledging a situation that would pierce the image of a "happy family" of homesteaders joined in worthy struggle and supported by the Catholic Church.

One homesteader described her initial involvement, which epitomizes some of the dynamics between men and women in the movement. In 1979 Lourdes met several activists and homesteaders. She became interested at a time when the city did not yet support homesteading and projects were starting without official approval. She was asked to organize a group of people so they could be instructed about homesteading and be assigned a building. The group that Lourdes organized did not include any men.

LOURDES: We go there Saturday, Kevin is there and Thomas is there. When they see us arriving they see all these women and Kevin said: "Is this the group? All of them women?" I said: "Yes. We are here." So we had the meeting. Kevin start talking about the idea of taking over a building illegally and then forcing the city to sell the building to us. He said: "We have a building that we are going to assign to you, but the building has other members already, they are males, but they are not here today." So we set up a meeting for the following Saturday when these guys are going to show. The following Saturday the guys don't show up, we show up. The meeting is postponed. We set up a meeting five times. The fifth time, Thomas told me that we have to cancel because the guys are not there. I said: "No, buster, we no canceling this meeting. You take me with my group to the building that you say you have and when your guys materialize you bring them to the building and we are going to work there. Because I am becoming suspicious that you are not going to take us over there because we are women and we have been showing up." Thomas admitted that this was true, and then he said: "Okay, let's go." He brought us to this building, right here. And this building was full of garbage, up to here [Lourdes stands up and holds her hand as high as her shoulder] floor by floor by floor. It was incredible. We said: "Ooooh weeeee!" Thomas said: "Are you willing to do it?" We said: "Absolutely." Then he said: "The first thing to do is put a door in place." We said: "Okay, what do we have to do?" He said: "Get a door." Thomas was just standing there. We said: "Alright," and went and got hammers and took a door and we put it there the best we could and we put a lock. Thomas did not believe it. Then he said: "When are you going to start?" We said: "Next Saturday." When he arrived Saturday, we were already here. He cannot believe that we were here. He cannot believe it. He can tell you. With us he learn a big lesson.

Lourdes's building was one of three in the original homesteading movement. The Community Land Trust concept and much of the subsequent political strategy of people involved in the homesteading movement was shaped by the homesteaders in her building in conjunction with a few other homesteaders and activists. One of the two other buildings dropped out of homesteading and was taken over by another housing development program. The other building was completed but is having difficulties with internal management.

Leadership in homesteading took several forms. One was leadership within the building; another within RAIN; and a third at a more amorphous level of the community. Within the building there were two kinds of leadership; one involving day-to-day rehabilitation work, and the other related to the handling of bureaucratic and financial matters. More often than not they were linked in that a person with a leadership role in one area did so in the other as well. In most of the buildings women did this work. Women played a more visible and active role than men in the organization and management of a homesteading group, financial oversight, and contacts to community organizations, lawyers, and city agencies. Women also played a more visible and active role than men in the Community Land Trust RAIN, making up more than 70% of the leadership. The following description of a building meeting reflects the general dynamics in the building: Carmen, backed up by Jim, who acted as construction supervisor, provided much of the leadership; the other members' participation varied from active interest to passive non-involvement.

> *June 28, 1991*: Carmen [at that time the building president] was chairing the meeting and provided most of the information. [The building was considering bids by contractors and had to make difficult choices about the continuation of rehabilitation work, the manner of which would affect the size of their eventual mortgage.] Aside from Carmen, there were three other women in attendance and two men. Rita was secretary and Leona was treasurer. Rodrigo and José were not present. The women sat in a circle facing Carmen, and Jim sat in the back on the window sill. Ramón came late, rejected the chair that Carmen, offered to him, and went to the back of the room and stretched out on some beams. Jim made a few joking comments, but essentially neither Ramón nor Jim made any contributions to the discussion. Carmen and Rita repeatedly yelled at Ramón and tried to prod him to say something. Leona and Rita asked questions and voiced concern about the likelihood of an increase in their eventual mortgage. Carmen translated most of what was said into Spanish for Dolores, who did not herself get involved in the discussion.

I attended other building meetings and RAIN meetings in which there were several individuals, usually women, who were informed about the matters at hand and actively involved in the discussion and decision making, whereas others appeared lost and lacked information about matters even in their own buildings.

A closer look at the leadership in individual buildings and in RAIN reveals another dynamic. RAIN and the early homesteading effort was propelled to a large degree by activists and vocal homesteaders. Several leaders of the early homesteading effort had firm roots in the activism of the late 1960s and early 1970s. The group of homesteaders during the early to mid-1980s represented a diverse mix of ages and ethnic and racial backgrounds, more easily labeled and self-identified as poor and working-class people with relatively limited educational backgrounds. In the mid-1980s there was a kind of interregnum during which some earlier leaders began to withdraw, in part for personal reasons and in part in the hopes that the movement had acquired a firm enough foundation to generate leaders from among all homesteaders in a more equitable fashion. Younger, more educated people began to predominate in homesteading. This also applies to the shift in leadership, which became characterized by a preponderance of younger, more educated, single women.

One activist explained this trend by using the analogy of a vacuum. He argued that a vacuum of leadership developed as earlier homesteaders who helped to spearhead initial efforts withdrew, dropped out, or became tired. A new group of people moved into this vacuum. I believe the analogy in this case is not entirely satisfactory. The homesteading movement as a whole underwent important changes in the years from 1978 to the early 1990s, relating to (1) the politics of housing on the Lower East Side, (2) the increasing socioeconomic pressures on homesteaders, and (3) the concept of low-income cooperative housing conversions. These changes are reflected in the change in leadership.

In numerous instances and in overall developments in homesteading, leadership and passiveness were complementary components that masked the underlying sense of powerlessness of all involved. Leadership became concentrated among a smaller number of people as the homesteading movement weakened. The fact that women played a central role in buildings and in RAIN is not surprising given the nature of the problems being addressed. Delgado argues that many community organizations and progressive organizations are composed predominantly of women—which is not to imply, however, that women will be in positions of leadership in such organizations (Delgado 1986).

Nonetheless, leadership among homesteaders initially consisted of a more representative sample of people and a more even distribution of men and women and different age groups. One activist said they had envisioned a "participatory model" that embraced and integrated those who could do the sweat-equity and the elderly, disabled, or homeless. Instead, involvement in homesteading has been narrowed to a group of mostly single, unaffiliated, upwardly mobile people. Homesteading, originally viewed within a broader vision of "community making," was changed and limited to an albeit laborious path to homeownership. Homesteading represented challenges to normative concepts of traditional gender roles in division of labor and leadership issues. Yet as the movement weakened or shifted in orientation, leadership changed, bringing more women to the fore at a time when this leadership itself lost influence and ability to act or effect change.

This development is analogous to allowing women to enter certain job categories once these have been devalued (e.g., secretarial work at the end of the nineteenth century). Nevertheless, women have played a central role in homesteading on the Lower East Side. They helped shape the initiative, gave it an early impetus, kept it going over long and arduous years, and have been providing a record. Women who stayed with the process over many years have acted as historians of their particular buildings and of the movement as a whole.

OWNERSHIP

Ownership was the cornerstone of homesteading. Originally, when the homesteading movement on the Lower East Side was formed, a concept of individual ownership was rejected in favor of a concept of control over housing by the community. This helped to inspire activists and homesteaders when first embracing the homesteading effort in the late 1970s and early 1980s. The city, in supporting homesteading, was not so much concerned with ownership by individuals or a community as with getting unmanageable properties off its hands. In the early 1990s more homesteaders began to talk about their rights as individual homeowners—rights that were based on having contributed labor and money to the rehabilitation of their units. Conversations with homesteaders reveal these varying notions, overlying and shaping each other, and the processes of change undergone by homesteaders in thinking about ownership. Three issues illustrate these contradictions. One is the evolving attitude vis-à-vis squatters. The second is homesteaders' involvement in RAIN. The third is the issue of Nazareth Home people in rehabilitated buildings.

On the Lower East Side in 1991, roughly 30 landlord-abandoned buildings were occupied by approximately 500 squatters (Nieves 1991).[2] *Squatters* are here defined as people who live in vacant buildings without paying rent. Some squatters go to great length to make their buildings habitable, but others simply use the buildings as shelters from wind and rain. Generalizations about squatters are not easy to make. There are single individuals but also families. Some squatters are employed; others are on the bottom rungs of the economic ladder. An anomalous case is Julius Feinstein, a familiar sight on the Lower East Side for more than a decade and described by some homesteaders with affection. Julius walked around the neighborhood with a group of black Labrador retrievers and lived in a series of abandoned buildings. He had been evicted from a housing project on the Lower East Side because he did not want to give up the animals. In 1993 a social worker found Julius a small room in the basement of a single-family house in the Bronx; he had to give up all the dogs except one.

There are numerous factions of squatter buildings. Some buildings remain politically unengaged. Others are politically active and participate in
demonstrations and other protest actions when threatened with evictions
or when their buildings are razed by the city. Several buildings on 8th Street
between Avenues B and C, also the site of a homesteader building, were
squatter buildings and were razed by the city in 1989. Squatters from these
buildings took their belongings to Tompkins Square Park, where they lived
until the city evicted them in June 1991. Ironically, the vacant rubble-strewn
lot on 8th Street became a tent city of squatters after the park was closed.

According to homesteaders, several homesteader buildings began as
squatted buildings. In effect, this meant not so much people living in the
buildings who later became homesteaders but people beginning to work
on a building before having the city's permission to do so. One homesteader
emphatically told me that the meaning of the term *squatting* changed over
the years.[3]

LOURDES: The squatter movement at that time was about rebuilding a community,
     making a community work, economically speaking, socially speaking, cul-
     turally speaking. . . . The idea of taking over buildings was not just that, not
     just to move people in; economic development had to go hand in hand with
     that. Then the concept of rebuilding went together with paying rent.

In the late 1970s, squatting was used to describe an effort by people in
the community to take control of empty buildings with the goal of forcing
the city to sell them so they could be rehabilitated and transformed into
affordable housing. Homesteaders refer to this history with pride.

LISA: They opened up this building in August of 1985 and I started working on it in
     October of 1985. That's just breaking through the doors. We didn't get site
     control until a year later. We really were here illegally. We would come in on
     Saturdays and try to fill dumpsters and do stuff, and every now and then the
     city would come by and cement-block the door, and we would come and
     would have to break through the cement blocks so we could continue doing
     the interior demolition and cart out all the garbage.

In this context homesteaders identified themselves with squatters while
resting on the self-assurance that they had nothing in common with the
squatters currently on the Lower East Side. Yet, on what is this distinction
founded? Squatters have been perceived as looking for a free ride, not
interested in serving the community. Homesteaders are perceived as self-
serving. It could also be argued that homesteaders, although they started
out with a notion of creating housing for the community, have evolved into
owners of apartments with little intention of looking beyond the concerns
of their own building.

Accusations of conspiracy were leveled against squatters, one being the
argument that many squatters were in reality gentrifiers, the other that

squatters were brought in to the community as a destabilizing element. Homesteaders used words such as *anarchists* or *radicals* to describe squatters. Again, one might argue that homesteaders present a mirror image to squatters in that homesteaders were accused of wanting to sell their apartments for a profit (i.e., contributing to gentrification of the area), whereas simultaneously homesteaders were perceived and often were self-represented as radicals who fought to keep the community from being destroyed via the city's strategy of "planned shrinkage."

MANUEL: At first I thought they sounded good, they took over the buildings. It seemed an excellent idea. The way ACORN did it. I went to several meetings. Then I started to see something different in their attitude. I thought that there were a lot of highly educated people, a lot of them weren't even from New York. I understand they brought a whole busload from California to start a building on, I think, East 12th; and this was a movement, they were calling for support. There was a mother with three kids living in an abandoned building with no water. I don't know . . . I would rather go to the shelter. I don't know which is worse. I don't know if it was destitute people from another state. It became a situation where they became our rivals; they want to squat those buildings, we want to tear them out. So we are different. They are so radical, they are out of it, they are not realistic. I thought at one point they were HPD plants to destroy the homesteading movement on the LES. They disrupted a lot of our meetings when we went in front of the Community Board, jump up and down and disrupt the whole thing. They were angry that we would not support what they were doing. But they don't eat at our restaurants, they are not interested in the community, they don't shop there, they are not people you might see at church or at any other community thing.

Homesteaders distinguished between "homeless" people—whether they lived on the streets, in shelters, or in vacant lots—and "regular" people—that is, homesteaders who were described as desperately in need of adequate housing. Research on the housing situation of homesteaders indicates their lack of adequate permanent housing—they lived doubled-up with other people and/or in unacceptable, hopelessly decayed, substandard housing. Nonetheless, homeless people in vacant lots or in the shelter system were seen as potentially more deviant than "regular" people.

This distinction was also evident in attitudes toward Nazareth Home people. The following comments echo the conspiracy theory about squatters and illustrate the ambivalence of homesteaders in completed buildings toward homeless people.

EDUARDO: You know we have a lot of homeless in that lot next door, and they are a source of much frustration in this apartment and in this building; you hear their music playing . . . not now, but loud, it bothers you, you have to close the window, turn on the air conditioner; but I don't know, I feel very much for people who don't have housing, I know what that is like. I don't feel too much for—and I'm going to hate how that sounds—white squatters, because I don't feel they have an interest in the community. If gentrification is one force, the white squatters are another force. There is a building up here on Avenue C which is being squatted mostly by white people, they are not really neighborhood residents. What makes me angry is we have such a need for housing in the neighborhood amongst Puerto Rican people, I don't even want to say Puerto Rican, community residents, and they are not getting it because people are squatting the building. I feel very much for the people in the lot next door, because those people are community residents who have taken and built up that shanty-town even though that shanty-town has been a source of tremendous problems for this building. The person who murdered S. came from there. We have had incidents of attempted break-ins from people in the lot. It's always the feeling that the children are not safe here. At night . . . there is a fight every night, because they are alcoholics and they fight every night. It gets to be unbearable at times. But homeless is not having a home and being in that lot over there. I don't really know if squatters are homeless, because I think they have another agenda.[4]

A film of a group of people living in such a shanty-town on the Lower East Side, *Inside Life Outside*, is a revealing commentary on the spuriousness of some of these distinctions.[5] In one scene, a resident from a building overlooking the shanty-town argues with people from the shanty-town. He says that they are "choosing to live there," that they should get jobs, that they should find apartments, and that he himself was living in an apartment for only $150 a month. The response from the people in the lot is to point out that people living in any of these buildings are just a small step away from being thrown out on the street, that it is impossible to find affordable apartments, and that this is their home, a place they have created themselves, and that they are not hurting anyone by living on the lot. The people from the shanty-town are Puerto Rican and describe themselves as residents of the neighborhood.

On a day-to-day basis, homesteaders pointed out squatters and squatter buildings to volunteers working on homesteading projects just as they pointed out tent cities on vacant lots and shacks built by homeless people. Squatters' protest activities were viewed with a great deal of ambivalence.

October 12, 1991: We stood in the basement talking to Concita, who was having problems with the water level, which kept her from blowtorching effectively. At one point there was noise on C and somebody called out, saying: "It's the squatters' march." I ran upstairs. Greg and Luis were looking out of the window at the procession of squatters with colorful signs marching by. Greg called them "squatorotos," was laughing about them, said they are "crazy, with their signs and making noise, white guys in dreadlocks." Later we took a break for soda and iced coffee, which Ramona bought, and were sitting at the basement stairs. Greg was again laughing at the idea of living in the building with "squatorotos" trying to chip away the cinderblock wall to get in and squat: "We would wake up and hear them and we would say, 'Hey, I am living here!' "[6]

Squatters were suspected of breaking into buildings to steal tools. In several instances homesteaders found messages from squatters scrawled on building walls mocking their effort. In one building the issue was of immediate relevance in that a neighboring building was being squatted. There was daily interaction, and homesteaders and squatters knew each other. In contrast to other buildings, a relationship of mutual tolerance had emerged over the years.

In one incident, volunteers echoed the sense of distance and estrangement from squatters felt by many homesteaders and other people in the community. A LESAC construction worker who was supervising work in a building asked the volunteers to knock on the door of the neighboring building. They were to inquire whether they might enter into the backyard shared by the two buildings in order to remove some debris from there. The volunteers were rather ill at ease and said: "But they're squatters, aren't they?" The LESAC worker laconically responded: "They don't bite, they're our neighbors." So with some trepidation the volunteers did as they were asked, and—to their great relief—nobody answered their repeated banging on the door and calling out.

Generally, people in vacant lots inspired more apprehension than did squatters. This fear reached a peak in the summer and fall of 1991, after homeless people had been evicted from Tompkins Square Park. The park was closed off on June 3, 1991, "for renovation." Many homeless people who had been living in the tents there initially settled on an empty lot on 8th Street next to a homesteader building. During the summer months the lot was a beehive of activity, while a makeshift shower was rigged to a water hydrant in the middle of the block. The homesteaders were very worried that their building would be damaged or even burned down. In October 1991 this lot was also cleared by the city and fenced in, and those who had been living on it were forced to move. Homesteaders' comments about the squatters next to their building ranged from pity to arguments that the squatters were somehow practicing deceit on everyone, that some had places to live elsewhere, and that many were crazy.

The Community Land Trust RAIN in its origins, development, and most recent history encapsulates many contradictions of the homesteading movement. The story of the origin of RAIN as told by homesteaders varies in relation to the nature and degree of involvement of the particular individual. However, all accounts share a utopian idealism about the meaning of RAIN for the homesteading movement and, more important, for the community as a whole.

CARMEN: Pretty much it was working-class people between 20 and 35 who saw what was happening with all the buildings that were empty. It was really bad in

1979. There were a lot of young people for whom there was no space, some were living with their parents, there was no place for them to go, or they could not afford it. So what happened was they said: "Heck, there are all these abandoned buildings, so we're going to go in and fix them up." They said: "It's tough out there, we can't do this by ourselves, there is no way we can get the money." Some of these buildings were bad. You should have seen the basement on 66 Avenue C; the buckets were weighing 70 pounds. These people said: "If we band together, we can have more power, we can find out what is going on with the city, we can educate ourselves, we can find out where we can get the money. The second thing we want to do is we are busting our chops off; there's no way we are going to allow people to come in and take it away." So these were the two main points originally.

Then it so happened that some of the people working in those buildings were Catholic, they went to church on Sundays, they were talking. LESAC became interested, saw the inspiration, saw that junkies and pushers were being pushed out of the buildings. So we thought they know about the government and the city and about raising money, and so that's the way we began to work with each other—as long as they have the same idea that these buildings should remain in the neighborhood. Now, the name RAIN—we had not decided what it was supposed to mean, but we wanted the group to be called RAIN, so over the years it evolved. When it finally incorporated by 1987, everyone understood that RAIN was Rehabilitation in Action to Improve Neighborhoods.

The main thing was we wanted to keep these buildings for people in the neighborhood forever. We didn't want the grandkids to come and say we are going to sell this for profit. Because then the money that poor people paid would be for nought.

Carmen stressed an image of people participating in the early homesteading movement that applied more directly to those who have been involved since the latter part of the 1980s. It was a description that applied to herself: young, upwardly mobile, single, having become a homesteader in the mid-1980s and in a leadership position in RAIN since 1989. Some homesteaders in relating "origin myths" of RAIN stressed an inclusive image of the people involved; RAIN was to empower not only a relatively small group of people rehabilitating housing but rather an entire community. The "participatory model" mentioned earlier was connected to a vision of homesteading and control over buildings that went beyond the immediate goal of rehabilitating a number of buildings. According to Lourdes, RAIN was a fictive organization used to impress the city administration into accepting the homesteading movement as a powerful voice in the community that was not to be easily dismissed.

LOURDES: Kevin came up with the strategy, saying that we have to give the impression that we were many though we were not. The way to do that was to create a coalition. Because *coalition* by definition means that there are many groups involved. Kevin and Thomas came up with the idea of a fake coalition and calling it RAIN, an umbrella organization that really didn't exist. So we had a meeting and we created RAIN and we elected people. M., who was the treasurer in this building, was the treasurer of RAIN; I was the vice president; my cousin was the president. We went to the city with this supposed coalition. We requested a meeting with HPD. So RAIN was created and it slowly became real.

RAIN appeared to be stronger while it was not yet incorporated, while it was still in the process of "slowly becoming real." Homesteaders described the "early days" of homesteading with nostalgia.

ELENA: What used to happen was once a month on Saturday all the buildings would shut down at four o'clock and every member would come to the meeting. Every member of every building would come to those meetings.

However, there was no fairy magic to make RAIN "real" like Margery Williams's "velveteen rabbit." RAIN's existence was contingent on the emotional commitment of homesteaders. One homesteader said: "What is RAIN? It is a nothing, a figment of our imagination." In the late 1980s, homesteaders began to withdraw their active support of and belief in RAIN. Several buildings were experiencing severe problems with funding, with the city, with former landlords raising claims to buildings, and—last but not least—with LESAC. RAIN, which had been central in the homesteading movement in the early 1980s, was perceived as useless in the face of many of these problems. Ideas about the objectives of homesteading were beginning to diverge. Factions among homesteaders were becoming more apparent. Most important, the notion of finalizing commitment to the no-resale policy, the ideological centerpiece of RAIN, assumed concrete shape for homesteaders who were about to buy their buildings from the city and hence became subject of internal debate.

At this juncture, several buildings refused to sign the no-resale policy and declined to join the Community Land Trust. RAIN was in no position to enforce anything. LESAC attempted to exert influence on homesteading projects by threatening to withhold all further support. Some buildings eventually signed the no-resale policy. A few of these buildings cut all ties with RAIN and LESAC and attempted to continue rehabilitation on their own. One was able to complete rehabilitation; others that were in less advanced stages of rehabilitation could not obtain adequate funding and other support and were unable to complete the work. One building was still in a state of limbo in 1993, an empty shell with its windows boarded up.

LOURDES: Some of the buildings began saying: "No, we are against the no-resale policy, we are not going to sign it." And it was too late to force them to do so. They already were so far ahead in the renovation of the building. That is what happened with 702, the one in the corner of 66 Avenue C. Those two were the first three buildings approved in the homesteading program. That building was part of RAIN, and they agreed in principle to the no-resale policy, low-income apartments, no one would profit from it. When they were almost close to finishing they said: "See you later, goodbye." The same thing happened with 10th Street and Avenue C. Same story again. They said: "Oh yes, we are for not-for-profit. We are going to go for the no-resale policy." When time came to sign it, they said: "No, we are not signing that shit."

Doubts about the no-resale policy also affected decisions made by buildings earlier in the rehabilitation process; however, such doubts were not yet readily apparent to other buildings nor publicized by such buildings or homesteaders. In the early 1980s a form of grant money from HUD was available that had a 20-year no-resale policy attached to it. A few buildings were offered this grant money. One building chose not to accept it.

LOURDES: How much money do you think we have to pay back? We have a mortgage of $130,000. Why do you think that happened? I tell you. There was money available from HUD. That money was money where you had to sign a no-resale policy for 20 years. That money was available. They were dying to give the money away. That building which is in trouble today, that money was offered to them. They did not want to take that money. It was $20,000 per apartment. We took that money; it doesn't have to be paid back.

In the late 1980s, homesteaders in completed buildings often expressed a mixture of feelings about the no-resale policy. During one such conversation a homesteader said that something seemed wrong if poor people work on a building for many years and then are told that they are not allowed to sell their apartments. In the same conversation this homesteader expressed doubts about another building member, saying that he had always suspected her of actually wanting to sell her apartment and not being sincere about her reasons for being a homesteader. The following unequivocal statement, by a homesteader who described her feelings about one building's hesitancy when they were confronted with formally joining the land trust, was an exception:

ELENA: They had signed documents all along that they were accepting technical assistance and money and this and that from LESAC, all predicated on their joining the land trust; and one day they wake up and suddenly don't understand the land trust? Drop dead! I just said to somebody: "Look, either the dude is lying or the dude is retarded, and he can choose. That is the choice."

Many homesteaders argued that it was not so much the no-resale policy per se that bothered them as the way in which LESAC and RAIN acted toward them. They felt they were being strong-armed into making a decision.

EDUARDO: RAIN is a political organization that basically could not do much for them. What could it do? It couldn't translate into anything tangible. It wasn't presented the right way. It was carried out with an ax. If you disagreed with the no-resale policy, you were put on the spot, you were made to feel like you were an enemy. To me it sort of resembled other political systems when people went against them they sort of got rid of you or they stopped your funding or they used you. I think the idea of the no-resale policy is a very good idea; but it was like they stuffed it down your mouth, and if you questioned it, it was wrong.

Alienation from RAIN became apparent in a rapidly diminishing attendance at meetings. In 1991 and 1992, RAIN meetings frequently did not have a quorum and thus could not conduct any business. Some homesteaders did not know who was on the board of RAIN or who the current president was. It had become irrelevant. Others who still were involved in RAIN and concerned with its development were alienated by the shift in leadership, which according to some had become elitist and cliquish.

By 1992, RAIN had become progressively weaker as an organization despite the directors' attempt to make it a businesslike entity. Its 1990/1991 annual report—like so many corporate annual reports—was a masterpiece in lending the impression that this was a healthy and growing organization. Yet RAIN could hardly claim to be speaking for all homesteaders, given that the majority of homesteaders could not be bothered to attend meetings. RAIN had also shifted in its orientation from an organization that attempted to bring together various elements and groups in the community to an organization that saw its primary goal as servicing its member buildings. Having become "real" in the sense of finally having been incorporated, it lost the element that earlier had made it real in people's imagination and hopes.

During those same years, the issue of Nazareth Home units emerged as another divisive element in the homesteading movement. This issue revealed various factions among homesteaders. It might be said that for homesteaders it was easier to express doubts about Nazareth Home units than about the no-resale policy, even though both were founded on similar ideological concepts. Further, the issue of Nazareth Home units emerged as a problem only once some buildings had been completed and homesteaders had moved in. RAIN echoed these conceptual shifts; in effect, RAIN provided much of the formal impetus behind attempts to revise the policy on Nazareth Home units. Debates in buildings and in RAIN about Nazareth Home also repeated a theme that had been a source of irritation with regard to the no-resale policy—that is, the argument that homesteaders were being strong-armed into accepting a deal that was increasingly perceived as undesirable.

EDUARDO: We were told that one of the conditions the building would have money was that because we would have homeless families. It really came to a head when the building was almost completed. And Tana was against it. I was against it also. I was working in school where a lot of homeless families come in, and I remember saying: "Look, you are really bringing a lot of problems into this building." But again, I felt I had given my word and thought that was much more powerful. Well, Nazareth Home did stay, the group didn't fight against the concept, because for one we wanted the money to finish up the building. But to this day it has been a problem as I told you, because we find that we have gotten people here who have really no appreciation of this building. . . . I want to say this in their favor, there have been a lot of very nice people too, but you don't always remember the nice ones.

According to homesteaders' accounts, several completed buildings were experiencing problems with Nazareth Home residents in both permanent and transitional units. Homesteaders complained that Nazareth Home people brought roaches into buildings, suspected them of drug abuse, were upset about unpleasant encounters with Nazareth Home people themselves or with family members or friends over infringements of building rules, described their annoyance about loitering on building stoops and their suspicions about lifestyles to the point of suspecting prostitution, and expressed aggravation about neglect and/or destruction of apartments.

Meanwhile, a debate was going on among RAIN members and homesteaders at large with regard to the ownership of Nazareth Home units.

MARINA: RAIN doesn't want the Nazareth Home people to have leases or shares, they want them as renters so they can act as landlords. Once you are a shareholder you can't be put out, it is very, very difficult. Nobody wants to move next door to somebody that they don't know. Nobody wants somebody who hasn't done a day's sweat to get into a nice apartment, which is unfortunate. I came into this program innocently thinking that all the buildings were going to have Nazareth Home apartments and that these people were going to be well received. And now, as people are moving in, I am hearing that they don't want Nazareth Home people there. I am not saying that the homesteaders are wrong. They definitely have a right to know who is going to be living in their building. They should have a say.

LISA: We have a woman from Nazareth Home, we expect her to be a shareholder. She has full inheritance rights and everything. We have no problems. However, the other buildings are having lots of problems.

ELENA: Nazareth Home is not an issue among most of the people in the building. It was a term and condition when you came here. I tell people right in their face: "You don't like it, leave." It may be an issue in other buildings, but my feeling is tough shit. It all goes back to the same thing, there was never any doubt that in return for LESAC's assistance—anybody who says there was is lying—there never was any question. Let me add that it isn't that I don't think it will be a challenge to integrate homeless families into the building, to deal with the transitional homeless. This is going to be a challenge. But as someone said: "This is the charity."

In 1991 the Nazareth Home issue was treated in a RAIN meeting as an entrapment that the homesteaders had been tricked into. One RAIN director instructed the few homesteaders who were attending the meeting to study legal papers about their buildings carefully, because the agreements about Nazareth Home units would be hidden and only referred to by the term *homeless housing*. According to the RAIN president, an agreement between LESAC, RAIN, and Nazareth Home had just been worked out according to which people in permanent Nazareth Home units were to get proprietary leases and become shareholders in the building, but that the unit would revert back to the HDFC (the building corporation) in the event of demise or departure of a resident. It was pointed out that the time period for an obligation to Nazareth Home varied from building to building and ranged from seven to ten years. In other words, the concept of a commitment to providing some units to homeless families had been transformed into a notion of an inconvenient but fortunately time-bound obligation in connection with a source of funding that would otherwise not have been available.

The three issues discussed above—attitudes toward squatters, the history and development of RAIN, and the situation with regard to Nazareth Home units—ultimately all pertain to conflicting concepts of ownership within the context of a community. As homesteaders became property owners, their notions of property and community underwent transformations that led them to reject some of the premises originally embodied in RAIN and the early homesteading movement. The two other concepts considered in this context—work and gender roles—also underwent transformations in conjunction with the acquisition of property by homesteaders. The contradictions revealed in these processes of transformation were linked to and expressed conflicting notions of community.

DIFFERING CONCEPTS OF COMMUNITY

House rethatching in the Andes takes place as the dry season is giving way to the growing season. This seasonal shift involves a corresponding change in social relations from an emphasis on private appropriation by individual households during the harvest to an extensive and institutionalized interhousehold cooperation that will prevail throughout the growing season. (Gose 1991: 39)

Gose is concerned with illustrating the way in which house rethatching in the Andes produces a ritual imagery that gives form to, and is animated by, a tension between private appropriation and interhousehold cooperation. Like house rethatching in the Andes, homesteading was perched on the fault line between domestic life and the community. Homesteading presented homesteaders again and again with conflicting notions of community. The nature of the work process provided concrete expression and confirmation of a concept of a community based on sharing, reciprocity, communal control of resources, and the rule of custom rather than law (the notion that moral judgment of homesteaders and self-selective processes on part of homesteaders alone suffice to control behavior). Simultaneously, homesteading provided a catalyst for rejecting this same notion of community. Over the course of homesteading, such rejection took the following forms: a restatement of objectives (owning one's apartment rather than creating housing for control by the community), an assertion of a "pragmatic realism" in the face of a punishing market economy (buildings have to look out for themselves), an increasing reliance on formal procedures and a perceived need for a "more businesslike approach," and a notion of a right to return to one's private life. The eventual outcome was a virtual closing of doors, a gradual or not-so-gradual withdrawal from RAIN, and a reassertion of a notion of community as a tool in time-bound situations that can be discarded when no longer required.

Can one interpret homesteading on the Lower East Side as a form of community building, or is it to be seen as a replication of a status quo in which private ownership of residential space becomes the mainspring of homesteaders' involvement, in conjunction with an emerging class consciousness of property holders? There is no easy answer. House building—or, more precisely, building an apartment—is a metaphor both for construction of a private home and for the revitalization of a community. These need not be diametrically opposed; however, in the homesteading movement the tension between them strained the movement to and beyond the breaking point. This reflects a parallel tension in society.

The following account encapsulates the ideological conflicts contained in the homesteading movement. During the early part of my fieldwork I arrived at a building on a Saturday, to find the homesteaders engaged in clearing out a groundfloor space in order to demolish the rotting walls and ready it for reconstruction. However, this particular space was occupied by an old man, Ramón, who had a bike repair shop there. Without knowing the context and indeed without knowing much about homesteading at all, I found this to be a very disturbing scene. I watched the homesteaders carry mountains of rusty bikes, bike parts, tools, and unidentifiable items from this dank and dark space out onto the sidewalk and place it all in the dumpster. This occurred in grim silence while the old man occasionally wandered in and out, watching the proceedings, mumbling, and sucking his knuckles. At the end a thick piece of plywood was nailed over the hole that had served as an entrance.

The "shopsteader" Ramón's presence in the building presented various legal and practical problems in regard to the homesteaders' attaining legal title to the building and their plans to lease some of the ground floor as commercial space. Three years after the homesteaders began to work on the building, Ramón had not been removed despite two efforts by the city and one by the homesteaders themselves to evict him. Subsequent to each eviction he broke back into the space and reopened for business. To complicate matters, Ramón had run his bike shop for 15 years and was well known in the community, with a degree of support from various groups. The homesteaders of this building and other buildings—the majority of whom, like Ramón, were Puerto Rican—were by no means united in their perception of the matter. They were, however, unified to some extent against the pressure exerted on them from the disparate voices of criticism in the community as well as the pressure from the Catholic Charities organization that had been arguing for allowing Ramón to remain in the building—this would have meant giving away the space to a nonpaying tenant, whose presence according to some homesteaders presented risks of arson and crime.

It is worthwhile to note that it was impossible to clarify whether Ramón was spending his nights in this space as well as occupying it during the daytime when he "opened for business." Ramón himself at times stated that this was his home; at other times indicated that he was staying with a friend, someone who came by frequently to socialize with him. Many homesteaders emphasized that Ramón did not live in the space, in this appearing to find confirmation for their argument that eviction was acceptable. A minority of homesteaders argued to the contrary.

Thus, the issue continued to smolder over several years, and notions of ownership of property and rights associated with such ownership were pitted against other notions of a shared sense of poverty, powerlessness, and vulnerability to the dynamics of the free market. In the fall of 1991 the city again acted to evict Ramón. A city marshall appeared, took all of Ramón's bicycle materials out of the space, ripped up the floorboards, and placed a lock on a piece of plywood over the entrance. To lend greater emphasis to this action, a sign was painted in red letters on the brick wall outside the building: "No floor." For several months on sunny days Ramón continued to sit on a crate outside the building talking to passers-by, while the homesteaders continued to work on the other side of the building, with little more between them than a water-logged basement and a piece of plywood. In 1993 the building was nearing completion, and Ramón had left his perch and disappeared.

Homesteaders' conflicting notions of community are reflected in the following comments about Ramón:

EDUARDO: He [Ramón] has been in that building for years, he has an identification with it, I think he should have a place there. I don't know how small it will be or what, but the building is going to have to work him in. He is there just by right of default if nothing else, because you know he runs that bike store, and for him it's his life. And in a sense he has watched out for that building. But that is a double-edged sword, because just like S. you are getting into problems, because he has a criminal record. He is a marginal person. But what I feel is communities are not about everyone who is a college graduate. We've got to have our marginal people. They are part of our community. . . . Most neighborhood residents would not squat a building; it would be someone coming in from the outside.

In other words, when individuals or groups of people are not considered a threat to a building, building members are willing to include them in their image of the community. For Eduardo, the issue of Ramón was once removed and hence not a real problem. Similarly, Julius, the squatter who owned several dogs, was tolerated because he did not infringe on space that anyone in the area wanted to claim for themselves. Meanwhile, politically active squatters were described as outsiders and perceived as a threat. The city administration and homesteaders made somewhat odd bedfellows with regard to their views about squatters.

The story of Ramón illustrates conflicts between homesteaders and "marginal people" of the area, conflicts between the Catholic Church and homesteaders, and conflicts between the city administration and "marginal people." What is perceived as unfair eviction and cruel outcroppings of gentrification (the image presented by people in the neighborhood who demonstrated against homesteaders' attempts to evict Ramón) is seen by homesteaders as the attempt to claim what is rightfully theirs by virtue of "sweat" poured into the building and as a justifiable protection of property, which in itself is viewed as a building block in community revitalization.

It is redundant to speak of fragmentation in discussing the concept of community in an urban environment, or for that matter in other environments. Such fragmentation can be illustrated in any number of ways. One example is that on a particular block none of the homesteaders in a building knew or even cared who was working on a building across the street. In the context of homesteading, the lines separating "us" and "others" were sharply drawn. In other contexts, the notion of community might be more inclusive.

For some homesteaders, the tension between the needs of the community and individual lives was ultimately not a problem.

LOURDES: What I say to you is the following. The building is like a micro-environment of society. Society cannot function in a vacuum. Everyone has to carry their load. The society has compassion and understanding about drug abuse and drug abusers. We don't put them in jail; we help them to get rehabilitated. But we also understand that we cannot allow them to be robbing people, destroying property to buy the drug in order to fix themselves. What I am saying is that a building, a collective, is no more important than an individual, but that an individual is not more important than a collective and there has to be a balance. If an individual is threatening the collective, the collective has to do something about that.

CONCLUSION

In the context of a community as a construct constantly undergoing change, homesteading was a creative dynamic. Normative concepts of gender roles, work, and ownership were contested in homesteading, inextricably linked to conflicting concepts of community. Processes of transformation were fragmentary, bound and defined by pre-existing values and norms as much as by an evolving socioeconomic and political context. Homesteading provides lessons informing future efforts—for instance, a more complex understanding of the power and pervasiveness of mainstream values in conjunction with a harsh economic reality.

On a winter night in 1992, Lourdes showed me the waterlogged basement in her building. She pointed out a patch in the brick wall at the back of the basement and explained that the opening to the backyard would be there. Somewhat wistfully she said: "We will have a garden there." Lourdes began working on the building in 1979. That is a long time to wait for a garden, not to mention for a habitable home; but when I left that night, the garden was vivid in my mind, filled with peppers, tomatoes, sweet peas, and sunflowers.

NOTES

1. From a poem by Jorge Lopez, "Pesetas de Embuste" (Counterfeit Quarters) (Algarin and Piñero 1975); translation by Miguel Algarín.

2. This is an approximate figure. Squatters certainly are not eager to advertise their presence in a particular building, and neither HPD nor the local precinct are able to state with any certainty the number of buildings occupied by squatters. Also, the figure depends on the precise definition of *squatting*, that is, whether one includes people who seek shelter in abandoned buildings without undertaking any alterations to the structure.

3. The terms *squatter* and *homesteader* were appropriated by different groups of people. Some groups, described as squatters in the press and by HPD, may describe themselves as homesteaders. A woman living in an abandoned building on 13th Street said: "We're called squatters and we call these buildings squats, but I think of ourselves as homesteaders" (Kaufman 1989).

4. In December 1990 a resident in this building was killed in his apartment. His life before moving into the rehabilitated apartment, which he had helped to build, illustrates the grey area that many homesteaders try to present as a sharp line separating homesteaders from homeless people. For a number of years he lived in a local flophouse. He lost his job as a welder two months before his death. He had a drinking problem that worsened over time. He was often seen socializing with homeless people in the shanties in the vacant lot next to his building. However, homesteaders in the building spoke about his contribution to the building work and his technical and engineering skills.

5. *Inside Life Outside*, filmed and produced by Sachiko Hamada and Scott Sinkler in 1988 (New York: West Glenn Films), covered two and a half years in a shanty-town on the Lower East Side.

6. On October 12, 1991, squatters in Lower East Side buildings staged a protest march through the area to protest recent evictions carried out by the police that were expected to be followed by more evictions. The description "squatorotos" used by Greg is derived from the squatters' own rallying cry to "squat or rot."

7

SOCIAL MOVEMENTS, COMMUNITY ORGANIZATIONS, AND PRIVATE LIVES

There in their little cells, divided by partitions of brick or board, they sit strangers. . . . It is a huge aggregate of little systems, each of which is again a small anarchy, the members of which do not *work* together, but *scramble* against each other.[1]

The history of homesteading on the Lower East Side has been shaped by the dynamic tension between individual lives and general developments inside and outside the neighborhood. Constructions of concepts of community, whether formally embraced by a group or an organization or informally expressed by individuals, are idiosyncratic and simultaneously reflective of common processes. I analyze the homesteading model devised on the Lower East Side and individuals' constructions of homesteading and community, and I compare these with other community organizations involved in housing-related efforts in order to shed light on the intersections between (1) differing political and ideological agendas, (2) historical developments, and (3) private lives in contestation and construction of concepts of community. Homesteading—with its concepts of a Community Land Trust, cooperative housing, and cooperation in rehabilitation work—involved ideas intrinsic to particular notions of community. Activists initially viewed housing as a basis for organizing a more comprehensive social movement; subsequently they moved away from this notion. Individual homesteaders' constructions of concepts of community were subject to internal contradictions and evolved over time. Finally, various community organizations active in housing make claims on how a community should be organized and maintained. Although their respective organizational structures and purported objectives differ, there are several instructive parallels to the organizations involved in homesteading on the Lower East Side.

ESSENTIAL TEXTS IN HOMESTEADING ON THE LOWER EAST SIDE

Three texts give concrete expression to the goals and aspirations of this housing movement. One is a position paper used by LESAC; another an instruction manual for homesteaders; and finally, a text that contains the principles of the Community Land Trust as set forth by the Institute for Community Economics (ICE).

LESAC Position Paper

The position paper prepared by Howard Brandstein for adoption by LESAC in May 1984 provides insights into the goals set by community activists for the neighborhood:

The goal of community empowerment suggests a cooperative model for future development. This model is defined by shared ownership of property and equal voice in decision making for residents. A cooperative model could apply equally to the organization of buildings, community gardens and open spaces, and even economic ventures. Its aim is to foster a *productive* relationship between community residents and the land they inhabit by empowering those residents to initiate, manage, and assume responsibility for development. . . .
More broadly, homesteading may be understood as a logic of action that connects community residents to buildings and land establishing a physical space or "infrastructure" for community social and political life. The principles of homesteading may therefore be applied as well to the construction of community parks and planting of gardens on vacant lots, the development of community centers, and the organization of cooperative businesses. (Brandstein 1984: 5, 17)

This is a sweeping vision of the role homesteading was intended to fulfill on the Lower East Side. The crucial element in this passage, aside from the emphasis on a cooperative model and a notion of property as shared and not to be alienated from the community, is the concept of homesteading as a "logic of action" that extends far beyond the single issue of housing into the social and economic life of the community.

Homesteaders Instruction Manual

The previously articulated concepts appear in less abstract language in a small "how-to" manual prepared for distribution among homesteaders in the early 1980s. This manual, written in cooperation with LESAC and RAIN by the inner-cities program Save the Children, provides practical suggestions and a basic philosophy of homesteading. Several aspects are interesting in terms of what homesteading has succeeded in accomplishing, and some are interesting in terms of what it has not.

The manual emphasizes the theme of inclusiveness: Today's homesteaders are male, female, young, old, single, married, some with children, some without children. Some have physical disabilities, some are homeless, others on welfare, but the over-riding factor for all these people is their willingness to contribute their talents and energy to achieve their goal of decent and affordable housing for themselves and their families. (Save the Children 1982: 2)

This model envisions a process whereby disabled or less skilled members are not penalized for being unable to contribute an equal amount of sweat labor. The attempt to make homesteading an integrative process and hence a critical stepping-stone for the creation of an integrative community also emphasizes the importance of volunteer labor. The manual points out that volunteer labor is necessary to the success of homesteading projects and argues that benefits move in both directions. It represents a vision of a community that transcends all boundaries.

Volunteers benefit from their involvement in return. For example, the high school students enrolled in job training classes received valuable skills and experience that helped them find jobs. . . . The European and African students gained a broader view of life in the United States. The ex-offenders had a chance to see how a community works together and how their efforts could have a positive impact on the community. (Save the Children 1982: 32)

The manual also emphasizes the cooperative learning experience, which provides low-income residents with a way to solve their own housing problems and to gain skills in construction and property management, and "a mechanism to create decent, low-income housing and neighborhood stabilization." More important, the manual implies that homesteading involves a lifetime commitment and that it provides a training program for future management of buildings and a different approach to other problems. "They use the construction skills for one or two years, but they need the management skills for life" (1982: 2). Being in charge of one's own housing is a stated goal; the implied goal is empowerment, and community organization is seen as the key to such empowerment. Organizing tips emphasize that the project must be approached like any other business, and that a professional approach is essential to the project's survival.

Issues of ownership and production of housing in a market economy are mentioned in the manual, but with a careful attempt not to dictate ways to consider these issues. Thus, the manual addresses the issue of assigning value to sweat-equity labor and to cooperative shares in an oblique way:

Arriving at a final policy may depend largely on members' willingness to compromise and "get the job done" rather than the degree to which they're compensated for their efforts. If these issues are dealt with early, procedures can be written into the Membership Agreement and subsequent disputes avoided. (Save the Children 1982: 39)

As far as the no-resale policy is concerned, the manual remains equally vague; but in essence the point is clear:

Many homesteading groups have broken apart trying to resolve this issue. Your commitment to maintaining low-income housing should be discussed thoroughly in the beginning and the final decision written into the Membership Agreement at the very early stages of the project. You should make sure that your resale policy is acceptable to your sponsor in order to avoid any misunderstandings or conflicts. (Save the Children 1982: 41)

The last sentence is a reminder of the fragile relationship between a sponsor organization and a group of homesteaders. In the case of LESAC, there were repeated incidents wherein LESAC threatened to withdraw its support from a particular building unless that building acted according to LESAC's wishes.

Community Land Trust Principles

The Community Land Trust movement in the United States inspired the homesteading movement on the Lower East Side and supplied it with a concrete model for realizing some of its goals. Although the Community Land Trust model of ICE is flexible and can be adjusted in accordance with a given local situation, certain basic characteristics have been put forth as guidelines:

A community land trust is a nonprofit corporation created to acquire and hold land for the benefit of a local community and to provide permanent access to land and housing at affordable rates for low- and moderate-income people. It is committed to:

1. a democratic structure that includes both community and land trust residents in its membership and board of directors;
2. meeting needs of those most excluded and oppressed by prevailing and speculative real estate markets;
3. an active ongoing development program which attempts to meet other community needs;
4. providing ownership and management opportunities for residents;
5. shared equity based on property value created by residents as well as that created by the community at large;
6. a continuing program of member and public education.

(Matthei 1987: 3)

In terms of an evaluation of the Lower East Side Community Land Trust RAIN, points 1, 3, and 6 are of particular interest. Evidence indicates that with regard to these, RAIN has been least successful and is foundering as a result. This is to be understood in conjunction with the "logic of action" proposed by Brandstein, which, just like the ICE model, envisions a movement that is much broader than one focusing solely on the creation and control of affordable housing.

"People Reform"

Social programs that try to change behavior of poor people enter a highly charged arena of ideological conflict. The following statement by a theologian in the Catholic Church was cited at the top of the position paper prepared for adoption by LESAC in May 1984: "The right to property must never be exercised to the detriment of the common good" (Brandstein 1984: 1). Differing notions about the nature of the relationship between exercising a right to property and the common good are played out in conflicting agendas on "people reform" in the homesteading movement. Efforts at "people reform" are situated within a context of explicit and implicit ideological frameworks, which affect and distort each other. Analysis also suggests that the recipients of such efforts are active interpreters of the ideological frameworks imposed on them.

The no-resale policy attached to RAIN buildings was an ideological cornerstone of the homesteading model devised by social activists during the late 1970s. Another crucial factor was that the model was inclusive. Housing was to be created and made permanently available not only to a particular group of low-income people directly involved in sweat-equity labor but also to a broader range of people, cutting across ethnic and racial lines and including the elderly, disabled, and people from city shelters. The model also envisioned that labor would be treated not as a commodity but as a community property, to be shared and made available to those in need. Some construction work was planned as training experience for young men and women from the neighborhood. Work done by homesteaders was not to be compensated in monetary form. Disabled individuals, elderly, and people from shelters placed in the buildings at a later date were all to be treated as full members regardless of the amount of labor contributed by them.

According to the LESAC homesteading model, self-help involves drawing on the resources of neighbors and the community in order to address larger forces affecting that community. Owners of property are portrayed as helpless unless they cooperate with each other to maintain control over such property and maintain it for the community. The following quote from the LESAC position paper illustrates its conceptual approach:

Schooled in the theory and everyday reality of "competition," neighborhood residents (as all members of society) have been educated, for the most part, in the basics of "getting" and "having." An education in cooperation, on the other hand, will emphasize the basics of "doing" and "sharing." Education in this new sense is both political and practical; political in that we learn the true meaning of self-government while becoming conscious of the larger forces affecting our community, and practical in the everyday practice of the "techniques" of cooperative living in a not-for-profit setting. (Brandstein 1984: 6)

The agenda pursued by federal, state, and local administrations involved a different set of ideological parameters. Practical considerations (e.g., lack of funds for housing) were reinforced by a political climate that favored governmental withdrawal from local and national issues of a social welfare nature. Researchers under contract to HUD in 1969 defined self-help as "participation by an individual in any or all phases of the process regarding his own dwelling, with the primary intention being to reduce the amount of external assistance required for the completion of the process" (see Bratt 1989b: 28). This report expresses the notion of individual betterment through reliance on one's own resources.

The moderate income family with aspirations for higher status consolidates its upward mobility. . . . The capable but disadvantaged minority family [will establish] itself in the wider society. . . . The family incapacitated by prolonged unemployment discovers or rediscovers hope and opportunity. . . . The indigenous and unambitious self-helper consolidates his independence and improves his condition. . . . The aspiring but extremely poor independent self-helper realizes his own opportunities and consolidates his improved status. (quoted in Bratt 1989b: 28)

For city, state, and federal administrations, homesteading (1) was convenient, (2) did not cost a lot of public money, and (3) returned otherwise useless vacant buildings to the tax base. Moreover, the concepts of self-help and self-reliance fitted in beautifully with predominant ideological thought of the 1980s. The notion that poor people needed to be taught the principles of property management and realization of a project and the benefits of long-term commitment, stability, and hard work as paths to independence and economic security had profound resonance during the years of the Reagan administration. An additional attraction of homesteading was that it placed the burden of responsibility for failure anywhere but with the government.

The perceived need to rehabilitate not only buildings but also people is implied in various comments on the part of HPD officials. HPD argued that although homesteading is not cost-effective, the city had been in support of it because of the social benefits involved. At the same time, this embrace of so-called social benefits glosses over the fact that rehabilitated buildings not only would be returned to the tax rolls but also would help pay for citywide sewer and water system repairs in the form of exorbitant water rates. Further, training poor people in the principles of property management would draw them onto the economic treadmill of loans and mortgages.

Participant observation illustrates how proponents of differing agendas have appropriated concepts such as empowerment, self-help, sweat-equity, ownership, and community. For instance, although sweat-equity as a concrete experience is intended to provide a sense of shared struggle and common purpose in the construction of community-controlled housing, it is also used to instill a sense of pride in individual ownership and to provide a training ground for future property holders. Both interpretations come into play in efforts by community organizations and city agencies alike to control and manipulate their clients' behavior with the simultaneous objectives of creating a stable, bill-paying group of tenants and politically active, community-oriented residents.

Both conceptual plans of reform—that of activists, predominantly educated, middle-class individuals; and that of the administration—have been imposed from above. At this point it is too early to predict the final outcome, given the fact that several buildings in this effort were only completed in the spring of 1995. However, it is apparent that the outcome is not going to be what either party originally intended. In other words, the target population, low-income people from the Lower East Side, have not readily accepted either one of these agendas.

The contradictions between the two agendas are reflected in homesteaders' comments. They have expressed fears about having provided sweat labor for buildings that may again end up on the open market unless protected through some sort of Community Land Trust arrangement. At the same time, they have argued that something was wrong with a model that resulted in poor and low-income people not being able to profit from their labor by selling their units on the open market.

Homesteaders have resisted what they perceived as insidious efforts to trap them into fiscally detrimental situations. Homesteaders in some buildings have refused to accept low-interest loans from the state on the grounds that signing the loan agreement was tied to signing an agreement allowing homesteaders to take out mortgages on their apartment units. This was perceived as potentially disastrous for buildings belonging to a Community Land Trust. One homesteader described the agreement as a "self-destruct button built in by the state."

Homesteaders themselves spoke about the need for learning the principles of property management. One homesteader, who had been actively involved for five years, said: "These are poor people. They don't understand the concept of ownership." On the other hand, homesteaders became irritated with HPD rules about the maximum amount of sweat-labor hours homesteaders could put into a building. They felt that the city administration treated homesteaders like children by implying that homesteaders could not assume responsibility for how much time they put in without jeopardizing their employment.

Some efforts at training homesteaders as future property owners and business managers focused on the need for businesslike conduct during building and organizational meetings. The homesteaders manual suggests a format for meetings and encourages homesteaders to follow it. Robert's Rules of Order are suggested as a reliable formal method that ensures everyone's ability to express their opinions in a structured and hence by implication constructive environment. Meetings that I attended reflected this "lesson" in that participants appeared to observe the formalities as if they were "playing school"; more heated and ultimately more decisive discussion of controversial matters occurred before or after meetings were adjourned and when some participants had either not yet arrived or already departed. A similar disjunction occurred with regard to training sessions run by ICE, which provides educational, technical, and informational resources to community organizations. Only a minority of homesteaders attended these sessions, a significant factor being the location out of state and the required time involvement. Other homesteaders at times expressed doubts about the practical value of such sessions, in effect shrugging them off as "cute" but of little relevance to what was really going on. Their reactions implied that as far as they were concerned empowerment had definite limits, and that it was a delusion to believe that real change in any of the underlying power structures could be affected by attending such educational sessions.

In the final analysis, the impact of efforts to effect behavioral changes among low-income people may be elusive because most homesteaders originally involved in the effort in the late 1970s have been replaced by new generations who came to the effort with different ideological preconceptions. However, the manner in which people in the neighborhood portray events of the last two decades suggests that homesteaders were not easily manipulated, even though they were subject to wider social and economic forces.

INDIVIDUAL CONSTRUCTIONS OF HOMESTEADING AND COMMUNITY

Over the course of my fieldwork I became aware that there were several levels at which the various actors—homesteaders, LESAC and HDI, activists, and even volunteers—were being and/or perceived themselves as being manipulated. This awareness was sharpened by the contrast to my original impression of a group of people, community organizations, and ultimately a community asserting control over events and developments.

This shift in perspective is analogous to the process of many homesteaders becoming alienated from homesteading and everything associated with it. After several years of involvement, homesteaders began to feel they had been used as tools in a process over which ultimately had little control. One example is the situation at a building discussed previously (Chapter 5). It involved a dispute over whether the homesteaders must accept a particular party as a commercial tenant and as a full shareholder in the building. According to homesteaders, LESAC engaged in a form of blackmail, trying to force them into accepting something by withholding technical assistance at a critical stage in the building's rehabilitation.

Other examples relate to membership in RAIN. Homesteaders from several buildings described the way in which the buildings became RAIN members as a form of manipulation on part of LESAC. According to homesteaders, in several instances LESAC threatened a particular building with withdrawal of all assistance unless the RAIN documents were signed. In the highly polarized atmosphere of the late 1980s, other homesteaders reacted with anger after hearing such descriptions and argued that home-steaders in those buildings knew full well what was expected of them upon accepting LESAC assistance. Nonetheless, the feeling of having been ma-nipulated or conned in some way was pervasive and contributed to the increasing fragmentation among homesteaders.

Some homesteaders argued that LESAC used homesteading to build up the organization's position in the housing arena and abandoned home-steading when it no longer served this purpose and instead had become a liability. According to proponents of this perspective, LESAC by the late 1980s was starting to withdraw from active support of homesteading projects and was considering other options within the housing arena.

Homesteaders were not the only ones who felt they had been used as pawns. Activists described the Catholic Church as having been a tool of sorts, brought into homesteading through their efforts. They had hoped that the Church by virtue of its power and influence could help turn the homestead-ing movement into something far more effective and far-reaching. In fact, neither LESAC nor HDI were equipped to deal with the complexities of homesteading in the arena of low-income housing development.

One might argue that volunteers who worked on the buildings in the mid-1980s and early 1990s also were tools beyond the labor power they provided. Volunteers were used for garnering publicity for homesteading and served in furthering the image of a housing movement that was connected to the larger world and, therefore, was worthy of support. Of course, various corporations were more than happy to exploit volunteerism for boosting their corporate image. On numerous days, teams of volunteers from a particular corporation spent more time with the firm photographer than they did working in the building.

Another perspective on homesteaders as tools used by LESAC and by the city was provided by an individual living on the Lower East Side who was not himself directly involved with the homesteaders. Calvin lived in an occupied building, as opposed to one homesteaded through an officially sanctioned program. He had been working on his building for ten years. According to Calvin, he and other people in occupied buildings felt that the homesteaders sold out to the city and to LESAC. He argued that in return for financial and technical assistance, homesteaders allowed themselves to be controlled politically and economically. "I don't like LESAC; they manipulate people." As an example Calvin pointed to the LESAC rule that homesteaders were expected to put in the same amount of time, and that latecomers to a building had to work on another building later to make up the sweat hours. According to Calvin, this created bad feelings and killed enthusiasm. "People like to work on their own." He said that what LESAC was doing amounted to a kind of slavery and exploitation. He claimed that some people bought their way out of that rule by paying someone else to do their work.

During my fieldwork I was aware of only one such suspected incident. It is not easily proven that this was an exception. However, although there was a lot of absenteeism on the buildings I was observing, I never was aware of someone else doing the work for a particular homesteader. In terms of the amount of sweat labor that homesteaders were expected to contribute, this issue was handled flexibly and haphazardly, particularly during the last few years. The hours put in by any one individual were not recorded meticulously or consistently. Peer pressure combined with a process of self-selection provided an informal system of ensuring that individual homesteaders did their share of the work. Nevertheless, Calvin's comments reverberated in my mind as I thought of homesteaders who had expressed bitterness about a situation wherein low-income people were expected to work on buildings without compensation and yet were not allowed to profit by selling the fruits of their labor for profit.

Homesteaders and others tentatively put forth the argument that homesteading was an inexpensive way for the city to renovate buildings, implying the possibility that these buildings would eventually—because of tenants' difficulties in keeping up with costs—be recycled into the market. Although I could not establish a concrete basis for substantiating this dire prognosis, and although it is still too early to tell whether any of the buildings might actually default on their mortgage and other payments, this type of discourse reflects the mood of a number of people involved in homesteading directly or peripherally. One activist whom I told about Calvin's comment agreed that indeed homesteaders had been tools in the process, but for somewhat different reasons:

LOURDES: He [Calvin] is right in the sense that the homesteaders were a tool for saving this neighborhood. The goal was to create a community for low- to moderate-income people.

For Lourdes and other activists, homesteading had never been an end in itself. Homesteading was to be a way to defeat plans of the city administration of the late 1970s and early 1980s for leveling the neighborhood and transforming it into an area for luxury housing for the downtown financial district. The tensions between various political agendas, efforts at imposing these agendas onto the target population, and homesteaders' self-perceptions as pawns in a large game, the dimensions and rules of which were barely discernible, all contributed to the fragmentation of the homesteading movement on the Lower East Side.

Homesteading, Community Organizations, and Private Lives

During a RAIN meeting on September 7, 1991, developments concerning two buildings, 340 and 344 East 4th Street, were discussed. These buildings had been scheduled for rehabilitation work, LESAC had obtained site control, a group of homesteaders had been formed for each building, and debris removal had begun. However, in 1991 LESAC notified the homesteaders in the two buildings that their projects could not proceed. LESAC argued that there were not enough funds to complete these buildings as homesteading projects, claiming that most city and state funding was designated for the construction of housing for the homeless. The homesteaders in these two buildings were advised that apartments would be made available to them in several other buildings already under construction.

Nearly everyone attending this meeting expressed outrage over LESAC's actions. However, their reasons differed. The homesteaders from the two buildings were extremely angry that they were being pushed around after having already invested as much as two years in these buildings; they also were concerned that appropriate replacement units in other homesteaded buildings would not materialize. Others expressed outrage over the construction of housing for homeless people, which was concentrated in two buildings side by side on a single block. Someone argued that these buildings would ultimately be lost to RAIN as potential member buildings. According to this homesteader, buildings designated exclusively as housing for the homeless could not join RAIN because they would be managed by a managing agent rather than by the residents themselves. This distinction later turned out to be spurious, as several homesteader buildings have chosen managing agents.

As I listened to the comments made by RAIN members and homesteaders about "homeless housing," "housing for regular people," "people doubled-up," and "homesteaders," I began to think about the intersections of private lives, homesteading, and the various community organizations, encapsulated in such shifting definitions of self and others. During the early 1990s the perceptual lines between "us" (homesteaders) and "them" (people from shelters placed in homesteaded buildings through the Nazareth Home program, and squatters in vacant lots and in occupied buildings) became more sharply drawn. Simultaneously, there was an increasingly noticeable process of withdrawal into private lives. Once homesteaders moved into a completed building, they almost literally closed the door to the world beyond their individual units. One activist told me in 1990 that over the course of several years of involvement, individual homesteaders experienced a shift in self-orientation. He argued that "the system as a whole forces people to change their thinking from a communal orientation to a me-orientation." Although this was meant not so much as a value statement but as a statement of fact, it is important to understand that the process of withdrawal has various components.

At a very simple level, one might say that a number of homesteaders got what they set out to get. The goal was to obtain a decent, affordable apartment; to achieve this goal certain strategies were followed, including cooperation with others in a common struggle. Once that goal was achieved, the need for cooperation in a common struggle no longer appeared relevant.

The process of withdrawal also reflects mental and physical exhaustion. A commitment over many years to a project, at times seemingly hopeless, is exhausting. Homesteaders talked about being tired of attending meeting after meeting, having their lives on hold, having no time to do anything but struggle with the project. Many looked toward the time of moving into their units as a point at which they could finally resume their "own lives."

During a conversation in 1993, one activist talked about his own life. He pointed out that as people grow older the need for security and stability increases. "People evolve. They need to go on." Christopher said that in some ways he is not quite sure why he became involved in homesteading. "It seems like a ride, a bit like having been taken for a ride as much as having chosen it." For this homesteader as well as for others, homesteading had become part of their personal past. It was over. Meanwhile, the vision of homesteading as a continuing way of life that extends beyond the construction of housing no longer had concrete reality, if indeed it ever did.

The perception of homesteading as a thing of the past was reinforced by one homesteader's description about an incident in the early 1980s. Christopher and two other homesteaders had laid claim to a building over which LESAC had not yet obtained site control. They were arrested in the process of nailing a door over the entrance of the vacant building. As the arrest took place, people in the neighborhood watched with great interest. Christopher later heard that these people, who knew him and associated him with housing, suddenly thought he was a drug dealer trying to set up business inside that building. In prison the three homesteaders were asked by other inmates why they had been arrested. When they explained they had been arrested for "taking a building," they encountered nothing but blank amazement. Christopher talked with a curious detachment about the irony of being taken for a drug dealer by people in his own neighborhood and the incomprehension on the part of his prison cellmates. The episode had been consigned to the past.

Activists experienced a particular set of shifts beyond the feelings of exhaustion and disillusionment. Independent actors in a vibrant movement became dependent employees of an organization. LESAC became increasingly institutionalized and reoriented itself away from homesteading, and activists became alienated from the organization and from many other homesteaders. One activist described the final shift away from the organization and from the homesteading movement as liberating. It was time to go on.

Many people who were active in homesteading at one time are no longer involved. Activists and homesteaders who have played leading roles are now practically invisible. Yet their work in terms of the initial effort and in terms of actual rehabilitation was the foundation for other people's efforts. Some early homesteaders are nearly forgotten; others are viewed with disdain. An example is one of the original homesteaders whose building eventually decided against joining RAIN. This homesteader, along with his building, is considered to be "a renegade," a traitor of sorts, regardless of the fact that since then many others have followed him in questioning the process.

Personal lives are not on hold over the course of homesteading; people suffer personal upheavals such as loss of a family member, divorce, and unemployment. Some who were actively involved in the earlier years of homesteading have gone on to other arenas; one homesteader went to the South Bronx to become involved in housing and community matters there. Another moved out of his apartment and is now renting it to someone else. Yet another resident one day simply packed up and left the city, to the dismay of other residents in the building who were left to figure out what to do with the suddenly vacant unit.

Frequently the process of individuals' disassociation from homesteading was furthered if not caused by political power struggles within various organizations, LESAC, HDI, and RAIN. These power struggles took various forms. Some people merely did not get credit for work they had done. Others were accused of wrongdoing. Some were fired, some decided to leave. According to homesteaders and activists, LESAC repeatedly chose to blame one or another employee for financial troubles instead of critically examining its own organizational structure and the decision-making people within it. Disillusionment was deepened by the realization that LESAC was pursuing aims that paralleled those of homesteaders only for a limited time. LESAC's final withdrawal from the homesteading arena was not only the result of greatly reduced sources of funding for homesteading and the decreased availability of abandoned buildings on the Lower East Side; it also reflected a shift on part of the Catholic Church into a politically more promising housing development field, the Lower East Side Mutual Housing Association.

According to activists, perhaps the greatest blame to be laid at the doors of LESAC in terms of its treatment of individuals associated with the organization was its failure to train and make room for new leaders from among the homesteaders and thus make the concept of community empowerment a concrete reality. One homesteader, who was not only associated with the early efforts but went on to become an active and loyal LESAC employee, was cited as an example of this failure on the part of LESAC. An interlocutor described Luke as the original "model target"—Latino, low-income, without a high school diploma, oriented toward the church, articulate, respected in the community, committed, an individual who should have been groomed to become a leader. Instead, in the early 1990s—according to my interlocutor—LESAC permitted a situation to occur as a result of which Luke was lost to homesteading. LESAC was not able to pay salaries for several months, and Luke ran out of money. He approached a LESAC official and asked for help. The LESAC official did not do anything about the situation. Luke quit and is now driving trucks in Pennsylvania.

Withdrawal from homesteading and the attendant shift in self-identification and identification by homesteaders and others cannot be reduced to a reassertion of normative values with regard to concepts of property, ownership rights, and private lives. The intersections of individual lives, homesteading, and community organizations are complex; and developments are not predetermined or inevitable. A comparison of the structures and dynamics of other community-based organizations offers some insights and explanations for these developments.

COMPARISONS WITH OTHER ORGANIZATIONS

In the housing development arena there are many organizations with differing models and strategies for the construction and management of affordable housing for low-income people. LESAC, a Catholic Church–based organization, was different from other organizations in terms of internal organizational and hierarchical structures as well as focus. Nonetheless, analysis of other community organizations indicates parallels in their respective developments.

Some organizations invite comparisons to homesteading on the Lower East Side under the auspices of LESAC because of their seeming similarities. Others invite comparison because developments within them illuminate shared weaknesses and difficulties. For this reason, the following organizations are briefly considered: Habitat for Humanity, Mutual Housing Associations, Banana Kelly, ACORN, Los Sures, Inner City Press/Community on the Move, and Adopt-A-Building, Inc. In addition to Adopt-A-Building,

organizations that have been active in tenant advocacy, housing development, and management on the Lower East Side include Cooper Square
Committee, It's Time Agency, and Pueblo Nuevo.[2]

Whenever I described my association with homesteaders on the Lower
East Side, people would say: "Oh, like Habitat? Isn't that what Jimmy
Carter was doing?" Indeed, certain aspects suggest this comparison. Both
Habitat for Humanity and the homesteading program sponsored by LE-
SAC involve the use of sweat-equity labor in the construction of affordable
housing for low-income people. Habitat for Humanity also attaches resale
restrictions to deeds on houses or apartment buildings. Despite these
shared characteristics, the programs are rather different. Habitat for Humanity was founded in 1977 as an ecumenical Christian housing organization that works in partnership with low-income families and individuals to
build decent, affordable housing. In 1991 Habitat had over 600 affiliated
projects in communities across the country and over 100 sponsored projects
in 30 developing countries. There are three Habitat affiliates in New York
City, two on the Lower East Side. Habitat began renovation of a 19-unit
building in late 1983 on East 6th Street and completed it in late 1986. It began
its second project in July 1987.

Habitat does not operate with any government funds; money is raised
through individual donations, church donations, and foundation grants.
There are also in-kind donations. The majority of Habitat affiliates are
single- or two-family houses; apartment buildings are rare. In 1991, fully
10,000 houses were built through Habitat efforts. Habitat provides tenants
in completed projects with no-interest mortgages, generally to be paid off
over a 20-year period. According to one Habitat official, the use of volunteers on building projects is one way by which Habitat manages to keep
costs down and maintenance and mortgage payments at an affordable level
for low-income people. Habitat has been reasonably successful in constructing single-family homes predominantly in rural areas. The difficulties
Habitat has encountered in urban areas are similar to those experienced by
other housing development organizations; the official said that the process
takes too long, turnover is too high, and fund raising for large projects is
far more difficult than for single- or two-family homes. When asked about
building management in completed projects, the official stated that Habitat
has not experienced any difficulties. Essentially, building management has
not been a focus of Habitat. It is too early to say whether this will become
a problem for apartment buildings in urban environments. Given the
experiences of other housing organizations, it is likely that such problems
will arise in Habitat buildings as well.

A Habitat brochure describes the building of communities as its central
goal: "Building relationships and communities is just as important as
building homes." Habitat's approach to the realization of this goal is based
on the creation of individual building cooperatives rather than support

networks and relationships with local organizations. On the Lower East Side, Habitat has remained distanced from other developments and organizations and has interacted with the Community Board only to secure its support in obtaining site control. Habitat has not attempted to play a role in the community beyond the completion of its own projects. In sum, Habitat is a single-issue organization and does not attempt to act as a community organization.

A Mutual Housing Association (MHA) is essentially an umbrella term covering a range of models of tenant and community control of housing.

These Mutual Housing Associations are nonprofit organizations that build, rehabilitate, or convert existing housing, as well as sustain operations at the buildings they own. Membership in the association is restricted to residents of buildings owned by the association, those on a waiting list for such a unit, and representatives of neighborhood organizations, financial institutions, businesses, local government, and others from the religious or local philanthropic communities. A majority of the board members are residents or waiting residents, and development or purchase of the buildings is accomplished through substantial up-front capital grants with as little reliance on debt financing as possible. (Bratt 1989b: 194)

Several MHAs have been formed on the Lower East Side. One, the Lower East Side MHA, organized its members before beginning to select and rehabilitate apartment buildings. The members have been involved in the planning process from the outset. As a result, the MHA has had to struggle to keep future tenants interested and actively involved in the project. Over the course of many delays in the renovation process, the level of distrust and alienation among tenants has risen. Another group, People's MHA, completed rehabilitation of its first set of apartment units without involving future members. This created different kinds of relationships between tenants, community representatives, and other parties on the board—and different problems. Residents are more likely to treat the MHA as a landlord than as a cooperative association for their benefit with representatives from among their own ranks. It has been argued that a MHA is able to function more successfully when members have a long history of involvement with the community and have played an active part in the formation of the association. According to the Neighborhood Reinvestment Corporation, which has helped sponsor the formation of MHAs, a potential difficulty faced by smaller MHAs is that a MHA cannot become fully self-supporting unless it links 500 apartments or more.

The Cooper Square MHA set up a Community Land Trust. In this model, private resale of units is prohibited; residents must sell their units back to the Community Land Trust at no profit. The People's MHA and the Lower East Side MHA own the buildings, and residents pay monthly charges to cover the costs of operating and managing the buildings.

Supporters of MHAs argue that the establishment of a MHA is not just about housing; there would be far simpler ways to accomplish that end. Instead, MHAs are supposed to help refashion a sense of community and rebuild and create democracy; the process of developing and successfully managing a MHA is seen as a training ground toward that end (Neuwirth 1992). Critics argue that rents may increase beyond levels affordable to residents, despite restrictions on increases that parallel rent stabilization regulations. Another concern is that MHAs as a form of privatization—with the MHA owning the building and the units in them—will result in yet another landlord/tenant relationship wherein tenants lack control over their housing. These critics argue that the only acceptable model would be cooperative ownership through a Community Land Trust combined with 99-year leases to residents. Other possible problems concern the increasing rift between those who manage the buildings and hence act as landlords and the residents themselves, notwithstanding the fact that some of the residents are directly involved in the management.

Many conflicts and debates concerning MHAs on the Lower East Side are as much about political control and turf as about ideological differences. The Cooper Square Committee has been under attack by various groups and organizations with regard to its MHA. One is Pueblo Nuevo, which has been competing with Cooper Square for years; others, such as LESUTA (Lower East Side United Tenants Association), are linked to political campaigns of the New Alliance Party and its leader, Lenora B. Fulani, and politicians such as City Councilmember Antonio Pagan. LESUTA has been charging Cooper Square with favoritism in placing tenants in rehabilitated buildings, secret plans to raise rents beyond levels affordable to tenants, and fraudulent means of obtaining residents' approval for their plans.

The Banana Kelly Community Improvement Association, now one of the most well-known community groups in the South Bronx, started as a small urban homesteading group on Kelly Street in the 1970s. Supported by Community Development Block Grants, government contracts, and corporate support, it has become a Community Development Corporation that manages 26 buildings with more than 1,000 tenants. Banana Kelly now acts as a housing developer as well as a manager and landlord. The organization has tried to be closely involved in the personal lives of tenants. It attempts to address problems of poverty, drug abuse, violence, and unemployment and to build a sense of community by focusing on tenants' behavior. One such attempt is the Family and Community Enrichment (FACE) program, which involves training sessions that residents are required to attend. Sessions are designed to address behavioral choices, to emphasize the importance of social values in everyday life, and to help people reflect on, plan, and act on choices made. For Banana Kelly, empowerment means instilling community values and weaning tenants from welfare and social services. "We teach people: 'Don't buy into that stuff, reach into yourself

for the answers!' " (Glazer 1992). Compliance with the buildings' requirements is enforced by a lease rider signed by tenants, according to which
they agree to submit to certain behavioral standards and to attend training
sessions.

From 1982 to 1991 the organization was run by Getz Obstfeld, who
developed a reputation for not being amenable to sharing power with other
individuals in the organization. Further, because he was a white male
heading a community group in a predominantly African-American and
Latino neighborhood, his leadership was increasingly subject to question.
His position was taken over by Yolanda Rivera, who was brought up in the
South Bronx. She has been the driving force behind the recent shift of
Banana Kelly to an emphasis on personal and community improvement,
with the term *value clarification* functioning as a leitmotif. Ostensibly the
leadership of Banana Kelly, headed by Rivera, is now more indigenous to
the neighborhood that the organization tries to serve. This fact notwithstanding, one must ask whose values are being imposed and who has the
right to impose them.

Banana Kelly's "value clarifications" effort implies that an inability to
achieve goals on part of the poor is a personal deficiency owing to a lack of
values or misplaced values. This in turn is thought to lead to a lack of
self-esteem and antisocial and self-destructive behavior that hurts the
individual and the community. The earlier model used by Banana Kelly was
based on a concept of self-help that implied that lack of self-esteem is due
to a lack of livable-wage employment opportunities, poor housing and
community services, and a feeling of powerlessness. *Self-help* is defined as
a way to understand how the system works and to take charge of circumstances that are within people's control (e.g., a dirty street, garbage that
needs to be picked up, or an abandoned building). The model aimed for
ongoing participatory control over particular circumstances.

In its efforts to train and re-educate tenants, Banana Kelly is replicating
some of the preconceived notions about poor people from the last few
decades that attributed the reasons for their poverty and related difficulties
to their *own* behavior, to the virtual exclusion of any other contributing
factors.

Los Sures, otherwise known as the Southside United Housing Redevelopment Fund, is a community-based housing group that has been in
existence since 1972. In the Southside area of Williamsburg in Brooklyn, Los
Sures has been active in tenant organizing, low-income development, and
housing development. As Los Sures became more successful over the years,
reflected in the dwindling number of abandoned buildings in the area, it
has experienced difficulties as a result of attempting to fill several roles at
the same time. Los Sures has been acting as a large-scale housing manager
of buildings that it has helped to renovate. This pushes the organization
into the difficult role of landlord.

Even though Los Sures has continued to be active as an advocate and tenant organizer, the organization has become more institutionalized. Los Sures strives to encourage community involvement. However, it is having difficulties in this regard. It is rarely able to fill all 50 spots for members on its board. Moreover, there has been a considerable shift in the distribution of ethnic and racial groups in the neighborhood. Formerly, Puerto Ricans were in the majority, but now Dominicans are in the majority; there are also sizable contingents of Mexicans and other Meso Americans and South Americans. This shift is not reflected in the leadership of Los Sures.

Los Sures is attempting to reorient itself in terms of its increasingly prevalent role as housing manager as opposed to housing developer. In this effort to develop new areas of activity, Los Sures is exploring joint ventures with other community organizations and is also working on bridging the relationship between Latinos and Hasidim; but housing continues to be a top priority. The organization has made consistent efforts to hire and train community residents (see Oder 1992).

Inner City Press/Community on the Move is the name of a publication and a group in the Bronx that has been active in tenant organizing, job creation efforts, community gardens, and cultural efforts such as classes and theater performances. The group is best known for taking over abandoned buildings and attempting to renovate them without assistance or legal sanction from the city. Work on the buildings progresses painfully slowly. The families working on the buildings are predominantly Latinos who live doubled-up in nearby public housing. Each family contributes $45 in dues on a monthly basis, which is not enough to cover major construction work.

As far as the city administration is concerned, this group operates without legal title to the buildings. It also obstructs the planned renovation of the buildings under an HPD initiative to renovate city-owned buildings for the homeless from welfare hotels and shelters. The city argues that Inner City Press has jumped the line ahead of people who are patiently awaiting their turn. Meanwhile, Matthew Lee, the leader of the group, argues that there are enough abandoned buildings in the Bronx for a variety of reha-bilitation efforts. Furthermore, those individuals and families living dou-bled-up rather than in the city's shelters are not eligible for units under renovation for the homeless (Turetsky 1990).

Inner City Press is beginning to abandon its radical stance and increas-ingly attempts to work through the system rather than against it. For instance, on the basis of the Freedom of Information Act, the group has been filing requests for lists of buildings assigned to the various HPD programs and have attempted to avoid occupying buildings that are already slated for government-financed rehabilitation. In 1990 the group applied for Housing Trust Fund money from the state for a third project they had started. The group also negotiated with Con Edison to get buildings legally connected to electricity. However, between 1990 and 1992 city officials evicted a total of 87 families from 4 buildings (Mitra 1993). In 1994, Inner City Press took the city to court over its choice of developers for two abandoned brick buildings in the Bronx, from which the city had evicted 31 Inner City Press families and which it then turned over for development as low-income housing. The State Supreme Court has upheld the group's right to sue. In this instance, Inner City Press is trying to use the system in its fight rather than going outside of it.

The Association of Community Organizations for Reform Now (ACORN) began as an organization of welfare recipients in Little Rock, Arkansas, in 1970. Since then it has grown into a national organization with chapters in 26 states. Delgado, a long-time organizer of ACORN, describes it as a "mass-based, multi-issue, multi-tactical, community organization" (Delgado 1986: 3). Everything that affects its constituency of low-income and poor people (e.g., welfare policy, redlining, environmental issues, school closings, utility rates, the job market, general city services, health care, and housing) can become the subject of an ACORN campaign. ACORN tactics take their inspiration from confrontational direct action of the 1960s. The association also has been marked by a self-analytical stance and a flexibility that allows new strategies to be devised in accordance with evolving circumstances.

ACORN's organizational structure is based on a dichotomy of organizers and leaders or staff and members. In principle, organizers are supposed to do just that, organize people and train leaders; leaders are supposed to make decisions regarding which issues to target and how to go about doing so. In practice this is more complex (Delgado 1986). Delgado draws attention to various aspects of the dichotomy such as the prevalence of white, middle-class males on the staff and the prevalence of Latinos and African Americans among the members and leaders. Essentially, ACORN membership is 70% female and 70% Latino and African-American (Delgado 1986: 191). Yet the sheer number of women members and leaders in local ACORN affiliates, not unusual for community organizations, does not reflect the issues addressed. Issues such as daycare, equal wages, and reproductive rights have been ignored. Similarly, the organization has not succeeded in developing a staff infrastructure that is supportive of people of color.

ACORN, as much as other grassroots and community organizations, suffers from an internal contradiction that is exacerbated as the organization matures. Organizers want to establish themselves politically and create a firm power base. Yet these goals at times override the purported goal, which is to address the needs of constituents (Delgado 1986).

Interfaith Adopt-A-Building, Inc., a politically active community organization, has been involved in tenant organization and assistance to early sweat-equity projects (Lawson 1984). Its efforts helped urban homesteading to be embraced by the city administration. During the late 1970s and early 1980s, Adopt-A-Building was a key organization in the Joint Planning

Council, which became an influential voice for critical needs and aspirations of the community on the Community Board and in the city administration. Two publications sponsored by Adopt-A-Building attest to the organization's role during those years (Interfaith Adopt-A-Building 1978; Zarza and Cohen 1979). During the late 1980s, the organization narrowed its activities to act predominantly as a housing manager.

Distinctions between the approaches of various housing development groups and organizations are blurred. On the Lower East Side this point becomes particularly clear. Squatters, homesteaders, and housing activists have cooperated and pursued the same goals at various times (e.g., in protest marches against landlords who have been warehousing apartments). In fact, the Mutual Housing Association of New York (MHANY) evolved out of a squatting campaign organized by ACORN. During the mid-1980s, squatting and other confrontational tactics were successfully utilized by ACORN with regard to 2,000 abandoned city-owned buildings in East New York. As a result MHANY was formed, and 58 city-owned buildings were turned over to the housing association, with the likelihood of more to come. Inner City Press/Community on the Move in the Bronx is currently undergoing a transition from being (1) a group in direct confrontation with the city by renovating abandoned buildings without a license to do so, to (2) a group that is aspiring to city and state funding and legal sanction for its activities. At the same time, there are squatter groups on the Lower East Side that do not seek city assistance and perceive such an action as a form of selling out.

When comparing these community-based organizations, certain key points can be discerned. As an organization matures, it undergoes various transformations with attendant problems of internal organization and leadership, its ability to retain an actively participating constituency, its orientation and purpose, and its position vis-à-vis comparable organizations and the city administration. An activist from It's Time Agency said that organizations on the Lower East Side age just as individuals do. "They tend to become institutionalized and rigid and do not realize that they are no longer on the cutting edge."

Situations or conditions that have lent impetus to an organization during its early phase change and evolve, in part as the result of activities by the organization. This leads to shifts in direction and focus. Organizational ideologies are not straightforward; rather, they encompass contradictory concepts. As an organization matures, such contradictions become more apparent and contribute to fragmentation of allegiance among staff and constituents.

Bratt (1987) names four major dilemmas faced by community-based housing programs. One is the conflict between private ownership and accumulation on the one hand, and social control and access on the other. Two, local residents are targeted as clients; this conflicts with the goal of providing open access and/or occupancy according to need. Three, an organization is torn between the need to maintain a community and tenant orientation and the need to act as a developer and landlord. Four, the organization needs to provide services to the original target group in the face of potential neighborhood change and a redefinition of the organization's objective and clientele.

One of the greatest challenges faced by community organizations is to maintain an actively involved constituency. This most essential characteristic, the element that makes an organization truly community-based, must be finely balanced with the need for some form of ongoing leadership. Each organization, depending on its internal structure, faces this problem differently. ACORN is an example of an organization that has attempted to maintain a highly active constituency. It has been more successful than others in having its organizers and staff maintain a low profile. However, Delgado has shown that this dichotomy of staff and members presents a form of hidden leadership that does much to determine which issues are targeted by ACORN campaigns as well as which strategies are utilized (Delgado 1986).

Maintaining constituents' interest in participatory politics presents a fundamental dilemma (Davis 1983). Strategies that make use of confrontation are more likely to stimulate involvement; the same strategies can contribute to disrupting the organization beyond the point at which it can function successfully. Yet strategies that avoid confrontation may become boring and cause members to lose interest altogether.

In theory, a community organization must be organized in such a way that others can eventually step into the shoes of the organizers and act for themselves. An activist said that one of the main roles of an organizer, for housing or labor or any other cause, is to "organize himself or herself out of a job" (White 1993: 8). Organizers want to shape and guide an organization in a particular direction. At the same time, a central goal is to help people in a given community to create their own structures of leadership and to devise strategies independently.

A problem with the imposition of planning and ideology from above is that people are more likely to drop out when they see others becoming involved. This is in part due to weariness on the part of those dropping out; they may feel they have done their share and the time has come for others to do their turn. In part a dynamic is at play where people withdraw as leaders emerge, who in turn are perceived as "replicas of the system in which the uninvolved feel helpless" (Freidenberg 1991: 72). It is important not to overemphasize the role played by individual leaders or point to individual leadership as major explanatory factors for organizational and ideological shifts. Although such leadership is certainly instrumental, an individual does not act in a vacuum; there is a relationship between any one individual leadership figure, the people or the organization affected by changes, and the management of that organization or the local administration. As organizations mature, they often have difficulty in grooming successors to one or two charismatic leaders while at the same time a previously actively involved constituency is gradually withdrawing.

Community organizations become bureaucratized and institutionalized with time. This may strengthen them in certain ways; among others, it may help an organization in accessing various sources of funding, and it may help in providing access to various forms of political representation. However, it may also result in a greater distance from its original power base, its actively involved constituency. Meanwhile, a shift in orientation (e.g., from that of a housing developer to that of a housing management agency), may contribute to increasing alienation of an organization from its clients.

Some organizations such as UHAB, Banana Kelly, and Los Sures have become more involved in issues of education and social control at a time when state and local administrations are withdrawing from direct involvement. Banana Kelly attempts to address some of the seemingly intractable problems of poverty, violence, crime, drug abuse, and unemployment by examining behavioral patterns within the community itself. It is one of six community organizations in the South Bronx that are participating in a program backed by several foundations to improve the quality of life in their community. The program covers a vast array of issues such as plans for a new Bronx supermarket, offices for primary care doctors, immunization programs, home health care, and building maintenance. Many efforts are made to encourage community participation. A central element of the program is the controversial self-esteem training program, which appears to imply that poor people are more emotionally troubled than the rest of society. The danger in this and similar efforts to "reform" poor people and to hold them accountable for their actions is that the approaches ignore the underlying causes of unemployment, housing problems, and other characteristics of poverty in urban environments.

However, the program described above illustrates the potential strengths of a multi-issue focus, both in terms of encouraging involvement on part of community members and in terms of the political currency it represents. Community activists have noted a shift in funding patterns toward favoring comprehensive, integrated programs in neighborhoods such as the one in which Banana Kelly participates (Glazer 1993). The program also illustrates an important point about community organizations; they are dependent vehicles subject to shifting levels of resistance and support on the part of local, state, and federal administrations as well as shifting amounts of funding from both private and public sources. In other words, failure and success of a particular community organization is not to be explained solely through internally generated causes.

A final point, which becomes apparent when comparing various community organizations, is that these organizations compete with each other for turf in a neighborhood and for funding—particularly when their agendas overlap. Such competition grows increasingly apparent as organizations become more interested in playing a role and exerting influence in electoral politics (Delgado 1986).

LESAC AND RAIN

On the Lower East Side, all these aspects have played a role in the transformations of both LESAC and RAIN, which are further compounded by two factors. One, homesteading from the very beginning was dominated by the Catholic Church. Two, the Community Land Trust RAIN, although in theory a community-based and independent organization, did not fully develop while under the tutelage of LESAC and, hence, the Catholic Church. At the time when RAIN began to assert itself as an independent organization and distance itself from LESAC, the process of disintegration of the homesteading movement had already started. Hence, RAIN never succeeded in properly establishing itself.

LESAC underwent a transformation over the decade of its involvement in homesteading that parallels some of the changes in comparable organizations. These include a shift toward institutionalization; financial, political, and administrative problems with realization of projects; role conflicts over the issue of a housing developer acting as a housing manager; a shift in focus away from homesteading toward an interest in alternative vehicles in the arena of housing development such as MHAs; and finally, the failure to groom leaders from the community to take over from LESAC. One homesteader described it as a process of becoming mainstream. Indeed, during the early years LESAC was supportive of strategies and positions that appeared to bring it more in line with squatters than with housing developers. Later on, as political, financial, and internal ideological problems mounted, the organization attempted to reshape itself into a more professional, streamlined, business-oriented housing developer.

By the late 1980s, LESAC had come under increasingly heated attack by homesteaders with regard to its handling of funds used for contract work on rehabilitation projects; in response, a person knowledgeable about computer programs and bookkeeping was hired. He spent much time trying to organize records for the various buildings but was less involved in day-to-day activities in individual buildings. During those years, the late 1980s and early 1990s, LESAC was less willing to be actively involved on behalf of any or all of the buildings with regard to problems they were experiencing (e.g., conflicts with contractors, internal building disputes, and conflicts with the city administration). Homesteaders would say: "LESAC is basically not interested in us anymore; they have abandoned us." For some homesteaders, the point of LESAC's gradual disengagement was finally brought home over the sequence of events concerning two buildings that originally had been designated as homesteading projects but became projects for housing for the homeless (see Chapter 6).

The development of RAIN in some ways is more dramatic and, as such, emblematic of the homesteading movement. Starting out as an idea embraced by a few enthusiastic activists and homesteaders, it was fashioned into a battle cry and symbol of unity and revitalization of the community. It became a successful means of bringing homesteaders together on a regular basis. Before RAIN became formally incorporated, it provided a profoundly compelling vision for the future.

The subsequent transformations, resulting in the near eradication of RAIN by 1993, are connected to leadership issues, participation, shifts in ideological orientation, and changes affecting homesteading that were external to RAIN. The shift in leadership from the original founders to a second generation of RAIN members was due to a strategic choice on the part of early activists. According to one activist, it became a choice between remaining at the center of the movement or attempting to gain influence at a wider political level such as the Community Board and, ultimately, electoral politics. The original founders succeeded in this goal to an extent; several new appointments on the Community Board attested to this success. The subsequent RAIN leadership confronted a growing number of difficulties, especially diminished participation on the part of homesteaders, shifts in the nature of the relationship with LESAC, and a changing orientation among RAIN members as far as the goals of homesteading were concerned. Eventually, RAIN became more exclusionary in its politics and did not actively pursue participation by a broad range of community members and organizations. RAIN leaders were accused of being elitist and of exacerbating (if not causing) the ideological fault lines that were dividing homesteaders into several political camps. The vision that initially inspired homesteaders had lost much of its shine, and RAIN could not compensate for this loss (e.g., in terms of technical, financial, legal, or administrative assistance to member buildings). Participation in RAIN meetings dropped further; often, meetings did not have a quorum. By August 1993 one homesteader described RAIN as "hibernating." Another said: "It is very weak, barely existing; there hasn't been a RAIN meeting in months."

One homesteader gave as an example of RAIN's development the fact that 66 Avenue C is not a member building. This building had been considered a flagship of homesteading. It was one of three original buildings on which work began in 1979, and the first to reach completion under the LESAC homesteading program. Several leaders associated with the early years of the program were homesteaders in the building. The LESAC office was established on the ground floor, and the Casa Adela (a restaurant) occupied the remaining commercial space. On Saturdays homesteaders, volunteers, and others associated with the projects would be busily going in and out of the building, and many would step next door for a coffee or for lunch. The building was not brought into the Community Land Trust when the homesteaders bought it from the city because RAIN was then not yet formally established. It was assumed that this would occur as soon as RAIN became incorporated. However, as one homesteader described it, somehow nobody ever got around to the paperwork. This homesteader claimed that RAIN was repeatedly approached about the matter but was too disorganized to follow up on it. Whatever the actual sequence of events behind this outcome may have been, it is profoundly ironic that this particular building should not be a member of the Community Land Trust, when much of the impetus behind the creation of RAIN had come from homesteaders within it.

Ideological shifts in RAIN centered around the issue of ownership and the notion of inclusive versus exclusionary politics. According to Davis, as people acquire property their politics of ownership change (Davis 1983). In the context of a market economy, in which real estate is a valuable commodity, a Community Land Trust embodies a fundamental contradiction. As an alliance based on shared interests, a Community Land Trust is a source of strength to those who own nothing. However, once the Community Land Trust has been the successful means of establishing control and ownership over a piece of property, it becomes an obstacle by virtue of the fact that it prohibits individual resale.

Some changes in RAIN can be traced to individual building histories. As homesteaders began to move into completed buildings, there were corresponding shifts in the demands placed on RAIN (e.g., assistance with building management) and a decreased interest in the political agenda that had initially inspired the Community Land Trust. The agenda, of course, was to ensure the availability of decent, affordable housing to low-income and poor people in the community.

One story (which, like any other story, has several sides to it), concerns the dispute over the building on 6th Street housing the Community Center and the RAIN office. The Community Center, which owns the building, applied to become a RAIN member. According to one RAIN director, the application was rejected because the building had too many unresolved financial issues. The RAIN director argued that such a building could present a potential danger for the organization. However, according to others, the Community Center was rejected because of a shift in policy away from the notion of broad community representation to an emphasis on a more narrowly defined group of residential property owners. The "truth" behind this outcome may well be a combination of these arguments; but indisputably in the early 1990s, many homesteaders described RAIN as practicing exclusionary politics, failing to pursue new members actively, and failing to ensure that RAIN represented a cross-section of the community. One homesteader said: "RAIN does not reflect the community, only in terms of ethnicity, but that is where it ends."

During a RAIN meeting in the fall of 1991, there was discussion about whether RAIN should become a formal affiliate of the Institute for Community Economics (ICE). ICE acts as an information base, provides education and training resources as well as assistance on various levels, and addresses issues of public policy on behalf of its members. Affiliates have access to workshops at a discount, technical assistance services, and information on CLT movements. According to ICE, a Community Land Trust must comprise a mix of participants reflecting not only the building owners—or, in this case, homesteaders—but also individuals from the community at large and community organizations. More precisely, RAIN would have to comprise one-third homesteaders, one-third technical assistants (such as LESAC or HDI), and one-third community representatives and organizations. At the time of the meeting, RAIN consisted only of homesteaders and technical assistants. During the sparsely attended meeting, a RAIN director cautioned against a membership in ICE because of a clause in the ICE stipulations. According to this clause, an affiliate of ICE must ensure that *everyone* in the community be invited to become a member. The RAIN director said: "We don't want just any Joe Blow." A homesteader argued that the benefits of being an affiliate might not outweigh this point. She also suggested that interpretation of the clause according to which the Community Land Trust should be "open to those in the community who meet the requirements" might be a matter of semantics. The decision to join ICE was deferred pending further research; RAIN has not become an ICE affiliate in the interim.

CONCLUSION

An attempt to reconstruct the histories of people associated with homesteading provides poignant illustrations of the tremendous difficulties and length of time involved. Many homesteaders dropped out, became ill and tired, died, disappeared, lost faith in the process, got divorced, or moved out of the city. Looking at the organizations involved reveals other casualties. RAIN is practically invisible, LESAC has closed its office. Nazareth Home, Inc., is still involved with the buildings because it has an interest in particular apartment units that are designated for Nazareth Home clients. One activist implied that some of the developments described above were foreseen or at least feared.

LOURDES: And one of the things the JPC [Joint Planning Council] realized very early—and everybody who was in the housing movement down here—was that we cannot create a community full of private buildings owned by small corporations that eventually—inevitably—will become interested in profit. That is the danger, the potential danger of homesteading, which later on was proved.

This development cannot have been surprising to activists and social scientists concerned with Community Land Trusts in the early 1980s. They had foreseen that Community Land Trusts might become "new exclusionary 'dealers' of property" (Davis 1983: 2).

The temptation is for the community to turn inward, defending itself against the outside world instead of challenging the working of that world. There is a danger, in other words, of CLTs contributing to the fragmentation of protest—a "ghettoization" of conflict that leaves basic political and economic structures of the larger society untouched. (Davis 1983: 3)

According to Mollenkopf, among others, housing is an unlikely base for a political movement. Homeownership not only encourages politics of exclusion but also can become a means of social control, making people quiescent and politically impotent (Mollenkopf 1983: 296). However, he also argues that "the contradiction between accommodative and accumulative interests may also be less protective of the capitalist status quo than has been assumed heretofore" (Mollenkopf 1983: 304). This latter point, the one most debatable because least concretized, is the subject of the next and concluding chapter.

For some individuals, homesteading on the Lower East Side was based on a model of a community that went far beyond the provision of housing. Cooperative organizational structures, integration of all members of the community, and a productive relationship between community residents and the land they inhabit were to be the empowering foundations for residents to assume responsibility for the development of their community. Others saw in homesteading a partial solution to housing problems in urban environments where there are large amounts of deteriorating and abandoned housing stock. Neither of these conceptual notions has been realized. An explanation of why this is so, and a final assessment of homesteading on the Lower East Side, must incorporate a contextual analysis that goes beyond a consideration of the particular organizational histories of LESAC and RAIN.

NOTES

1. Thomas Carlyle, "Journal of 1831," in Charles Eliot Norton, ed., *Two Notebooks of Thomas Carlyle* (Mamaroneck, NY: Paul P. Appel, 1972), 210–211.

2. Cooper Square Committee has been active as a tenant advocacy group in the East Village for several decades. It has also been involved in fighting gentrification of the area and in mapping out alternative plans for deteriorating and abandoned buildings. Since 1987, Cooper Square Committee has actively supported the concept of Mutual Housing Associations.

Pueblo Nuevo has been active on the Lower East Side since 1970, predominantly as a building management organization. In its first project it built 172 apartments at 210 Stanton Street. It has also acted as an administrator of 7A buildings. A 7A building is a privately owned building placed in the care of a court-appointed manager, or "7A administrator," because the landlord has been found liable for dangerous neglect. In 1994, Pueblo Nuevo was operating 42 buildings on the Lower East Side.

It's Time Agency has been active in tenant organizing and advocacy on the Lower East Side and in Chinatown for over 20 years. Its focus is on protecting buildings from deterioration and abandonment. The agency also works with the Public Housing Administration to ensure that services are delivered to tenants.

8

CONCLUSION

The voice of weeping shall no longer
be heard in [this city], nor the voice of crying.
No more shall an infant from there
live but a few days, nor an old man
who does not round out his full lifetime.

They shall live in the houses they build,
and eat the fruit of the vineyards they plant;
They shall not build houses
for others to live in
or plant for others to eat.

Isaiah 65: 20, 21, 22

In the early 1970s when Chino Garcia and Bimbo Rivas thought about a new name for the Lower East Side, they considered "La Mancha," that famous setting for the brave pursuit of ideals. Eventually, they chose a name closer to their hearts. Using the often-derided "Spanglish" to fashion "Loisaida" out of "Lower East Side," they expressed, embraced, and challenged the oppression and internal fragmentation of Puerto Ricans in America. Thinking about the homesteaders of Loisaida after my conversation with Chino Garcia, I kept visualizing tiny figures tilting at windmills.

Seventeen years have passed since homesteading on the Lower East Side was first formally begun as a successor to earlier sweat-equity efforts. As many as 17 projects for rehabilitation through homesteading had been planned under the auspices of LESAC. Of these, 13 have been completed and 4 have been redesignated to different housing rehabilitation programs. However, in 1995 construction had not begun on 3 of these buildings; the fourth, 206 Clinton Street, was completed in the spring of 1995. A total of 148 units, including 30 units for homeless people placed in the building, 17 units for elderly and disabled people, and 11 commercial units, have been produced. Less than a quarter of the homesteaders originally involved in the process are now living in the completed buildings. Most buildings are experiencing problems that range from annoying to serious. None of the buildings has a strong financial reserve to meet unexpected expenses. The Community Land Trust RAIN is not in a position to intercede effectively in the event of serious problems. The notion of keeping housing permanently affordable for low-income people through the resale restriction imposed by RAIN is actively embraced by only a minority of homesteaders, although it has not yet been overturned. Given the continued depressed economy in New York City and the shrinking labor market, low-income residents of homesteader buildings—faced with mortgage payments, nonpaying commercial tenants, exorbitant tax assessments, and increasing costs of living and building maintenance—are situated precariously, their newly won status as property owners notwithstanding. In terms of the need for affordable housing, the addition of these 13 buildings over a period of 17 years cannot be considered even a drop in the bucket. Is that the outcome of all the time, money, and dedication invested in homesteading on the Lower East Side?

The question of the "failure" or "success" of homesteading, however one wishes to define it, must be posed differently; any attempt at a response must consider the context at both the local level and that of society and governmental policy.

ASSESSMENTS OF HOMESTEADING AND COMPARABLE EFFORTS

An analysis of this housing effort provides clues for understanding why such an initiative, seemingly built around the values of self-reliance, independence, and hard work, has not been more successful in a political climate that proclaims the merits of these very values. Analysis further reveals why and how governmental anti-poverty policies have failed to effect changes among the very groups that programs associated with such policies purportedly address. Ronald Reagan's famous one-line comment about anti-poverty policies and the War on Poverty was: "Poverty won." In other words, governmental efforts to combat poverty were deemed a failure and a waste of money. Programs for welfare, housing, job training, education, and others came under attack and were seen as contributing to the problem rather than ameliorating it. Whatever the failings of anti-poverty policies may have been, the result of this perspective—tremendous cutbacks across the board in practically all social welfare programs during the Reagan and Bush administrations—were disastrous, plunging more and more Americans into poverty and homelessness. In the mid-1990s, the question regarding the failings of anti-poverty policies still stands. In fact, it has attained even greater urgency in light of an administration that seeks to redesign the approach to entrenched poverty yet (1) is painfully aware of the pitfalls of social programs and governmental action, and (2) is stymied by a powerful Republican majority in the Senate and Congress with a clear-cut agenda to remake, if not eradicate, many components of the social welfare network. Furthermore, shifts at both the state and local levels (i.e., the election of a Republican governor and a Republican mayor) will have an even greater and more immediate impact on anti-poverty programs in New York City and the Lower East Side.

Defenders of anti-poverty programs have argued that such programs are blamed for problems beyond their control. Indeed, programs addressing unemployment often appear insignificant in the face of worldwide restructuring of industry and production. By the same token, a program that attempts to address the need for affordable housing struggles in a context of a disintegrating labor market, wage stagnation, and growing numbers of single heads of families who are more vulnerable to factors that cause poverty. These contribute to the loss of housing; the availability of affordable housing is not itself a solution to poverty. The problems are too entrenched and overwhelming for any single program to have a lasting effect.

Another perspective is gained when we consider the extent to which programs, however broadly conceived, have actually been implemented. Critics of these programs have argued that financing of the War on Poverty never kept pace with its rhetoric. For example, in 1977 New York City in conjunction with HUD declared portions of Loisaida to be National Urban Homesteading Demonstration Areas, thereby making federal loans available to community residents who had developed renovation plans for vacant buildings on demonstration sites. The area covered lots on land south and east of Tompkins Square Park extending to Avenue C and down to Avenue D at 4th and 5th Streets. As the result of a HUD contract, an extensive study of Loisaida with recommendations for neighborhood revitalization and self-determination was prepared in 1979 (Zarza and Cohen 1979). Yet the developments in Loisaida do not by any means reflect consistently strong administrative and financial support.

HUD plans for homesteading in other cities, and the results of a few demonstration projects in various places with half-hearted administrative support, indicate a similar gap between rhetoric and implementation. Borgos argues that homesteading was never really given a chance. He points out that despite supposedly addressing the need for housing among low-income people, the HUD-supported homesteading program was actually structured to favor higher-income applicants:

The act that emerged from Congress in 1974 was, like the Homestead Act of 1862, a compromise. On the critical matter of homesteader selection, the legislation required that "special consideration" be given to the applicants' need for housing and their capacity to make the required improvement. The inevitable tension between the "housing need" criterion, which favored lower-income applicants, and the "capacity to repair" criterion, which favored higher-income applicants, was left unresolved. Although the houses were to be provided by the federal government, management of the program was entrusted to localities, which were given wide discretion over homesteader selection and other aspects of program administration. . . . As the program was implemented in the years following its enactment, the issue of homesteader selection was conclusively resolved in favor of middle-income applicants. (Borgos 1986: 432)

The most stringent criticism of anti-poverty programs has been that such programs do not aim to actually reduce poverty, but merely to cushion its effects. According to Williams, such programs are remedial efforts defined by "the criteria of profit and internal convenience rather than decisively against them" (Williams 1973: 294). Temporary housing, health care, and nutritional assistance are provided while root causes of poverty remain unaddressed. Such programs have been accused of reinforcing dependency on the state and have received criticism from both liberal and conservative camps, albeit for different reasons. This difference is illustrated by the concept of empowerment that has been popular during the past decade. Those with more conservative perspectives have argued that empowerment of the poor is the antidote to dependency on the government and hence the solution to poverty. For instance, Jack Kemp as secretary of HUD proposed to empower the poor largely through resident management of public housing and sales of public housing units to tenants. Those with more liberal perspectives have argued that empowerment was appropriated by conservatives and became a code word for abandonment by federal and local governments of poor and low-income people. Although they embrace the concept of empowerment, liberal advocacy groups and individuals believe it must be accompanied by a substantially larger commitment of federal resources than was the case during the Reagan and Bush administrations (see Bratt 1991). The so-called bandaid approach to poverty has been derided as doing little more than to provide jobs for a vast bureaucratic establishment and to still the voices of protest about the government's inactivity. This perspective implies a level of conscious manipulation, if not conspiracy, by the establishment to maintain an impoverished underclass for both economic reasons and political control.

When seeking to explain the failures and successes of anti-poverty programs in general and the history of homesteading on the Lower East Side in particular, one must not look for easy culprits. An explanation must take into account all the points raised above as well as additional ones. Among these is the fact that the bureaucratic establishment—including

HUD and HPD, among others—is not a monolithic body. Within HUD and HPD there are conflicting agendas, just as there are on the Lower East Side. Also, there is much bureaucratic confusion within an organization such as HPD, as well as in the relationship between HPD, HUD, and the federal government. As one HPD official put it, HPD "is not exactly centralized." Within HPD alone there are many programs addressing housing rehabilitation, but they are not coordinated within a single overarching plan. Thus, implementation of programs suffers not only from lack of sufficient funding but also from bureaucratic tangles, lack of coordination, and the consequences of tentative or experimental approaches in the form of demonstration projects that do not receive full support. Furthermore, local, state, and federal policies often are overwhelmed and unable to catch up with economic shifts that have depressed the wages of workers with few or no skills and continue to result in the elimination of jobs. However, governmental policy is just one—albeit critical—component; the others involve the dynamics of the economy and the local setting with its particular history and individuals, who are anything but passive recipients of programs.

Two recurring criticisms stand out. One is the tendency to focus on a single issue to the exclusion of others. The other relates to the difficulties of imposing a program from above with attendant failure to groom local leaders and to coordinate successfully with indigenous movements and self-generated efforts. A third problem, not as often recognized, is that bureaucracies such as HPD and HUD often develop a particular program as a reaction to situation rather than as a result of an initiative by the administration. The resulting program may not fully incorporate or recognize the dynamics or potentials of the local effort that spurred its own development.

The problems encountered throughout the LESAC homesteading program are to be seen in that context. Homesteading on the Lower East Side grew out of a strong, locally based effort that attempted to gain city, state, and federal support. Such support was fragmentary. As the economy worsened and funding for homesteading dwindled, the fragmented and largely reactive approach of the administration had increasing repercussions at the local level, compounded by divisions and conflicts internal to the homesteading movement. Currently, hardly anyone—both from the administration and among homesteaders and activists—seems sorry to see the effort brought to conclusion with the completion of most buildings in the original program.

For HPD, homesteading essentially was an experiment that will not be further pursued, given the disjunction between (1) the investment of time, effort, and money, and (2) the results. Between 1980 and 1994, a total of 45 buildings with 365 units were completed in New York City under the auspices of HPD's homesteading program. Now HPD has discontinued the program. One HPD official bluntly stated that homesteading is not an effective way to solve the pressing housing crisis. By its own admission, HPD embraced homesteading initially because—among other reasons—it appeared to be a way by which the city could relieve itself of the burden of managing buildings.

An assessment of homesteading by the Housing Development Institute (HDI) was cautious, presumably in part because at the time of my fieldwork HDI was still actively involved in several homesteading projects. One HDI employee argued that a purely financial analysis of homesteading would be misleading, because the program represents something other than an economic solution and that the benefits of homesteading could not be counted in terms of dollars and cents. Nonetheless, he claimed that home-steading compares favorably to straight market-rate rehabilitation projects. He argued that homesteading is often unfairly derided for taking too much time; he claimed that other forms of gut/rehabilitation work also take time, on the average at least two to three years. In light of the length of time it has taken for most LESAC projects to be completed (six to eight years or more), this argument is hardly convincing.

In 1993, the HDI employee cited an average unit cost of $70,000–75,000. Meanwhile, during an orientation session of volunteers on a LESAC build-ing conducted by homesteaders and a LESAC employee in early 1989, the average per-unit cost was said to be $80,000–90,000. All attempts at present-ing a more rosy financial picture of homesteading aside, the HDI employee conceded that in homesteading—as in construction in general—there are always unexpected factors that raise the cost beyond original estimates. While pointing out that a calculation of the actual sweat-equity labor contribution in monetary terms would be at best a rough estimate, he named a figure of no more than 10% of total cost. He admitted that homesteading slows down the process but emphasized that there are compensating factors, saying that "learning is expensive." He did not present an outright negative assessment of the value of homesteading, but he was voluble in listing some of the problems, such as internal conflicts, lack of participation by homesteaders, and disillusionment—of homestead-ers, activists, and his own. In his opinion the issue of growing importance was building management of completed projects. This is an issue that both HDI and LESAC largely avoided until the late 1980s, in part because they did not want to be forced into acting as building managers and landlords. For several years LESAC operated on the assumption that RAIN would become involved and run training classes for homesteaders on building management. RAIN did not do so, and problems began to arise in com-pleted buildings.

According to a UHAB employee, homesteading definitely costs more than standard contracted gut/rehabilitation work. The UHAB employee stated that an average two- to three-room apartment rehabilitation through contracted labor would cost approximately $80,000 whereas the same unit would cost $90,000 or more if homesteading were involved. She pointed to the cost of correcting mistakes made by inexperienced homesteaders during the process as accounting for most of this increase. A cost increase not included in the $90,000 calculation results from the cost of insurance that accumulates over the years. This added cost is considerable, given the length of time it has taken to bring homesteading projects to completion. HPD, LESAC, HDI, and UHAB agreed on one point: sweat-equity labor does not save money; there were differences of opinion only on how much more expensive it might make a project in the long run. This conclusion is ironic and profoundly saddening in light of some animated discussions I have attended during which homesteaders were trying to determine how much of the rehabilitation and buildup labor they could do themselves, thereby saving money and reducing the mortgage they would eventually carry. In retrospect, the attitude expressed by UHAB as well as by HDI officials—that saving money is not the purpose of sweat-equity, that its only purpose is to develop people—appears condescending and patronizing.

Being the local sponsor, LESAC bore the brunt of accusations and complaints about homesteading from all sides. Accusations cover a broad range of errors, omissions, and commissions. LESAC was accused of pushing its ideology down people's throats through the medium of RAIN. It was also accused of being an inefficient administrator. The organization was accused of mislaying, losing, and even misappropriating money; of being a power broker that made deals with various groups to the detriment of homesteaders; of abandoning homesteaders; and of embracing the MHAs that in turn were suspected of being a cover for eventual for-profit development. Some accusations were founded on truths, some were incorrect, some were exaggerated. However, that is not the issue here; at this point, LESAC's perspective is being considered.

For LESAC, homesteading turned out to be a vastly more complex undertaking than had been anticipated. The disparities between LESAC's many roles—business administrator, sometime fund raiser, construction consultant, developer, quasi-landlord or managing agent, mediator, supporter of the notion of housing for low-income people and of the Community Land Trust, and simultaneously a not-for-profit organization trying to survive in a profit-driven environment—became too great. One might also argue that LESAC and HDI had looked to homesteading as a vehicle by which to develop the Catholic Church's role in low-income housing on the Lower East Side. As it happened, in part due to LESAC's own failure to expand homesteading at a time when this could have been achieved, homesteading turned into a narrow and increasingly conflict-riddled dead end, promising to saddle LESAC with a gamut of problems from a comparatively small number of buildings. The closed office on Avenue C eloquently expresses LESAC's final assessment of homesteading as much as the realization that a project was brought to an end, however unsatisfactory that end may be.

However, assessments of what has been achieved need not simply consider homesteading at best a learning experience and charming vignette of Lower East Side history, or at worst a waste of time and money. Marcuse (1987), Schuman (1986), Mollenkopf (1983), and Bratt (1989a, 1989b), among others, have provided assessments of comparable and related efforts.

In political rhethoric, the concepts of self-help and community-based housing efforts at times are used as if they are interchangeable or interdependent. These are in fact two separate concepts with different sets of ideological parameters; this becomes apparent in situations where an attempt has been made to bring the two concepts together, as in the Lower East Side homesteading movement. Consideration of assessments of self-help and community-based housing efforts must take into account what exactly is being assessed; further, care must be taken to distinguish between assessing effectiveness of particular programs and their ideological content.

The least sanguine assessment of the transformative value of community-based self-help efforts is provided by Marcuse. As discussed in Chapter 2, Marcuse emphasizes the state's manipulative role with regard to community action. Following his line of argument, self-help efforts and other forms of citizen participation provide the state or local administration with a useful tool for social control, while not effectively altering the distribution of power, resources, or services in a neighborhood (Marcuse 1987). Hence, feelings of self-confidence and empowerment that develop through self-help efforts obscure the fact that the power of central political leadership really is unabated.

Schuman discusses four potential benefits that have been and are being claimed for self-help housing: (1) reduced construction and operating costs, (2) employment and skills training, (3) control of urban land, and (4) strenghthening of community and individual identity (Schuman 1986). Although he finds that all these potential benefits have been realized to some extent, he is wary of applying this approach to the need for affordable housing. In particular, the notion of reduced construction cost, itself highly debatable, glosses over the fact that a central problem for buildings is the mortgage rate. High mortgage payments on rehabilitated buildings cannot easily be met by people with low incomes. The second purported benefit is also debatable. Training in building trades may well have applicability in building maintenance of owner-managed buildings; but given a depressed economy (particularly with regard to construction), and competition from construction unions, self-help training is not likely to result in permanent employment.

If the pitfalls of self-help housing are predominantly economic in nature, the shortfalls stem from its failure to challenge the structure of the economy. The root of the dilemma is the privatization of the housing question, the attempt to solve a collective social problem—the provision of decent, affordable housing—at the level of an individual building. (Schuman 1986: 468)

Mollenkopf provides an assessment of what he calls the "neighborhood movement" in terms of the history of activism from the 1960s to the present. He argues that a number of tangible results as well as other developments provide the critical foundation for movements to come. Among these he names discouragement of large-scale clearance projects, a shift in planning practices toward inclusion of citizen participation, and a new emphasis on rehabilitation and preservation (Mollenkopf 1983: 210–211).

Mollenkopf further argues that neighborhood activism has helped to develop a veritable vocabulary and rhetoric of action, an organizational infrastructure for participation in political life at the grassroots, and "a new set of alliance patterns in urban politics" (Mollenkopf 1983: 211). His arguments are compelling, particularly in light of the fact that in 1975 there were less than 10 statewide community organizations in the United States, and by the mid-1980s there were over 8,000 such organizations in 50 states (Delgado 1986: 3). However, it is necessary to keep in mind that rhetoric can be appropriated by proponents of differing political agendas, that organizational infrastructures can be appropriated as tools for social control; and that a number of newly emerging alliance patterns, such as those between community organizations, major foundations, and city administrations, should not be accepted uncritically—even though these are not necessarily the kinds of alliances that Mollenkopf had in mind. For instance, Community Development Corporations (CDCs), community-based nonprofit organizations, have become the subject of debate and criticism because of their relations with city administrations.[1] New York City has been a major source of funding for CDCs, which may affect their willingness to engage in confrontational politics (Sullivan 1991). Some CDCs receive funding from major foundations and corporations, such as the Prudential Insurance Company, the Lilly Endowment, and the Rockefeller Foundation (Turetsky 1991). One might argue that we are moving from a circuit of accumulation as it is contained in the vast social welfare bureaucracy to a privatization of poverty—poverty transformed into a private corporate industry.

According to Bratt, there is a certain justice in the three main criticisms of community-based housing programs (Bratt 1989b: 203–205). One, they do not really alter fundamental causes of housing problems and homelessness and have little or no effect on institutional relationships or traditional business patterns within the private housing industry. Two, self-help programs are seen as encouraging federal complacency and inaction. Three, sweat-equity cooperative conversion programs have been criticized for their implicit acceptance of the market system, whereas community organizations have been criticized for encouraging groups to think and act as for-profit developers. In sum, however, Bratt's assessment of the potential and actual benefits of community-based housing programs is positive, despite their relatively small scale and limited impact (Bratt 1989b: 195–196). Among other considerations, Bratt argues that community-based groups are more likely than private developers to undertake nonmarket projects; but perhaps more important, they provide potent symbols indicating "that socially oriented solutions are feasible" (Bratt 1989b: 204). She points out that many benefits of community-based housing are qualitative, including an array of nonhousing benefits and a positive impact on a given community (Bratt 1989b: 205).

Self-help initiatives and community-based housing efforts are equally vulnerable. Control of urban land by not-for-profit community organizations and housing cooperatives of low-income people is diametrically opposed to the private real estate sector's perspective of the city as an opportunity for investment. Community control over housing through various forms of cooperative, nonprofit models is likely to erode unless tenants are able to meet carrying costs. Self-help initiatives that do not build strong cooperative support systems will eventually result in the recycling of housing into the market, to the detriment of those who created or rehabilitated housing units but do not have the economic resources to maintain them.

On the Lower East Side, the disparity between the ideological parameters of self-help and those of a community-oriented approach to housing have provided the symbolic and rhetorical setting in the context of which the dynamics of the market economy–dominated housing sector could be brought to bear. As a result, housing cooperatives have been created that are to all intents and purposes isolated from each other and vulnerable to market forces.

TRENDS AND DIRECTIONS FOR FUTURE DEVELOPMENTS

Although predictions about future developments must be made with great caution, certain policy trends and patterns among community-based organizations are discernible.

Probable trends and developments as far as local and state policies are concerned are taking shape in the context of a public and administrative reaction to more than a decade of efforts, however questionable and fragmentary these efforts were, toward community control of housing development and housing management. In 1992, one out of every four formerly city-owned buildings sold to community groups and low-income, tenant-run cooperatives was on the brink of fiscal collapse (see White et al. 1992). Further, Bratt has pointed out that the foreclosure rate for nonprofit developments is two to four times higher than it is in for-profit developments (Bratt 1989a). Such figures provide ammunition to the argument in favor of greater reliance on private for-profit development and privatization as opposed to community control. Hence, privatization efforts have again acquired political currency and public support, and various forms of community and tenant ownership and control are blamed for many of the troubles in low-income housing. One illustration of this trend is the city administration's decision to phase out the Community Management Program (CMP). The Community Management Program had inspired high hopes when it was set up in 1978 on the strength of Community Development Block Grants. The program had worked with and relied primarily on nonprofit neighborhood groups. The city provided funding for the renovation of abandoned buildings, a community group oversaw the renovation, and once the building was completed, tenants were meant to become the owners, assuming responsibility for taxes and maintenance. In those cases where tenants did not become the owners, the respective community group took over from the city and became the landlord. HPD argued that the program was too costly, time-consuming, and did not produce or renovate enough housing units. Meanwhile, according to a UHAB employee, among others, the city was never serious about tenant ownership; if it had been, tenants would be the major decision makers in the program. In many instances, the envisioned partnership between tenants, the respective community management organization, and the neighborhood did not materialize; community groups turned into unsatisfactory managers of buildings, and the notion of tenant ownership receded into the background.

The Community Management Program was officially ended as of July 1, 1995. The Neighborhood Ownership Works (NOW) program that was to replace CMP is also being phased out. The Guiliani administration is sponsoring three programs for the privatization of city-owned properties. In addition to renewed support of the Tenant Interim Lease (TIL) program, the city is supporting the Neighborhood Entrepreneurs Program (NEP) and the Neighborhood Revitalization Program (NRP). NEP provides support to small businesses and for-profit organizations to acquire buildings and act as landlords. NRP's central thrust is on selling residential properties to community organizations and then providing assistance with obtaining loans for rehabilitation. Any pretense of support of tenant ownership, still the purported goal in the Community Management Program, has now been dropped. These programs reinforce the city administration's disengagement from low-income housing rehabilitation as well as management of residential properties in low-income neighborhoods.

Although criticisms of the Community Management Program and its short-lived successor, the NOW program, are academic at this point, these developments provide illustration of arguments by Mollenkopf (1983) and Bratt (1989a; 1989b) about real and potential strengths of community organizing and grassroots activism. In 1992 and 1993, low-income housing groups and community organizations marshalled efforts to resist the phase-out of the Community Management Program and its replacement with the NOW program and to come up with an alternative proposal that would give community organizations and nonprofit housing groups more input.

The NOW program was supposed to use for-profit contractors to restore buildings and then sell the property to community-based nonprofit groups. According to its critics, the program did not take into account any of the lessons learned in the past, particularly the need to incorporate tenant organizing into processes of rehabilitation or construction work in order to "create community-controlled, low-income housing that withstands the test of time" (Mallin and Glazer 1992). The respective community organizations were to be actively involved in the process only after a project is completed and about to be handed over. According to critics, this would result in community organizations being reduced to cleaning up after for-profit developers with no interest in the community. Even more than the Community Management Program, the NOW program would force community groups to assume the standard landlord role to the detriment of their other activities. It is doubtful whether the developments under the Guiliani administration with the renewed emphasis on privatization of city residential properties and disengagement from active involvement in rehabilitation efforts will provide nonprofit housing groups with more input. Yet it is noteworthy that a coalition of nonprofit community organizations and national organizations succeeded in making its voice heard in the course of these debates. An alliance between the Enterprise Foundation and the Local Initiatives Support Corporation (LISC), national organizations that channel corporate investment in housing tax credits to rehabilitation efforts run by nonprofit community groups, provided the coalition with the necessary force to involve the city in reconsideration of its programs.

The Enterprise Foundation and LISC have, however, been criticized for creating another layer of bureaucracy that controls funding at the expense of grassroots community organizing. Further, their projects are structured in such a way as to exclude Mutual Housing Associations, limited-equity co-ops, or other tenant ownership or management arrangements. The projects must be run as rentals; meanwhile, a community group that sponsored a renovation project may buy the building after 15 years and convert it to tenant control. A criticism of this arrangement is that community organizations are not sufficiently involved in the buildings before being permitted to buy and take over control of them. This is another example of the way in which community organizations find themselves becoming building management groups and developers, while their roles as tenant organizers and advocates are curtailed (Turetsky 1991).

The following two factors are also critical to future directions. HPD has tended to be reactive rather than pro-active and, hence, would act more in response to a problem at its doorstep rather than according to a clearly defined long-term plan. The other factor relates to the increasing coalescence of Community Development Corporations (CDCs) as more durable and having access to a greater range of resources than do nonprofit community-based organizations, which focus mainly on housing issues (Bratt 1989a: 281). Both factors foster a tendency on the part of the city administration to relieve itself of cumbersome real estate and associated building management problems. This is one of the reasons for HPD's cooperation with nationally-based organizations and CDCs as well as community organizations, particularly when they offer to troubleshoot contentious issues (e.g., social control of residents or awkward and time-consuming building management).

These trends, (i.e., greater encouragement of privatization and for-profit low-income housing development, and the emergence of increasingly powerful corporate bodies that are positioned between community organizations and local administrations), are reflected in (1) community organizations' projections for future development, and (2) strategy recommendations on the part of activists. One emphasizes coalitions and involvement in electoral politics as well as utilization of confrontational strategies. Another emphasizes multi-issue approaches and concentration on a particular locality. Finally, issues of labor and employment are increasingly seen as critical to the success of any efforts, particularly housing-related ones.

At the level of individual buildings, homeowners are beginning to see the need for coalitions. In New York City a coalition of low-income homeownership cooperations or HDFCs (Housing Development Fund Corporations) such as the homesteader buildings on the Lower East Side was formed in 1994. In April 1995 the coalition included only 14 actively involved buildings and 50 affiliates out of a total of approximately 1000 HDFCs in New York City. However, this coalition is a repository of information for HDFCs in need of assistance, and it might become an important organizational and lobbying tool.

Activists on the Lower East Side have pointed out the need for building coalitions between community-based organizations in order to expand resources and broaden the constituency. Activists have also debated the question of increased involvement in electoral politics. One activist was convinced that a shift in the mid-1980s away from grassroots-level work to an involvement in the Community Board and electoral politics was detrimental to the continued impact of homesteading.

Delgado, a longtime activist and social scientist, believes that isolated efforts on the part of community-based organizations are not likely to succeed; he suggests that both penetration of the electoral arena and continued development of a major movement mobilization are necessary. He argues that there is a need for multilevel coalitions that offer a diverse tactical repertoire in which disruptive actions are used to complement the electoral thrust (Delgado 1986: 231). Meanwhile, Piven and Cloward have noted that community organizations' class makeup and orientation tend to develop upward and away from poorer constituents, who may have lent original impetus to an organization's development. They also found that over time, community-based organizations opt for a reduction of militant tactics, move toward bureaucratization, and place more emphasis on state regulatory agencies as targets than they do on corporations (Piven and Cloward 1979: 38–39).

Some recommendations on the part of activists (e.g., greater emphasis on coalitions, and a recognition of the importance of electoral politics) had already been realized to some extent, for instance on the Lower East Side and in the South Bronx. On the Lower East Side, one of the reasons for activists' and homesteaders' initial success in marshalling reluctant support by the city administration can be traced to a relatively broad-based coalition of community organizations and interest groups that culminated in the Joint Planning Council. During the early to mid-1980s, the Joint Planning Council was involved in the struggle over the cross-subsidy plan for the disposition of 500 in rem properties held by the city (see Abu-Lughod et al. 1994: 311–332). In this context, housing units to be created through home-steading represented only a minor bargaining chip. The homesteading effort was left to fend for itself, while vocal and active leaders attempted to gain a more influential role in the Community Board and ultimately in electoral politics. The weakness of homesteading in the latter part of the 1980s stems as much from this shift in strategy as from other factors, both internal and external to the movement.

Activists for the most part did not need to learn the lessons from the failure of the Great Society and Model Cities anti-poverty programs of the 1960s to be wary of large-scale efforts. This distrust notwithstanding, in recent years activists and community organizations have placed greater emphasis on a concentration of efforts and the notion of coalitions. The coalition of six community organizations in the South Bronx, including the Banana Kelly Community Improvement Association, with several founda-tions is an example of a multilevel, broad-based approach to community development. Generally, community-based organizations as well as activ-ists are aware of the pitfalls of single-issue campaigns. On the other hand, it is easier to organize and marshall support around a single issue.

Activists as well as administration officials have begun to focus more on the critical relationship between jobs and housing. Activists on the Lower East Side who were involved in housing efforts discussed with increasing frequency the difficulty of obtaining adequately compensated employment and the vagaries of the labor market. Some activists shifted their activities to involvement in work programs and local organizations with a focus on labor and related issues, such as the Chinese Staff Workers Association. Repeatedly, activists stated that they felt it would be easier to organize people around labor than housing. This implies that the most important factor is organizing people, and that the precise issue used as a vehicle for such organizing efforts is not as important. Delgado also argued that the idea of being organized is more important than the particular issue being worked on; the organizing experience is seen as a way "to understand how power and politics operate, to grasp both the essentials and limitations of collective action, and to feel a new sense of self-esteem" (Delgado 1986: 202).

Public agencies were not oblivious to the link between labor and housing or to the paradox posed by the concept of self-help. The goals of reducing the cash cost of rehabilitation and providing homesteaders with a way to build up equity in their units were not easily reconciled with the realities of building rehabilitation and homesteaders' lives. Rehabilitation projects realized solely with unpaid "sweat" labor would take too long; homesteaders could hardly afford to quit their jobs in order to work without compensation on their buildings on a full-time basis. In some cities, sweat-equity and homesteading programs were combined with publicly funded training and employment programs. But such attempts to combine training and job creation with low-income housing development were pursued only tentatively in short-term experimental models; they foundered on administrative and organizational aspects and a precarious and shrinking job market.

While grafting an employment program onto what was already a highly ambitious experiment in reversing housing abandonment tended to dilute the self-help principles and complicate the administrative and organizational aspects of homesteading, it explicitly recognized the relationship between jobs and housing. The participants in sweat-equity were primarily minority youths between 16 and 25 years old, the bulk of them "hardcore unemployed." Construction work was both an appropriate and socially respected potential source of employment. Moreover, and this was only dimly perceived at the outset, regular wages for at least most of the would-be occupants were essential to the long-term financial viability of the rehabilitated housing developments. (Kolodny 1986: 450)

Local job training programs in New York City, such as the federally funded Job Training Partnership Act, have been subject to criticisms as ineffective, if not corrupt. The Department of Employment has acknowledged cases of fraud within the city's $90 million job training program. More important, critics have argued that the requirements of these programs encourage quick job placement, even in jobs not likely to last or pay a decent wage. The emphasis is on getting people off welfare quickly without a long-term perspective regarding job security or possibilities for advancement. A much broader and more comprehensive effort is called for, resulting in more intensive training services and safeguards against "creaming" more advanced students. Another program that appears to be more promising was founded in the 1970s: under the YouthBuild program training lasts a year and is full-time, and participants are paid for their work.

It is also expensive: $20,000 a year for each participant. Although this program has a good record in placing graduates in jobs, it addresses only a tiny percentage of those in need of training and assistance. Also, it does not alter the reality of a shrinking job market, particularly on the lower end of the wage scale.

On the Lower East Side, the Department of Employment had supported a training program for high school dropouts in conjunction with home-steading. Called Youth at Work, it was a one-year program including coursework and construction training. In July 1991 one group was celebrat-ing its graduation at the Emmanuel Presbyterian Church at 6th Street between Avenues C and D. This group of young men and women had spent a great deal of time working on one building, although I had observed them on other buildings as well. The program was designed in the mid-1980s; one of the activists centrally involved in planning—and in fact the author of the program—was also a leading activist in the homesteading effort. Another activist and homesteader involved in the program pointed out that the real difficulties begin *after* graduation, when graduates try to enter and survive in the job market. A program without follow-up in terms of place-ment and continuing support would not be very successful.

Homesteading on the Lower East Side is remarkable in that it attempted to combine some aspects of self-help with a community-oriented approach while also acknowledging the importance of the labor market. Nonetheless, in summary, the weakness of housing movements in general and of the Lower East Side effort in particular can be traced back to the following critical factors: a separation of housing from other factors of the economy and society, a forbidding economic context, a tortuous bureaucratic jungle, and profound ideological contradictions within local and federal admini-strations as well as community organizations. Both in theory and in prac-tice, the need for housing is all too often decontextualized and treated as a separate item, as "property" that is detachable from other factors of the economy and political and social considerations. This decontextualization is reflected in and exacerbates the ideological contradictions of homestead-ing. Different constructs and concepts such as the Community Land Trust RAIN, sweat labor, community, and property become actors on a stage that hides underlying dynamics and structures.

CONCLUSION

As a concluding assessment of homesteading on the Lower East Side, the above comments are rather open-ended, and perhaps that is the point. When considering the outcome of homesteading, one encounters contra-dictions at every level. In terms of its goals of stemming the wave of gentrification of the neighborhood, of preserving and creating housing for low-income people, and of creating a new foundation for a growing community, homesteading on the Lower East Side was only partially successful. Buildings were constructed and are now inhabited by low-income people from the neighborhood. Homesteaders who began by looking for a place to live have gone on from homesteading to activities on the block and in the community on a variety of levels in addition to taking an active part in managing their own buildings. Women homesteaders who emerged as leaders during rehabilitation are still involved in building management and community matters; yet they often do much of the work alone and without support from other members of their buildings—building management as a form of domestic "women's work." City blocks that featured drug shooting galleries and rubble-filled lots have been transformed by the presence of one or several rehabilitated buildings. This transformation is all the more concrete for having occurred over a long period of time with people from the neighborhood playing an active part. In other words, transformation could be observed as a physical process seemingly initiated and realized by people from the neighborhood rather than imposed from outside like a prefabricated product. The degree to which the changes on the Lower East Side are the product of gentrification or the product of homesteading combined with other community-based efforts is unclear; indeed, it is not possible or necessarily meaningful to draw a line between these processes, given that they are interdependent dynamics in a market-based housing arena.

For some homesteaders the impact of homesteading on the neighborhood over the last decade is concrete and visible. One homesteader described driving through the neighborhood in 1984 and going past 336 East 4th Street. He saw as many as 15 drug dealers sitting and standing around outside and using the building as a base for operations; now it is rehabilitated. However, another perspective was provided by a homesteader now living in a building between Avenues C and D on 6th Street, who argued that there has been a shift toward Avenue D; drugs and poverty have simply been relocated or forced into a different neighborhood or area of the city.

The change in appearance of Loisaida over the last decade is striking. There are now only a few open lots filled with rubble and weeds. Most remaining empty lots are firmly encased in shiny, new fencing. There are several new community gardens where even two years ago there were tent cities. Some vacant buildings have been demolished, others are being rehabilitated. A one-time chop shop and several former squatter buildings have been gutted. In December 1993 the shanty-town at Avenue D and 4th Street, called "Bushville," was razed by city bulldozers.

One might say the neighborhood is being "tamed," fenced in, sanitized, and cleaned up. Inevitably this raises the question of what will happen to those who had somehow managed to survive on the margins, now that the borderlines between those with a home and those without are being drawn in ever sharper outlines. Where will the inhabitants of "Bushville" go, credited with constructing some of the longest-lasting and most solidly constructed shanties in Manhattan? Where will the old homeless man go whom I have seen walking around Loisaida, waving his arms, sobbing, and laughing? Most current rehabilitation is done either by private developers or by companies on behalf of the city or in the context of MHAs. Yet the neighborhood has not been completely gentrified. Although homesteading has come to a halt, many buildings have been retained rather than demolished and have been appropriated by low-income people.

When considering the impact of homesteading on the neighborhood, it is important to look beyond the creation of housing and issues of control of housing property. For instance, a playground has been reclaimed by homesteaders and tenant managers on the block where the playground is located. Sauer Playground on 12th Street between Avenues A and B had been a place for drug dealers and addicts since the 1970s. The process of forcing the city administration to take steps to renovate and redesign the neglected property began with a first community rally in 1985 and was brought to triumphant conclusion in August 1993 when the playground reopened, complete with safety features, attractive sitting areas, and new playground features. Of course, this battle-on-all-fronts approach has many pitfalls, not the least of which are fragmentation and potential diffusion of efforts and the burn-out of individuals involved. One homesteader said: "We tried to do everything, anti-arson fights, anti-drugs, housing, gardens."

Sweat and empowerment, rallying cries of homesteaders, activists, community organizers, and even city administration officials, express the pitfalls and strengths of the homesteading effort on the Lower East Side. They evoke concepts of private, individual success and attainment of property as much as community cooperation and control of property. The notion of empowerment is made to appear concrete and vital while simultaneously masking underlying problems.

Bratt points out that empowerment consists of three interrelated dimensions: psychological, political, and economic empowerment (Bratt 1991). In her analysis of a Mutual Housing Association in Baltimore, she finds that "an impressive level of actual participation [in community activities] provides good evidence that political empowerment is occurring" (Bratt 1991: 178). She points out that the study did not consider voting behavior or external political activities and organizing; instead, it focused only on participation in Mutual Housing Association affairs. As far as economic empowerment is concerned, the general perception among members of the Mutual Housing Association appeared to be that things had stayed the same. "As a social experiment, mutual housing appears to be successful, creating a viable and secure community for low- and moderate-income families, and apparently, enhancing the feeling of empowerment among residents" (Bratt 1991: 180).

According to Bratt, residents' perception of their situation is of critical importance. She mentions a shift in perception from "slums of despair" to "slums of hope" (Bratt 1989b: 29). This is the danger contained in the concept of empowerment. The internalized perception of power cannot be taken as a substitute for such power, nor is the perception of a situation as hopeful a substitute for change. Otherwise, one returns only to the notion that what is wrong with poor people is their outlook.

Empowerment does not come with swinging a sledgehammer or holding a blowtorch, despite their symbolic impact. However, despite the deceptive overemphasis on the notion of empowerment as a sort of liberal-conservative "feel-good" soporific and the mistaken glorification of sweat, homesteading in all its dimensions provides a concrete experience of struggle and power through intimate knowledge of the process of housing rehabilitation. It is woven into remembered, shared history as a tangible spur to the imagination and a basis for future action.

The partial transformation of patterns of control over the development and maintenance of housing—and ultimately of the community—as envisioned by activists and initially embraced by homesteaders must be understood in conjunction with the reproduction of existing patterns and reinforcement of normative values. Neither transformation nor reproduction are complete and total. "Thus the dialectics of subject and object in *all* social contexts—whether of "simple" or more complex systems—generate both reinforcement *and* tension, reproduction *and* transformation" (Comaroff 1985: 6).

The problem of housing in America is defined by and dependent on the dynamics of capitalism. For this reason, Stone argues that the housing problem cannot be solved within a capitalist system (Stone 1986: 42). However, given the fact that no viable structural or political alternatives to capitalism presently exist, any solutions to housing must be framed in relationship to its central tenets, and the forces of the market must be taken into account. Neighborhoods, cities, corporate capital, industry, national and transnational conglomerates are interconnected in a giant global network. Withdrawal into an attempt at self-sufficiency at any level is an untenable proposition; equally untenable is passive acceptance of outside forces and dynamics. Individual building cooperatives are more likely to survive in coalition with others. Community organizations look toward linkages with other organizations, funding agencies, and administrative bodies. Activists consider shifts in strategy away from a single-issue approach to one using a variety of strategies and focusing on numerous issues.

"The community's strength on the Lower East Side is everywhere, but today the organizations that represent it are sleepwalking. The forces of the marketplace hold a strange, dreamlike spell" (Brandstein 1984: 19). When we consider the history of homesteading on the Lower East Side over the past 17 years, the forces of the marketplace are not so strange or dreamlike;

instead, the dynamics can be analyzed and explained regardless of the complexity of individual processes involved. Thus, they can be transformed.

In Chapter 2, I described one homesteader's reference to land-holding structures in the Middle Ages as a spiritual model for the Community Land Trust. In a description of open-field farming or "champion farming," in Northwestern Europe before 1800, Smith discusses the network of communal rights and restraints with regard to land and cultivation. He illustrates the interdependency of ownership and consumption on the one hand and production on the other:

And if the communal restraints tended on the one hand to reinforce the social bonds which held together the village community, they also influenced the appearance of the landscape in a number of important ways. It has already been seen that the use of the heavy plough encouraged cooperation in farming and communal cultivation of large open fields rather than individual cultivation of enclosures. . . . Arable land and meadow were therefore subject to common rights of pasture once the grain or hay harvest had been taken. . . . Communal rights made it difficult to contract out of the arrangements for cropping and to grow what each wished on his strips in the open fields. They made it difficult for any individual farmer to extract his lands from the intermingled strips of others and to reorganize them into a compact holding. (Smith 1967: 204–205)

Homesteading on the Lower East Side was originally framed around such an envisioned web of relationships, interdependencies, and cooperation. The model challenged normative concepts of ownership, consumption, and production of housing. Contrary to the original vision, it was eventually transformed into a concept of ownership that was detached from factors of production and the needs of the community. By virtue of its development and effects on the Lower East Side, homesteading provides a lens onto the dynamics of housing in a market economy.

In talking about this linkage and the interplay of market economy and market culture, Zukin argues that there has been an "increasing abstraction of value from productive labor, and the transfer of the dominant source of social meaning from production to consumption" (Zukin 1991: 57). The inner-city wastelands and the ruin of once thriving steel towns such as Homestead, Pennsylvania, reflect the reshaping of America's landscapes as much as the suburban mall, gentrified neighborhoods, and Disney World.[2] Although she argues that to ask local communities to generate change is a romantic notion, Zukin nonetheless sees a potential for reshaping America's "moral landscapes." Market culture is defined on the basis of ownership and consumption, yet markets and places are socially constructed by conscious actors. This offers the potential for a redefinition of market culture to one based on public value and citizenship (Zukin 1991: 274).

The poet Bimbo Rivas spoke for his people on the Lower East Side as much as for everyone struggling to survive—at risk of losing a home, without an income to make ends meet, lost and homeless—in an eloquent plea for work, asking for "a job, a simple job."[3] He knew that a roof over one's head is not enough.

> I don't expect the world to stop for me
> to stop its mission for my sake
> I only ask for a clearer path
> to put my brains and hands to work
> to prove my worth

Homesteading was as much about the creation of self-worth as about the creation of housing units. As Rivas knew, self-worth becomes a hollow phrase unless it is linked to jobs. In its attempt, however flawed, to integrate notions of cooperative production and control of housing, homesteading was a vastly ambitious project of community construction. For the remaking of America's inner-city landscapes, concrete and imagined, homesteading on the Lower East Side offers a compelling conceptual building brick.

NOTES

1. For extensive study and analysis of Community Development Corporations in various parts of the United States, see research done under the auspices of the Community Development Research Center of the New School for Social Research in New York City (Sullivan 1991).

2. Homestead, Pennsylvania, the heart of the American steel industry, has become a symbol of conflicts between labor and management, corporate mismanagement, and the radical restructuring of the economy (Serrin 1992). The first settler of what became Homestead, Pennsylvania, was Sebastian Frederick from Germany, who in the 1770s claimed a tract of approximately 300 acres. He was to all intents and purposes a squatter, hunting and fishing on land to which he had no title. Eventually he moved on to places unknown. The name derives from the name given by the first permanent settler, John McClure, who in 1786 obtained a deed to 329.5 acres of land in the area and called his farm the "Amity Homestead." To complete the ironic historical symmetry, John McClure was a trader, farmer, and land speculator.

3. From a poem by Bimbo Rivas, "A Job," in Algarín and Piñero, 1975.

BIBLIOGRAPHY

Abeles, Schwartz and Associates. 1970. *Forging a Future for the Lower East Side: A Plan for Action.* New York: Prepared for the City of New York Housing and Development Administration and City Planning Commission.

Abu-Lughod, Janet, et al. 1994. *From Urban Village to East Village: The Battle for New York's Lower East Side.* Cambridge, MA: Basil Blackwell, Ltd.

Algarín, Miguel, and Bob Holman, eds. 1994. *Aloud: Voices from the Nuyorican Poets Cafe.* New York: H. Holt.

Algarín, Miguel, and Miguel Piñero, eds. 1975. *Nuyorican Poetry: An Anthology of Puerto Rican Words and Feelings.* New York: William Morrow.

Alpern, Robert. 1973. *Pratt Guide to Planning and Renewal for New Yorkers.* New York: Quadrangle–New York Times Book Company.

Annez, Philippe, and William C. Wheaton. 1984. "Economic Development and the Housing Sector: A Cross-National Model." *Economic Development and Cultural Change* 32 (4): 749–766.

Arnstein, Sherry. 1969. "A Ladder of Citizen Participation." *Journal of the American Institute of Planners* 35 (7): 216–224.

Bach, Victor, and Sherece Y. West. 1993. *Housing on the Block: Disinvestment and Abandonment Risks in New York City Neighborhoods.* New York: Community Service Society of New York.

Baker, Russell W. 1989. "New York City Housing Shortage Prompts Squatters to Rehabilitate Housing." *Christian Science Monitor*, June 12.

Barlow, Elizabeth. 1969. *The Forests and Wetlands of New York City.* Boston: Little Brown.

Batista, Frank. 1990. "The Battle of Home Street." *Village Voice*, October 9.

Blau, Joel. 1992. *The Visible Poor.* New York: Oxford University Press.

Bookman, Anne, and Sandra Morgen. 1988. *Women and the Politics of Empowerment.* Philadelphia: Temple University Press.

Borgos, Seth. 1984. "The ACORN Squatters' Campaign." *Social Policy* 15 (1): 17–26.

_____. 1986. "Low-Income Homeownership and the ACORN Squatters Campaign." In *Critical Perspectives on Housing*, eds. Rachel G. Bratt, Chester Hartman, and Ann Meyerson. Philadelphia: Temple University Press.

Bowles, Samuel, David M. Gordon, and Thomas E. Weisskopf. 1990. *After the Waste Land: A Democratic Economics for the Year 2000*. Armonk, NY: M. E. Sharpe.

Brandstein, Howard. 1984. *Toward a Sheltering Community: Developing a Land Trust for the Lower East Side*. New York: Lower East Side Catholic Area Conference, position paper adopted by LESAC on May 1, 1984.

Bratt, Rachel G. 1987. "Dilemmas of Community-Based Housing." *Policy Studies Journal* 16 (2): 324–334.

_____. 1989a. "Community-Based Housing in Massachusetts: Lessons and Limits of the State's Support System." In *Housing Issues of the 1990s*, eds. Sara Rosenberry and Chester Hartman. New York: Praeger Publications.

_____. 1989b. *Rebuilding a Low-Income Housing Policy*. Philadelphia: Temple University Press.

_____. 1991. "Mutual Housing: Community-Based Empowerment." *Journal of Housing* 48: 173–180.

Bratt, Rachel G., Chester Hartman, and Ann Meyerson, eds. 1986. *Critical Perspectives on Housing*. Philadelphia: Temple University Press.

Bromley, G. W. 1902. *Atlas of Manhattan*. New York.

_____. 1910. *Atlas of Manhattan*. New York.

_____. 1930. *Atlas of Manhattan*. New York.

Brower, Bonnie. 1989. *Missing the Mark: Subsidized Housing for the Privileged, Displacing the Poor (An Analysis of the City's 10–Year Plan)*. New York: Association for Neighborhood and Housing Development; Housing Justice Campaign, August 1989.

Burns, Leland S., and Leo Grebler. 1986. *The Future of Housing Markets: A New Appraisal*. New York: Plenum Press.

Carlson, David B. 1978. *Revitalizing North American Neighborhoods*. Department of Housing and Urban Development, U.S. Programs: Book Grants and Housing Rehabilitation.

Carmon, Naomi, and Tamar Gavrieli. 1987. "Improving Housing by Conventional versus Self-Help Methods: Evidences from Israel." *Urban Studies* 24: 324–332.

Castells, Manuel. 1977. *The Urban Question*. Cambridge, MA: MIT Press.

_____. 1978. *City, Class and Power*. New York: St. Martin's Press.

_____. 1983. *The City and the Grassroots: A Cross-Cultural Theory of Urban Social Movements*. Berkeley: University of California Press.

Cavallo, Diana. 1971. *The Lower East Side: A Portrait in Time*. New York: Crowell-Collier Press.

Chandler, Mittie O. 1988. *Urban Homesteading: Programs and Policies*. New York: Greenwood Press.

Chodorkoff, Daniel. 1980. *Un Milagro de Loisaida—Alternative Technology and Grassroots Efforts for Neighborhood Reconstruction on New York's Lower East Side*. New York: New School for Social Research, Ph.D. dissertation.

Clark, Anne, and Zelma Rivin. 1977. *Homesteading in Urban U.S.A.* New York: Praeger Publications.

Collier, David. 1976. *Squatters and Oligarchs: Authoritarian Rule and Policy Change in Peru*. Baltimore: Johns Hopkins University Press.

Comaroff, Jean. 1985. *Body of Power, Spirit of Resistance: The Culture and History of a South African People*. Chicago: University of Chicago Press.

Cowley, John. 1986. "The Limitations and Potential of Housing Organizing." In *Critical Perspectives on Housing*, eds. Rachel G. Bratt, Chester Hartman, and Ann Meyerson. Philadelphia: Temple University Press.

Davidson, F. S. 1979. *City Policy and Housing Abandonment: A Case Study of New York City, 1965–1973*. New York: Columbia University, Ph.D. dissertation.

Davis, James H. 1975. "A Second Look at the Urban Homestead." *Landscape*, January: 23–27.

Davis, John Emmeus. 1983. "CLTs and the Politics of Ownership." *Community Economics* 2 (Fall 1983). Springfield, MA: Institute for Community Economics.

————. 1991. *Contested Ground: Collective Action and the Urban Neighborhood*. Ithaca: Cornell University Press.

————, ed. 1993. *The Affordable City: Toward a Third Sector Housing Policy*. Philadelphia: Temple University Press.

Davis, John Emmeus, and Chuck Matthei. 1982. "Community Land Trust: A New Approach to Home Ownership." *Shelterforce*, March.

Dear, Michael, and Allen J. Scott. 1981. *Urbanization and Urban Planning in Capitalist Society*. New York: Methuen.

DeCourcy Hinds, Michael. 1992. "Public Housing Ills Lead to Questions about H.U.D." *New York Times*, July 20.

DeGiovanni, Frank F. 1984. "An Examination of Selected Consequences of Revitalization in Six U.S. Cities." *Urban Studies* 21: 245–259.

————. 1987. *Displacement Pressures in the Lower East Side*. New York: Community Service Society of New York.

Dehavenon, Anna Lou. 1985. *The Tyranny of Indifference and the Reinstitutionalization of Hunger, Homelessness, and Poor Health*. New York: East Harlem Interfaith Welfare Committee.

Delgado, Gary. 1986. *Organizing the Movement: The Roots and Growth of ACORN*. Philadelphia: Temple University Press.

DeRienzo, Harold. 1992. "The Touchstone—Letter to the Editor." *City Limits*, June/July.

Deutsche, Rosalyn, and Cara Gendel Ryan. 1984. "The Fine Art of Gentrification." *October* 31 (Winter): 91–111.

Dickens, Charles. 1978. "American Notes." In *Dickens on America and the Americans*, ed. Michael Slater. Austin: University of Texas Press.

Dolbeare, Cushing. 1986. "How the Income Tax System Subsidizes Housing for the Affluent." In *Critical Perspectives on Housing*, eds. Rachel G. Bratt, Chester Hartman, and Ann Meyerson. Philadelphia: Temple University Press.

Drewes, Chris W. 1974. "Homesteading 1974: Reclaiming Abandoned Houses on the Urban Frontier." *Columbia Journal of Law and Social Problems*, Spring: 416–455.

Dripps, Matthew. 1852. *Map of New York City, South of 50th Street*. New York.

————. 1879. *Map of New York City, South of 50th Street*. New York.

Ewen, Elizabeth. 1985. *Immigrant Women in the Land of Dollars: Life and Culture on the Lower East Side, 1890–1925*. New York: Monthly Review Press.

Feagin, Joe R. 1986. "Urban Real Estate Speculation in the United States: Implications for Social Science and Urban Planning." In *Critical Perspectives on Housing*, eds. Rachel G. Bratt, Chester Hartman, and Ann Meyerson. Philadelphia: Temple University Press.

Folbre, Nancy. 1990. "Where Has All the Money Gone? Trickle-Up Economics in America." *Village Voice Literary Supplement*, April.

Ford, James. 1971. *Slums and Housing, with Special Reference to New York City: History, Conditions, Policy*. Westport, CT: Negro Universities Press (orig. ed., 1936).

Franck, Karen A., and Sherry Ahrentzen, eds. 1989. *New Households, New Housing*. New York: Van Nostrand Reinhold.

Freidenberg, Judith. 1991. "Participatory Research and Grassro Development: A Case Study from Harlem." *City & Society* 5 (1) (Spring): 64–75.

Gabel, Hortense W. 1970. *The New York City Rehabilitation Experiments*. New York: Report prepared for the City Housing and Development Administration.

George, Henry. 1979. *Progress and Poverty: An Inquiry into the Cause of Industrial Depressions and Increase of Want with Increase of Wealth; the Remedy*. New York: Robert Schalkenbach Foundation (orig. ed., 1879).

Giddens, Anthony. 1981. *A Contemporary Critique of Historical Materialism*. Berkeley: University of California Press.

Gilbert, Alan, Jorge E. Hardoy and Ronaldo Ramirez, eds. 1982. *Urbanization in Contemporary Latin America: Critical Approaches in the Analysis of Urban Issues*. New York: J. Wiley.

Gilbert, Alan, and Peter M. Ward. 1985. *Housing, the State and the Poor—Policy and Practice in Three Latin American Cities*. Cambridge: Cambridge University Press.

Glazer, Lisa. 1991. "The Chopping Block: How Budget Cuts Hit the Housing Department." *City Limits* August/September.

———. 1992. "Beyond Bricks and Mortar." *City Limits*, May.

———. 1993. "Making Connections." *City Limits*, February.

Glazer, Nathan. 1987. "The South-Bronx Story: An Extreme Case of Neighborhood Decline." *Policy Studies Journal* 16 (2): 269–276.

Gordon, David M. 1984. "Capitalist Development and the History of American Cities." In *Marxism and the Metropolis*, ed. William K. Tabb. New York: Oxford University Press.

Gose, Peter. 1991. "House Rethatching in an Andean Ritual Cycle: Practice, Meaning, and Contradiction." *American Ethnologist* 18 (1): 39–66.

Gruson, Lindsey. 1992. "Housing Aid Goes Unspent by Poor Cities—Conservatives Assail Idle Federal Billions." *New York Times*, June 15.

Hall, Helen. 1971. *Unfinished Business in Neighborhood and Nation*. New York: MacMillan Company.

Hardy-Fanta, Carol. 1993. *Latina Politics, Latino Politics: Gender, Culture, and Political Participation in Boston*. Philadelphia: Temple University Press.

Hartman, Chester. 1986. "Housing Policies under the Reagan Administration." In *Critical Perspectives on Housing*, eds. Rachel G. Bratt, Chester Hartman, and Ann Meyerson. Philadelphia: Temple University Press.

Hartmann, Heidi. 1981. "The Family as the Locus of Gender, Class and Political Struggle: The Example of Housework." *Signs* 6 (3): 366–394.

Harvey, David. 1978. "Urbanization under Capitalism: A Framework for Analysis." *International Journal of Urban and Regional Research* 2: 101–131.

———. 1985a. *Consciousness and the Urban Experience*. Baltimore: Johns Hopkins University Press.

———. 1985b. *Urbanization of Capital*. Baltimore: Johns Hopkins University Press.

———. 1992. *Social Justice and the City*. Colchester, VT: Blackwell Publishers (orig. ed., 1973).

Herbstein, Judith F. 1978. *Rituals and Politics of the Puerto Rican Community in New York City*. New York: City University of New York, Ph.D. dissertation.

Heskin, David Allan. 1991. *The Struggle for Community*. Boulder, CO: Westview Press.

Hopper, Kim, Ezra Susser, and Sarah Conover. 1986. "Economies of Makeshift: Deindustrialization and Homelessness in New York City." *Urban Anthropology* 14 (1–3): 183–236.

Hughes, James W., and Kenneth D. Bleakly, Jr. 1975. *Urban Homesteading*. New Brunswick, NJ: Rutgers University, Center for Urban Policy Research.

Institute for Community Economics. 1982. *The Community Land Trust Handbook*. Emmaus, PA: Rodale Press.

Institute for Policy Studies, Working Group on Housing. 1989. *The Right to Housing—A Blueprint for Housing the Nation*. Oakland, CA: Community Economics.

Institute of Public Administration. 1968. *Rapid Rehabilitation of Old-Law Tenements: An Evaluation*. New York: Prepared for U.S. Department of Housing and Urban Development, Office of Urban Technology, Low Income Housing Demonstration Program.

Interfaith Adopt-A-Building, Inc. 1978. *A Portrait of Loisaida*. New York.

Israelowitz, Oscar. 1991. *Guide to the Lower East Side*. New York: Israelowitz Publishing.

Jacobs, Barry G., Kenneth R. Harney, Charles L. Edson, and Bruce S. Lane. 1982. *Guide to Federal Housing Programs*. Bureau of National Affairs.

Jacobs, Jane. 1961. *The Death and Life of Great American Cities*. New York: Vintage Books.

Jacobs, Karrie. 1993. "After a Noon Breakfast, an East Village Ramble." *New York Times*, September 19.

Joyce, James. 1961. *Ulysses*. New York: Vintage Books.

Kaufman, Michael T. 1989. "Living in Legal Limbo in Manhattan's Ghost Housing." *New York Times*, May 11.

Kemeny, Jim. 1986. "Critique of Homeownership." In *Critical Perspectives on Housing*, eds. Rachel G. Bratt, Chester Hartman, and Ann Meyerson. Philadelphia: Temple University Press.

Kennedy, Shawn G. 1992. "When the J 51 Bubble Bursts." *New York Times*, February 9.

King, Wayne. 1973. "Homesteaders Combatting Urban Blight." *New York Times*, September 16.

Kolodny, Robert. 1973. *Self-Help in the Inner City: A Study of Lower Income Cooperative Housing Conversion in New York*. New York: United Neighborhood Houses of New York.

_____ . 1986. "The Emergence of Self-Help as a Housing Strategy for the Urban Poor." In *Critical Perspectives on Housing*, eds. Rachel G. Bratt, Chester Hartman, and Ann Meyerson. Philadelphia: Temple University Press.

LaSalle, Barbara. 1989. "An Average Day at Homesteading." *Homesteader*, November 2. New York: RAIN (CLT) Community Land Trust.

Laven, Chuck. 1984. "Self-Help in Neighborhood Development." In *The Scope of Social Architecture*, ed. C. R. Hatch. New York: Van Nostrand Reinhold, pp. 104–17.

Lawson, Ronald. 1984. *Owners of Last Resort: An Assessment of the Track Records of New York City's Early Low Income Housing Cooperative Conversions*. New York: Report prepared for the New York City Department of Housing Preservation and Development, Office of Program Management and Analysis.

Leavitt, Jacqueline, and Susan Saegert. 1989. *From Abandonment to Hope: Community Households in Harlem*. New York: Columbia University Press.

Lewis, John. 1984 "Homesteaders Get $ to Fix City's Buildings." *Daily News*, December 4.

_____ . 1989. "A Place to Call Their Very Own." *Daily News*, November 10.

Linger, Daniel T. 1993. "The Hegemony of Discontent." *American Ethnologist* 20 (1): 3–24.

Listokin, David, ed. 1983. *Housing Rehabilitation—Economic, Social, and Policy Perspectives*. New Brunswick, NJ: Rutgers University, Center for Urban Policy Research.

Listokin, David, Lizabeth Allewelt, and James J. Nemeth. 1985. *Housing Receivership and Self-Help Neighborhood Revitalization*. New Brunswick, NJ: Rutgers University, Center for Urban Policy Research.

Lower East Side Joint Planning Council. 1975. *Report to Percy Sutton, Borough President of Manhattan, May 13, 1975*. New York.

Maffi, Mario. 1994. "The Other Side of the Coin: Culture in Loisaida." In *From Urban Village to East Village*, eds. Janet L. Abu-Lughod et al. Cambridge, MA: Basil Blackwell Ltd.

Mallin, Erika. 1990. "Withstanding the Test of Time: The Homesteaders." *Pipeline*.

Mallin, Erika, and Lisa Glazer. 1992. "The End of an Era." *City Limits*, October.

Marcus, George E., and Michael M. J. Fischer. 1986. *Anthropology as Cultural Critique*. Chicago: University of Chicago Press.

Marcuse, Peter. 1982. "Triage as Urban Policy." *Social Policy* 12 (3).

_____ . 1983. "On the Political Contradictions of Self-Help in Housing." Papers in Planning. New York: Columbia University, Graduate School of Architecture and Planning.

_____ . 1985. "Gentrification, Abandonment and Displacement: Connections, Causes and Policy Responses in New York City." *Journal of Urban and Contemporary Law* 28: 195–240.

_____ . 1986. "Housing Policy and the Myth of the Benevolent State in Critical Perspective." In *Critical Perspectives on Housing*, eds. Rachel G. Bratt, Chester Hartman, and Ann Meyerson. Philadelphia: Temple University Press.

_____ . 1987. "Neighborhood Policy and the Distribution of Power: New York City's Community Boards." *Policy Studies Journal* 16 (2): 277–289.

Matthei, Chuck. 1987. "The Community Land Trust Movement Today." *Community Economics* 13 (Fall 1987). Springfield, MA: Institute for Community Economics.

Matulef, M. L. 1988. "Community Development: A National Perspective." *Housing* 45: 239–241.

Mavrides, Melanie J. 1993. "Low-Cost Houses in a High-Price Haven." *New York Times*, May 2.

McMurray, Amanda. 1990. "The Power of Choice and Homesteading." *Homesteader*, January 13. New York: RAIN (CLT) Community Land Trust.

Mitra, Steve. 1993. "The Squatters' Paradox." *City Limits*, October.

Mollenkopf, John H. 1983. *The Contested City*. Princeton: Princeton University Press.

Nelson, J. M. 1979. *Access to Power: Politics and the Urban Poor in Developing Nations*. Princeton: Princeton University Press.

Neuwirth, Robert. 1992. "Speculators Keep Out!" *City Limits*, February.

New York City Department of City Planning. 1982. *The Puerto Rican New Yorkers: A Recent History of Their Distribution and Population and Household Characteristics*.

———. 1987. *Population by Rate and Hispanic Origin by Selected Ages and Total Housing Units, New York City, Boroughs and Community Districts*.

———. 1984. *Community District Statistics: A Portrait of New York City from the 1980 Census*.

———. 1991a. *Planning New York City, 1991–1992*.

———. 1991b. *Population by Race and Hispanic Origin by Selected Ages and Total Housing Units, New York City, Boroughs and Community Districts*.

———. 1992a. *Community District Needs*.

———. 1992b. *Comprehensive Housing Affordability Strategy: Federal Fiscal Year 1992*.

———. 1992c. *Demographic Profiles: A Portrait of New York City's Community Districts from the 1980–1990 Censuses of Population and Housing*.

———. 1992d. *Socioeconomic Profiles: A Portrait of New York City's Community Districts from the 1980–1990 Censuses of Population and Housing*.

———. 1994. *Puerto Rican New Yorkers in 1990, Analyses of Demographic and Socioeconomic Characteristics of the City's Puerto Ricans, and Changes over Time*.

———. 1995. *Community District Needs*.

New York City, Department of Housing Preservation and Development. 1979. *Department of Housing Preservation and Development Handbook of Programs*.

———. 1989. *The 10 Year Plan*.

———. 1990. *Four Year Housing Program, 1991–1995*.

New York City Planning Commission. 1969. *Plan for New York City: A Proposal*.

Nieves, Evelyn. 1991. "Squatters and Friends March, But Tompkins Square Is Weary." *New York Times*, October 13.

Oder, Norman. 1992. "Southside Survivors." *City Limits*, November.

Ortner, Sherry B. 1989. *High Religion: A Cultural and Political History of Sherpa Buddhism*. Princeton, NJ: Princeton University Press.

Pfandler, Dennis. 1990. "Homesteader Prayer." *Homesteader*, January 13. New York: RAIN (CLT) Community Land Trust.

Pisani, Angelo. 1983. *A Study of Government Subsidized Housing Programs and Arson: Analysis of Programs Administered in New York City, 1978–1981*. Report prepared for the New York City Arson Strike Force, September.

Piven, Frances Fox, and Richard A. Cloward. 1977. *Poor People's Movements: How They Succeed and Why They Fail*. New York: Pantheon.

_____. 1979. "Who Should Be Organized? Citizen Action vs. Jobs and Justice.'" *Working Papers*, May/June.

_____. 1982. *The New Class War*. New York: Pantheon.

Plunz, Richard A. 1990. *A History of Housing in New York City*. New York: Columbia University Press.

Rabinowitz, F. F., and F. M. Trueblood, eds. 1973. *Latin American Urban Research*, Vol. 1. Beverly Hills, CA: Sage Publications.

Rapp, Rayna. 1987. "Urban Kinship in Contemporary America: Families, Classes and Ideology" In *Cities of the United States*, ed. Leith Mullings. New York: Columbia University Press.

Richman, L. S. 1989. "Housing Policy Needs a Rehab." *Fortune* 119 (7): 84.

Riis, Jakob A. 1970. *How the Other Half Lives*. Cambridge, MA: Belknap Press of Harvard University (orig. ed., 1890).

Roberts, Sam, and Fred R. Conrad. 1991. "New York in the Nineties." *New York Times*, September 29.

Rosenberg, Terry J. 1992. *Poverty in New York City, 1991: A Research Bulletin*. New York: Community Service Society of New York.

Rosenberry, Sara, and Chester Hartman, eds. 1989. *Housing Issues of the 1990s*. New York: Praeger Publications.

Ross, E., and Rayna Rapp. 1981. "Sex and Society: A Research Note from Social History and Anthropology." *Comparative Studies in Society and History* 23 (1): 51–72.

Sacks, Karen, and Dorothy Remy, eds. 1984. *My Troubles Are Going to Have Trouble with Me—Everyday Trials and Triumphs of Women Workers*. New Brunswick, NJ: Rutgers University Press.

Salins, Peter, ed. 1984. *New York Unbound—The City and the Politics of the Future*. Colchester, VT: Blackwell Publishers.

Sánchez, José Ramón. 1986. "Residual Work and Residual Shelter: Housing Puerto Rican Labor in New York City from World War II to 1983." In *Critical Perspectives on Housing*, eds. Rachel G. Bratt, Chester Hartman, and Ann Meyerson. Philadelphia: Temple University Press.

Sanders, Ronald. 1979. *The Lower East Side*. New York: Dover Publications.

Sanjek, Roger. 1990. "Urban Anthropology in the 1980s: A World View." *Annual Review of Anthropology* 19 (October): 151–186.

Sassen, Saskia. 1989. "Economic Restructuring and the American City." *Annual Review of Sociology* 16: 465–90.

Save the Children. 1982. *Urban Homesteading: A How to Manual*. New York: Save the Children's Inner City Program in New York City.

Schoener, Allon, ed. 1967. *Portal to America: The Lower East Side 1870–1925*. New York: Holt, Rhinehart & Winston.

Schuman, Tony. 1986. "The Agony and the Equity: A Critique of Self-Help Housing." In *Critical Perspectives on Housing*, eds. Rachel G. Bratt, Chester Hartman, and Ann Meyerson. Philadelphia: Temple University Press.

Schur, Robert. 1986. "Manhattan Plaza: Old-Style Ripoffs Are Still Alive and Well." In *Critical Perspectives on Housing*, eds. Rachel G. Bratt, Chester Hartman, and Ann Meyerson. Philadelphia: Temple University Press.

Schwartz, Harry (assisted by Peter Abeles). 1973. *Planning for the Lower East Side*. New York: Praeger Publications.

Senft, Bret. 1992. "The East Village." *New York Times*, June 14.

Serrin, William. 1992. *Homestead: The Glory and the Tragedy of an American Steel Town*. New York: Random House.

Shaman, Diana. 1993. "Tenements Are Rebuilt as Rentals." *New York Times*, October 22.

Sharff, Jagna. 1987. "The Underground Economy of a Poor Neighborhood." In *Cities of the United States*, ed. Leith Mullings. New York: Columbia University Press.

Skinner, R. J. and M. J. Rodell, eds. 1983. *People, Poverty and Shelter*. New York: Methuen & Co.

Smith, Clifford Thorpe. 1967. *An Historical Geography of Western Europe before 1800*. New York: Praeger Publishers.

Stafford, Walter W. 1985. *Closed Labor Markets: Underrepresentation of Blacks, Hispanics, and Women in New York City's Core Industries and Jobs*. New York: Community Service Society of New York.

Stegman, Michael A. 1988. *Housing and Vacancy Report, New York City*. Report prepared for the New York City Department of Housing Preservation and Development.

_____. 1991. *Housing and Vacancy Report, New York City*. Report prepared for the New York City Department of Housing Preservation and Development.

_____. 1993. *Housing and Vacancy Report, New York City*. Report prepared for the New York City Department of Housing Preservation and Development.

Sternlieb, George. 1974. *The Myth and Potential Reality of Urban Homesteading*. New Brunswick, NJ: Rutgers University, Center for Urban Policy Research.

Stone, Michael E. 1986. "Housing and the Dynamics of U.S. Capitalism." In *Critical Perspectives on Housing*, eds. Rachel G. Bratt, Chester Hartman, and Ann Meyerson. Philadelphia: Temple University Press.

Sullivan, B. 1982. *Analysis and Assessment of the Alternative Management Programs for New York City's In Rem Properties*. New York: Pratt Institute Center for Community and Environmental Development.

Sullivan, Mercer. 1991. *Up from the Underclass: Ethnography and Community Development*. Paper presented at the American Anthropological Association Meetings in Chicago, November 19–24.

Sumka, Howard J., and Anthony J. Blackburn. 1982. "Multifamily Urban Homesteading: A Key Approach to Low-Income Housing." *Journal of Housing* 39 (July–August).

Susser, Ida. 1986. "Political Activity among Working Class Women in a U.S. City." *American Ethnologist* 13 (1): 108–117.

Tabb, William K. 1984. *Marxism and the Metropolis*. New York: Oxford University Press.

Tawney, R. H. 1920. *The Acquisitive Society*. New York: Harcourt Brace Jovanovich.

Tilly, Charles. 1978. *From Mobilization to Revolution*. Reading, MA: Addison-Wesley.

Tobier, Emmanuel. 1984. *The Changing Face of Poverty: Trends in New York City's Population in Poverty, 1960–1990*. New York: Community Service Society, Working Papers.

Turetsky, Doug. 1990. "Rebels with a Cause?" *City Limits*, April.

_____. 1991. "The Go-Betweens." *City Limits*, June/July.

Turner, Joan A. 1984. *Building Boundaries: The Politics of Urban Renewal in Manhattan's Lower East Side*. New York: City University of New York, Ph.D. dissertation.

Turner, John F. C. 1977. *Housing by People: Towards Autonomy in Building Environments*. New York: Pantheon Books.

Turner, John F. C. and Robert Fichter, eds. 1972. *Freedom to Build: Dweller Control of the Housing Process*. New York: MacMillan.

Tyrell, Emmett, Jr. 1990. "Homesteading on the Liberal Plantation." *American Spectator Journal*, April.

Urciuoli, Bonnie. 1991. "The Political Topography of Spanish and English: The View from a New York Puerto Rican Neighborhood." *American Ethnologist* 18 (2): 295–310.

U.S. Congress, House. 1974. *Housing and Community Development Act of 1974*. 93rd Congress, pp. 1–2.

U.S. Department of Commerce, Bureau of the Census. 1970. *Census of Population and Housing*.

_____. 1980. *Census of Population and Housing*.

_____. 1987. *New York City Housing and Vacancy Survey*.

_____. 1990. *Census of Population and Housing*.

_____. 1994. *Statistical Abstract of the United States*.

U.S. Department of Housing and Urban Development, Office of Development and Research. 1978. *Baseline Analysis of the Urban Homesteading Demonstration*.

_____. 1979. *Urban Homesteading—USA*.

Varady, David P. 1986. *Neighborhood Upgrading—A Realistic Assessment*. Albany: State University of New York Press.

Viele, Egbert L. 1874. *Topographical Atlas of the City of New York Including the Annexed Territory Showing Original Water Courses and Made Land*. New York.

Ward, P. M., ed. 1982. *Self-Help Housing: A Critique*. London: Mansell.

Weinstein, Jerome I. 1990. "Homesteading: A Solution for the Homeless?" *Journal of Housing* 47 (May/June): 125–129.

Weitzman, Phillip. 1989. *Worlds Apart: Housing, Race/Ethnicity and Income in New York City, 1978–1987*. New York: Community Service Society of New York, Working Papers.

White, Andrew. 1993. "As Far as the People Will Go." *City Limits*, August/September.

White, Andrew, Lisa Glazer and Jonathan A. Lewis. 1992. "Drowning in Debt." *City Limits*, October.

Williams, Raymond. 1973. *The Country and the City*. New York: Oxford University Press.

Yanagisako, Sylvia. 1977. "Women-Centered Kin Networks in Urban Bilateral Kinship." *American Ethnologist* 2: 207–226.

Zarza, Daniel, and Harriet Cohen. 1979. *Loisaida: Strategies for Neighborhood Revitalization*. Washington, DC: Report prepared for the U.S. Department of Housing and Urban Development (Contract 4376).

Zukin, Sharon. 1991. *Landscapes of Power: From Detroit to Disney World*. Berkeley: University of California Press.

INDEX

Westmorelands Homesteads, 19
Whites, 2, 65, 115, 124
Williams, Raymond, 30–31, 170
Women, 5–6, 110, 115–21, 145, 156,
    183. *See also* Community organiza-
    tions; Homesteading; LESAC;
    RAIN

Work, concept of, 110, 135

Young Women's Settlement, 43
Youth at Work program, 113, 182
YouthBuild program, 181

Zukin, Sharon, 186

About the Author

MALVE VON HASSELL holds a Ph.D. in anthropology from the New School for Social Research. Currently working as an independent scholar, she has taught at Queens College, Baruch College, and Pace University. Her interests are in the urban anthropology of race, class, and gender.

ISBN 0-89789-459-6

9 780897 894593

HARDCOVER BAR CODE